Management Accounting for the Hospitality, Tourism and Leisure Industries

Debra Adams

(G) Goodfellow Publishers Ltd

(G) Published by Goodfellow Publishers Limited,
26 Home Close, Wolvercote, Oxford OX2 8PS
http://www.goodfellowpublishers.com

British Library Cataloguing in Publication Data: a catalogue record for this title is available from the British Library.

Library of Congress Catalog Card Number: on file.

ISBN: 978-1-911396-70-3

DOI: 10.23912/9781911396703-3806

Design and typesetting by P.K. McBride, www.macbride.org.uk

Cover design by Cylinder

Contents

Preface

This third edition of this textbook has been written during some of the most turbulent times experienced not only in the hospitality and leisure industries but within the world economic environment in general. The bounce back from the Covid years and the impact of the pandemic on the sector has created extensive demand for travel, tourism and hospitality experiences. Whilst revenue have surged to almost 2019 levels, the sector has faced increased challenges from rising operational costs and high levels of inflation coupled with a growth in interest rates, all of which combine to impact on the conversion to profit. It has become increasingly important for business managers and their teams to fully understand the drivers of revenue, market segmentation and the strategic management of costs in order to achieve target conversion to profit and return on investment.

Modern strategic management theory suggests that the speed of change is such that the traditional approach to strategic management processes with a linear step by step process can no longer be applied, and instead, an ongoing integrated approach is required. As a result, the requirement for strategic management accounting information to support the strategic decision making and control process has never been more vital.

Working with accurate information is at the heart of the decision-making process and the finance function is at the centre of the management of an organisation's data, producing not just the statutory accounts but essential daily, weekly and monthly updates for all the operational teams across the business. Traditionally the role of management accounting has been heavily biased towards the comparison of costs with revenues, focusing on the internal operations of the business. Accounts are, by definition, historical and inward-looking, and the process of accounting is governed by the underlying concept of prudence. However, there is a need in most organisations for accounting information to be produced with a strategic perspective in mind. This involves considering not just the internal operations but also the external environment and the impact of the competition.

If used effectively, the process of strategic management accounting can provide the financial information required to monitor existing business strategies and provide support for strategy formulation. Consequently, this book has been written to follow the chronology of the strategic decision making process with the aim of placing management accounting in the context of strategic decision making.

The chapters in Part 1 start with a review of the basic principles and practices of financial management and strategic management. They include an introduction to the strategic management process and an overview of rudimentary accounting practices and techniques. These chapters are intended for those who have limited knowledge of financial accounting. The chapters within Parts 2 and 3 are designed to provide a range of tools and techniques to support the processes of internal and external audit. The aim of Part 2 is to address the role of financial information in a strategic review of the environment. It examines the role of competitor accounting, strategic cost analysis and pricing. Part 3 covers the strategic process of internal appraisal, focusing on budgetary control, working capital control and performance measurement. Part 4 focuses on the determination of corporate strategy, providing chapters on financing, investment appraisal, risk assessment and cost of capital measurement. Part 5 concludes by considering the future of accounting in the hospitality, leisure and tourism industry with an overview of the importance of accounting for sustainability.

Generally, the approach adopted throughout the text is to demonstrate the financial technique under discussion with appropriate examples drawn from the sector. Some financial techniques have been given greater prominence than might be normally expected due to their particular relevance to the hospitality, leisure and tourism industry. Chapter 13, on business valuations, is such an example. Where possible the financial theories have been illustrated with practical insights based on research drawn from the industry sector and the author's own experience over many years associated with the UK hospitality and tourism industry.

This book is intended for undergraduate programmes and post graduate courses in hospitality, tourism and leisure management and related disciplines. This book will also be useful for middle to senior mangers working in the sector, particularly those engaged with management development programmes. A range of additional resources are available for facilitators and tutors. Finally, I am delighted that this book has been used for a number of years for both non-financial and accounting students requiring more knowledge about the hospitality, tourism and leisure industries. I hope that you enjoy this revised and updated third edition.

Debra J. Adams

June 2024

Acknowledgements

This book could not have been written without the support of a number of people across my network who have provided me with support and advice including my wonderful team at arena4finance.

My thanks also to all those who have purchased early editions of the book and have given their feedback – your support is much appreciated!

I would also like to thank my editor, Sally North, for her patience whilst awaiting the revisions to this latest edition.

Finally, a huge thank you to my family and loved ones for their continuing support throughout.

Part 1 Introduction

The aim of this text is to provide the reader with insight into the role of accounting information for controlling and managing a business enterprise in the hospitality sector. Every financial report tells the story of the business in terms of how it has managed to deliver the strategic aims of the enterprise. Following the period of massive disruption for the hospitality industry, created by the global pandemic in 2020 to 2022, it has never been more important to ensure that operational managers are provided with all the data and information they need to manage the business effectively. With the breaking down of departmental silos across the business, the finance department needs to ensure that the daily, weekly and monthly management accounts provide the one true source of information to be used by all the specialists in the business – Operations, Human Resources, Revenue Managers, Sales and Marketing and Asset Managers, for example. The aim of this first section of the text is to provide an introduction for the reader to the process of strategic management in hospitality organisations and also to financial management accounting. This approach assumes that the reader has little prior knowledge of these topics and aims to provide a basic level of knowledge before embarking on the application of management accounting techniques to the strategic management process. In today's world, organisational reporting and management information systems have a crucial role in providing managers with the insight to enable them to make strategic decisions about the future of the organisation, such as:

- ☐ How does our business need to adapt to meet the needs of the future?
- ☐ Which of our customers and markets are the most profitable and how can we retain and attract more?
- ☐ Which are our most profitable products and services?
- ☐ How do we develop strategic partnerships with customers, suppliers and competitors?
- ☐ What resources and skills do we need to develop in the organisation to meet the changing demands of the future?

Chapter 1 reviews a variety of definitions for the strategy process and relates these to organisational decision making. All organisations, regardless of size, need to make decisions about the activities in which they wish to engage, the objectives they seek to achieve and the route that they intend to follow, and these stages are introduced and discussed, providing the reader with a model to summarise the total process. The chapter concludes with a review of some of the key strategic issues facing the hospitality, tourism and leisure industries and specific issues relating to financial management. The changing structure of the hospitality industry is discussed at length including the move to asset light strategies favoured by the dominant brands and the integrative role of specialisms such as asset management and revenue management.

Chapter 2 develops the link between effective decision - making processes and the role of the finance function as the source of relevant and timely information for operational managers and supporting department managers such as sales and marketing and the revenue management function. At this stage the changing needs of the business are emphasised using models to illustrate the life pattern of a business.

A review of the essential concepts for the understanding and interpretation of the key financial statements is provided in Chapter 3. The chapter reviews current accounting techniques based on recommended practice for the preparation of the three key accounting statements; Income and Expenditure statement (Profit and Loss), Statement of Financial Position (Balance Sheet) and Cash Flow statements to familiarise the reader with the presentation of financial information. The reader will also be introduced to the Uniform System of Accounts for the Lodging Industry (USALI) – a recommended voluntary approach for the presentation of internal reporting and performance measurement for the hospitality sector. In this chapter the topic of International Financial Reporting Standards is introduced as well as a brief review of the importance of corporate governance and Environmental, Social and Governance (ESG) issues.

1 Introducing strategic management

About this chapter

The subject of strategic management is wide ranging and extensive, and many excellent textbooks have been dedicated to the topic. In this text the focus is on the application of accounting data and information for the purposes of strategic decision making. As a result, a broad overview of the subject of strategic management is introduced, supported by a range of frameworks to illustrate the strategic use of financial information for effective strategic decision making. This chapter includes a discussion of the following key areas:

- The decision-making process
- Definition of strategy
- Organisational structures
- Organisational objectives
- Information needs
- Current strategic issues for the hospitality industry.

Learning objectives

On completion of this chapter, you should be able to:

- Define strategy and explain the key elements of the strategic decision-making process
- Appreciate the impact of organisational structure on strategic decision making
- List the key business stakeholders and understand how their needs can impact on organisational strategy
- Gain an insight into the current strategic issues in the tourism and hospitality industries.

Introduction

In the first edition of this text, published in the nineties, this chapter opened with the statement that:

> *"For the modern hospitality business faced with the challenge of operating in increasingly diverse markets it is essential, therefore, that the processes of strategic management are as effective as possible. All organisations need to make decisions about the nature of their business activities to ensure that the resources are put to the best possible uses whilst ensuring that customer needs remain satisfied."*

Almost over three decades have elapsed since the first edition was released and in many ways this statement has more resonance than before. In recent years the international tourism and hospitality industries have been at the centre of a period of tremendous change ranging from the increasing level of customer expectations and the entrance of many diverse competing and disruptive accommodation products and services, such as AirBnB and the growth of the serviced apartments sector, through to the huge opportunities arising from the application of technology for data management and business intelligence. Challenges arising in the post-pandemic period have included changing market segment profiles and disruption to the supply chain and labour resources.

Strategic management is defined by Johnson et al. (2017) as '*the long-term direction of an organisation*'. In the 11th edition of the leading text, *Exploring Strategy*, they cite the definitions of many of the thought leaders from the field of strategic management who focus on elements such as 'Competitive strategy' Porter (1996) and 'Competitive advantage' Peter Drucker (1994). In today's business environment it is overwhelmingly clear that it is essential for every organisation to continually review its activities to bridge the gap between where it is now and where it would like to be, or indeed, needs to be to survive and meet the new challenges arising. This ideal position is unique to each organisation and is dependent on the long-term organisational goals and objectives which have been set over a period, during which the external environment will continue to change. As a result, it is no longer relevant to assume that the implementation of strategy will lead to a fixed point in the future. Instead, the organisation needs to continually monitor, control and adapt the business strategy to meet the needs of a changing landscape, and this process is reliant on the provision of accurate and relevant information about the business, as well as a reliable review of the external environment through bench marking and market analysis.

The hospitality, tourism and leisure sector is extensive and diverse with the overall purpose of providing food, drink, accommodation and a variety of leisure activities and experiences. The sector is often cited to include the following:

- Hotels
- Serviced apartments and extended stay accommodation
- Restaurants
- Pubs, bars and nightclubs
- Contract food service providers

- ☐ Membership clubs
- ☐ Events
- ☐ Casinos
- ☐ Travel services
- ☐ Tourist services
- ☐ Visitor attractions
- ☐ Youth hostels and student accommodation
- ☐ Holiday parks
- ☐ Self-catering accommodation
- ☐ Hospitality services.

Focusing on the hotel sector, there can be multiple classifications for a single or group of properties. STR, part of the CoStar Group, leading providers of data for the hotel sector define these as:

- ☐ *Chain* or *brands* which are visible to the customer;
- ☐ *Parent company* – the overall name of the company which may include numerous brand names;
- ☐ *Hotel operating company* – the company operating the hotel on behalf of other parties such as a brand and/or owner;
- ☐ *Owner* – the investor in the property who may choose not to operate it;
- ☐ *Asset management company* – represents the owner to ensure the hotel is being operated to maximise the potential of the investment;
- ☐ *Franchises* – chain hotel run by a third party where the chain receives a franchise fee;
- ☐ *Independent* – not owned or affiliated with a chain or parent company in the industry.

As we approach the mid 2020s the integration of hospitality into wider urban planning is already here. With over 70% of the world's population expected to live in cities within the next decade, hospitality services have a key role to play in the development of urban co-work and co-living spaces. Against this background of constant change, this text attempts to demonstrate how techniques for monitoring and forecasting the business position can assist managers in decision-making, with examples based on the needs of the sector, where meeting expectations for customer service and quality of experience is central to the business purpose.

What is strategy?

Leading theorists, Johnson et al (2017) describe three elements which they suggest combine to form the strategy for a business entity:

1. The long term time frame
2. Direction
3. Organisation

The time frame will be over a number of years – for some organisations at least a decade or more. During this period the strategy will continue to evolve and direction will be set based on long term objectives but the route to achieving these objectives could be continually emerging. Organisations are continually evolving with both internal and external stakeholders.

Organisational structure

The way in which an organisation approaches corporate decision making and strategic management processes will very much depend on the organisational structure. The term 'structure' used in the organisational sense refers to the way in which capital and human resources are arranged, and has considerable impact on the operation of the business.

A review of texts about organisational change reveals that organisations can be structured in range of different configurations. Organisational structures can be classified according to a number of characteristic features.

- The *classical style* is characterised by a strict hierarchy and clearly defined roles for each level. Such structures operate like a machine which is most effective under stable market conditions. However, such a structure is lacking in flexibility and is unable to react effectively in changing market conditions.
- The *behavioural* style places greater emphasis on personal responsibility and participation in decision making and, as a result, tends to stimulate greater commitment to organisational goals.

In a small business, decision making is highly centralised and there is often little need for formal procedures and policies. The organisational structure tends to be much simpler and, therefore, it should be easier to develop the vision statement into a set of relevant goals on which the business objectives can then set. However, as the business grows a decision–making hierarchy tends to be employed and the challenge is to create a structure which combines flexibility and responsiveness with the controls and procedures required to deliver the business objectives.

Frequently, as the organisation becomes larger and more structurally complex, it becomes increasingly difficult to align business objectives because organisations rarely function as total entities. Instead, there are various functional activities such as operations, marketing, finance and human resources which make up the whole, and the long-term corporate objectives need to be broken down into separate but integrated strategies for each functional activity. For many organisations the challenge is to break down the 'working in silos' approach to ensure integration and understanding of strategy and the overall business performance. The management accounting function has an important role to play in overcoming this challenge by producing the one true set of business information.

As the organisation becomes even larger it will tend to subdivide into much smaller areas of responsibility. This can be achieved by splitting the organisation into the separate divisions. The separate divisions may then each have its own set of functional activities. Where managers have a considerable level of discretion these divisions are known strategic business units (SBUs). Each SBU will normally have its own customers and market segment and most strategic planning may be undertaken at this level.

In today's world it is becoming increasingly clear that organisations are tending to move away from hierarchical structures favoured by the classical approach and are instead moving toward flatter structures achieved by 'de-layering' the organisation. Such structures are typified by the emerging market leaders in retail, such as Amazon and Apple.

Defining purpose

Defining strategy starts with stating the organisational purpose. Every organisation should have a clear vision for the future and this is usually summarised in the mission statement or its vision and values statement. Articulating the business mission is one way to ensure that employees are aware of the business vision. Some mission statements are several pages in length whilst other companies choose to summarise in one simple sentence.

Whitbread Hotels, the largest budget hotel group in the UK summarises purpose as follows:

Whitbread Hotels

Our purpose

To provide quality, affordable hotels for our guests to help them to live and work well and to positively impact the world around us. With no barriers to entry or limits to ambition, to provide meaningful work, skills and career development opportunities for our teams.

"Our ambition is to be the world's best budget hotel"

About us - Whitbread PLC accessed 28th November 2023

Hilton Hotels, one of the largest brands in the world chooses to create a mnemonic to reiterate the core values:

Hilton Hotels

'Our Values'

H – Hospitality – We're passionate about delivering exceptional guest experiences

I – Integrity – We do the right thing, all the time

L – Leadership – We're leaders in our industry and in our communities

T – Teamwork – We're team players in everything we do

O – Owners – We're the owners of our actions and decisions

N – Now – We operate with a sense of urgency and discipline

"We are a business serving people, and our Team Members extend their passion for hospitality beyond our hotel walls every day. " Chris Nassetta - President & CEO

Hilton Brands | Global Hospitality Company accessed 28th November 2023

Organisational objectives

In most organisations in the tourism and hospitality industry the setting of goals and objectives will be influenced by the people who control and work within the organisation. The primary purpose of all profit-making organisations has traditionally been to add value over and above the cost of servicing the cost of capital used. In practice this is creating sufficient profit to exceed the cost of the finance in the business. This is called the 'Expected Value Added' concept and is discussed further later in the text. The creation of value enables the demands of shareholders to be met by providing returns in the form of dividends and increasing share price as well as retained profit to reinvest in the business.

However, this fundamental objective is often complicated by the actions of those stakeholders, both internal and external to the organisation, with the result that actual activities pursued may conflict with the fundamental purpose of the organisation. Increasingly the time frame over which objectives are considered can also result in a conflict between short term returns and long-term investment.

The upscale brand Four Seasons provides a brief summary of their objectives:

Four Seasons

"Our objective is to be recognized as the company that manages the finest hotels, resorts and residence clubs wherever we locate. We create properties of enduring value using superior design and finishes, and support them with a deeply instilled ethic of personal service. Doing so allows Four Seasons to satisfy the needs and tastes of our discerning customers, and to maintain our position as the world's premier luxury hospitality company."

Mission Statement | Service Culture | Four Seasons Hotels and Resorts, accessed 28th November 2023

The profit motive

Adding value requires making a profit on goods and services by selling these at a price in excess of the total cost of delivering the product to the customer. Whilst most organisations aim to maximise profit growth and return on investment, the reality is that the profit maximisation motive is undermined by the objectives of those stakeholders who are able to influence the organisation the most. Economists argue that the pursuit of profit maximisation in a competitive environment leads to economic efficiency. However, whilst the concept of economic efficiency is clearly desirable it is also difficult to measure in practice. Therefore, the performance of a business is typically measured quantitatively using ratios such as return on capital employed, where profit is compared to the capital investment. The practical measurement of efficiency and effectiveness is much more difficult and is often a matter of subjective judgement. In today's world many businesses seek to address the sustainability agenda for a range of reasons, which will be discussed later in the text but the result is the emergence of the triple P's – Profit, People and Planet. Each stakeholder group will seek to gain influence over a different aspect of business performance and the extent of their influence will depend on the relative strength of that stakeholder group.

Stakeholders

The typical range of business stakeholders or interested parties is illustrated in Figure 1.1. The relative power of each of these groups in relation to the other is very relevant and may change over time.

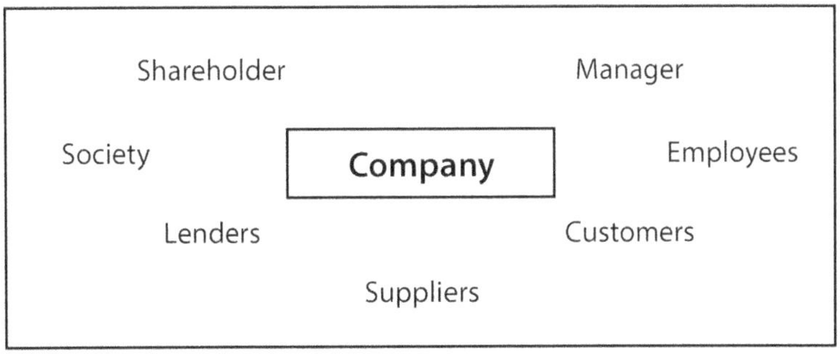

Figure 1.1: Business stakeholders

Quite clearly conflict can arise between the stakeholder groups resulting in a range of business strategies chosen to meet the demands of the most dominant groups. This means that the resulting objectives of the organisation are varied and certainly are influenced by factors other than profit maximisation because each stakeholder is deriving a different reward from the existence of the business. This concept is complicated further by the increasing separation of ownership and management of the hotel industry with the extensive use of leasing, franchising and management operating contract models preferred by many of the major players in the sector. Each of the stakeholders will now be considered in turn.

Shareholders

Shareholders are investors who have purchased a stake in the organisation. These organisations can be private i.e. not listed on a Stock Exchange or the capital markets. In the UK the investors purchasing shares in public companies are a combination of individuals and institutional investors. The nature of the investor will impact on their individual target levels of risk and return but typically investors in a large, international, well diversified organisation are essentially concerned with a competitive return on capital employed from their investment in the form of dividends and capital growth, the latter being the growth in the traded share price. These are obviously both functions of the profitability of the business and will therefore influence future business strategy. The need to pay out a reasonable dividend in relation to the investor's capital investment means that the business needs to make a level of profit sufficient to fund the dividend whilst allowing sufficient funds to remain within the business, in the form of retained profits, to finance growth. Failure to do this leads to shareholder dissatisfaction, with a possible fall in share price as investors disinvest, undermining market confidence in the company. The power of the shareholder group intent on pursuing the profit maximisation objective has led some business operators to review their dependence on the equities market, with the result that previously listed companies have returned to private ownership. Between 2005 and 2020, according to the OECD (2021), almost 30,000 companies delisted from global markets via conventional takeovers, share buybacks and leverage buyouts.

Managers

The management of the company have been engaged by the owners or the shareholders to maximise the profitability of the organisation and are rewarded with a salary and terms and conditions in return for achieving this. In practice, this concept can be undermined by the interests of the individuals in the management team and this is known as the *'agency'* problem. Consequently, managers pursue a profit level which they perceive to be in excess of the minimum acceptable to shareholders, but which also allows them to achieve their own personal goals. The leading managerial theorist from the nineties, O.E. Williamson (1995) listed these personal goals as being not only salary, but also security, status, power, prestige and professional excellence. As a result, the pursuit of profit maximisation through cost reduction could be said to be undermined because expenditure contributes to gaining power, status and prestige. Many of the non-monetary rewards have the benefit of being hidden from others within the business and external shareholders, and of course are not subject to taxation. The structure of the organisation is also relevant as this determines the level of influence exerted by the management group, emphasising the effect of ownership separate from control. In today's world in the hospitality industry, the separation of management and ownership is highlighted by the growth of asset lite strategies with the biggest brands owning only approximately 5% of the total branded real estate.

Employees

The strength of the employee group will depend on the nature of the workforce and the external environment. A highly skilled permanent staff has increased power compared to a poorly skilled part time work force. A powerful group will pursue objectives which include increased salaries, improved working conditions and effective lines of communication. Highly unionised industry sectors are subject to extensive employee influence on corporate strategy. The levels of unionisation in tourism and hospitality industries have traditionally been very low and the sector employs large numbers of part time and zero hours workers. However, increasing skill shortages in key areas such as food preparation and service has provided the workforce with the lever to demand improved working conditions, higher salaries and opportunities for professional development and training.

Customers

The power of the customer centres on the products and services being offered and the perceived value for money. That is the relationship between the benefits of purchasing the goods and services against the price of acquiring them. The strength of the consumer group will depend on the market conditions in which the purchase is to be made. Social media has provided a real time voice for this stakeholder with feedback and visual experiences freely posted on a range of platforms. Rating platforms such as TripAdvisor have become the voice of the consumer, with immediate impact on customer choice and decision making.

Suppliers

This group of stakeholders is essentially interested in guaranteed long term profitable custom from the organisation. At a practical level, suppliers are able to exert pressure for quick payment of outstanding invoices, thereby influencing business decisions relating to the management of working capital. In return the organisation will press for improved terms and conditions with regard to product quality and delivery patterns. The level of influence of this stakeholder group will depend on the reliance of the organisation on a supplier and the availability of the product required. Increasingly organisations are seeking to lower investment in working capital, in particular inventory, to reduce the cost of holding stock, including the use of the space. This topic will be discussed further later in the text.

Lenders

Lenders provide interest-bearing capital and want to ensure that the profits of the organisation are sufficient to service the cost of the debt, and that it has the ability to make capital repayments in the future. The debt holder may introduce covenants or restrictions on the business as well as taking part in the decision-making processes to oversee the management of the debt thereby influencing business strategy.

Society

The power of this group will be depend on the strength of opinion of the collective and the ability of the combined efforts to have a significant effect on the business. In recent times environmental issues have become more significant and organisations have been forced to adapt their policies and procedures accordingly. This has been the result of increasing public demand for change, coupled with the desire to avoid negative publicity.

Governmental influence in the form of legislation may affect the operation of the business. In the hospitality industry a recent example of governmental intervention effecting business operations has been the Food Allergen Regulations, where investment in operational processes and training has been required to meet government standards. Incentives in the form of tax allowances or grants may serve to encourage investment in certain industries and locations. Local or national government may show interest and attempt to influence business decisions, where strategy calls for large investment or the scaling down of operations resulting in widespread redundancies.

Aligning goals

It is possible for different stakeholder groups to have varied and possibly conflicting areas of interest in the organisation and each group will try to influence business strategy accordingly. In an ideal world, managers in the organisation should aim to reflect the objectives of the shareholders, and to a certain extent this does happen as managers who forget their responsibilities to shareholders are likely to lose their position in an efficient financial market. Where the personal goals of managers reflect the shareholder objectives, the implementation of business strategies to further these objectives is likely to be more successful. However, difficulties arise when manager and shareholder objectives are clearly in conflict. A situation may arise where shareholders wish managers to adopt a high risk, high growth strategy to produce additional profits. If the strategy fails and the business collapses the shareholders may be able to offset those losses elsewhere with little personal risk. However, the managers in the business face high personal risk if the business fails and may therefore be reticent about pursuing such a strategy. Goal congruence becomes even more difficult to achieve as the business grows, as conflict may arise within the management group itself.

Information needs

Strategic management accounting should be a decision support system providing relevant information to the appropriate decision maker. These decision makers are situated not only at the very top of the organisation but at various levels in the organisation, depending on the organisational structure. The business strategy must be implemented all the way down through the organisation and may result in several sub-strategies. The monitoring of the business strategy will take place at all levels in the organisation having been delegated to various managers at different levels. Therefore, the strategic management accounting system needs to provide information relevant to the needs of the user, rather than raw data, and the information needs to be presented in an intelligible form in sufficient time to be of assistance in the decision-making process. Essentially it is balance between the cost of providing this information against the benefit to be accrued to the organisation from taking a better financial decision. In recent years there have been extensive developments in the technology available to assist the presentation of fast and accurate information for decision making.

Current strategic issues

At the time of writing the UK hospitality industry, in particular the hotel sector, has experienced surging growth in revenue following spikes in demand arising from the impact of covid and the enforced periods of closure. Revenue growth has been coupled with a sustained period of increasing operational costs including the cost of food, salaries and wages and utilities.

Specific to the sector there are several factors which will impact on the strategic development of the international hospitality and tourism industries over the next decade presenting both opportunities and threats. These include:

- Continuing changing patterns of asset ownership
- Environmental issues and the greening of the sector impacting both operations and business valuations

- ☐ Information technology and the role of data management
- ☐ Changing consumer demands, preferences and requirements
- ☐ The increasing role of industry disruptors such as Airbnb and Snoozerroo
- ☐ The role of hospitality services in the growing co-working and co-living space.

Changing patterns of ownership

Traditionally ownership in the hotel and catering sector within the hospitality industry has been very dispersed, resulting in an industry which was dominated by independent owners and operators. This pattern has changed in the first part of the 21st century with a range of approaches for organisations to achieve growth without necessarily purchasing assets such as hotels. These strategies for growth include:

- ☐ Merger and acquisitions
- ☐ Franchising
- ☐ Management contracts
- ☐ Joint ventures
- ☐ Leasing assets

The first international hotel companies were formed in the late 1940s with the growth of American companies such as Hilton International, Inter-Continental and Sheraton. Large multinational companies have continued to grow and to expand throughout the world, posing a constant challenge to the independent operator who cannot always compete with the scale of the key functional areas of marketing, information technology, purchasing power and financing.

The separation of ownership of hotel and resort assets and their management is now widespread. This in turn has resulted in the growth of the phenomenon of the hotel management contract and hotel franchising arrangement. In the former arrangement the property is owned by investment companies, private equity groups or wealthy individuals and the property is managed by a hotel operator in return for a fee and possibly a share of the profits. Several of the major hotel operators now include managed hotels in their portfolio of properties. The nature of these arrangements mean that the accounting information emphasis is focused on revenue and gross operating profit maximisation, as these are normally the two figures on which the management fee is calculated.

Franchising now represents the most favoured form of hotel expansion, where owned properties are operated by the owner or a third party as part of a specific brand, and various hybrid arrangements have emerged. Franchising development in the UK hotel and restaurant industry has been focused on the development of brands. Hilton International was amongst the first to create branded segments but many other groups have followed this example on a world-wide basis including Ramada, IHG and Mariott. The use of franchising arrangements is not a new concept having been in use for many decades and is used to describe a business format which involves (DTI, 1998, p.2):

The granting of rights by a company (the franchisor) for a third party (the franchisee) to operate their business system using a common brand and common format for promoting, managing and administering the business.

There have been an increasing number of potential franchisees willing to pay a share of the revenue received for the right to operate under brand names and some of them have grown into considerable hotel companies in their own right.

Environmental issues

Many hotels and resorts have become much more focused on social responsibility, including managing and monitoring their impact on the environment. This has been driven by a range of key factors including the increasing requirement to report environmental impact data in the published annual report and the impact of climate and environmental issues on business valuations, as well as the social pressure to implement change. Due to the nature of their operations and extensive facilities, luxury hotels in particular are extensive users of resource consumption, impacting their carbon footprint, energy and water usage. The United World Tourism Organisation (UNWTO) states that:

Given the direct interactions between tourism industry operators, the environment, and communities the importance of ESG (Environmental, Social and Governance factors) in tourism cannot be overstated. In a practical sense, the importance of ESG to companies within the tourism industry can be clearly seen in areas such as customer acquisition, customer retention, managing risks and regulations, gaining access to sustainable financing or managing investor relations.

www.unwto.org/tourism-statistics/environmental-social-governance-tourism, retrieved December 2023.

Case study: ESG standards

There are over 600 different sustainability reporting standards, frameworks and guidelines available around the world. The good news is that these frameworks are converging and specific guidelines are emerging. At the current time the three largest ESG reporting frameworks are:

1. The **IFRS Sustainability Disclosure Standards** which were created in 2022 by the International Sustainability Standards Board (ISSB). These are worldwide standards which currently apply to 168 member jurisdictions, regulating more than 95% of the world's financial markets.
2. The **EU Corporate Sustainability Reporting Directive** (EU CSRD) set up by the European Financial Reporting Advisory Group (EFRAG) requires detailed reporting for reports for financial years commencing from 1st January 2024. The companies required to report include those listed on EU-regulated markets and unlisted companies or groups classified as 'large' in the EU. The data and non-financial information is required to be appropriately verified.

3. The **Securities and Exchange Commission** (SEC) governs public companies listed on the US stock exchange with focus on ESG reporting.

According to research from PwC (2024) companies should move quickly to implement the right infrastructure for ESG reporting. For the hospitality industry that may mean considering the role of ESG throughout the life cycle of hotel assets and disclosing information on ESG risks and opportunities that affect the value of a business.

Source: Adapted from https://www.pwc.com/us/en/industries/consumer-markets/library/esg-reporting-in-hospitality.html

Information technology

The past has already proven that the tourism and hospitality companies cannot afford to overlook the opportunities offered by the ever increasing potential derived from the use of information technology. The most exciting development in recent times must be the marketing and distribution opportunities offered by technological developments. It is estimated that over 65% of the world's population have access to the internet, providing access to markets in a way which has never been witnessed before.

It is already clear that the impact of the internet and multimedia technologies is having far reaching effects on the structure of the tourism industry in particular. The most significant changes have been in the way that tourism organisations communicate with clients and how they manage the distribution channels. There is a growing mass of literature on the usage of e-commerce in the industries and there have been a number of research studies on the subject.

Commentators originally assumed that the internet communication technologies would result in less business travel reducing the demand for business flights, accommodation and meeting rooms. However, prior to the pandemic in 2020 /21 in many cases the reverse had been the case with business travellers free to travel more widely whilst continuously in touch with the parent organisation and colleagues via various communication channels. Post pandemic, by the end of 2023 international tourism levels had recovered to almost 90% of pre pandemic levels.

Developments in information technology have impacted on the systems used to control businesses in the hospitality and tourism sectors. Financial controllers now have the opportunity to create their own business templates through their accounting systems, with the flexibility to create a new chart of accounts to suit the business need and take advantage of a variety of additional features for planning and control. Increased integration of these systems across the business with links to a common database means that typically data entry comes from other parts of the business operation, entered by operational staff. In practice this means that increasingly more time is spent checking that data has been inputted rather than inputting the data. With this increased flexibility comes the requirement for financial controllers and their teams to have a much more detailed understanding of the accounting policies and regulations which govern the preparation of accounts. Although in the accounts department physical book keeping at unit level is now highly automated in many ways, traditional book keeping skills are required more than ever in order to understand how these systems work.

Information technology has also created a range of opportunities with regard to procurement, including facilitating centralised purchasing allowing larger chains across the sector to leverage their size and purchasing power to achieve significant cost savings.

This section would not be complete without reference to the significant use of computerised yield management systems widely known as 'revenue management'. Developed originally for the airline industry, this tool is now used extensively across the sector, including in hotels and restaurants, to maximise both revenue and occupancy. Computerised systems replace the intuitive feel and allow for more complex computations of price and the impacts on demand.

Changing consumer demands

Despite the drop in travel and tourism during global pandemic of the early 2020s, the overall trends for the sector are buoyant. Travelers and visitors are seeking more personalised travel and hotel experiences, which means collecting data to focus on each guest's individual preferences and tastes. Business travel is often combined more frequently with leisure, breaking down the traditional groups for segmentation.

In Chapter 8 we will consider some of the performance measurement tools used in the tourism and hospitality industries to monitor performance in these key areas.

Changing role of the finance function

In the last few years, it has been clear that, across all sectors of business, the role of the finance function is changing. The continuing introduction of automated processes for the collection of data, book keeping and maintenance of records releases the unit financial controller from the 'bean counter' type role from the past. Increasingly, finance directors and controllers are required to make the leap to respond more directly to the imperatives of the business agenda and provide support to the business operators. In the hospitality and tourism industries they are key members of the management team and act as architects in the planning process. The finance specialists in the hospitality industry in particular have in the past been more likely to be qualified by experience rather than through formal examination. This pattern is now changing and increasingly qualified accountants are very much in demand to support the business. This trend is discussed more in the final chapter of the text.

Key financial issues

There are a number of key financial topics which have particular relevance for the hospitality and tourism industries. These issues are specific to an industry which is dependent on the use of long term assets and subject, as a result, to a high proportion of fixed costs. The topics include:

- Accurate valuation of property and assets
- Valuation of brands
- Information needs arising from changing patterns of ownership management contracts and franchising
- Performance management and benchmarking.

All of these aspects are addressed in later chapters of the text.

Summary

The purpose of this chapter has been to introduce the concept of strategic management and to highlight the importance of tailoring information systems to provide relevant information to assist the manager in the decision-making process. The key strategic issues for the hospitality and tourism industry have also been introduced at this stage.

Questions

1. Why is the development of corporate strategy important for the operators in the tourism industries?
2. What are the key challenges facing the hospitality and tourism industries over the next 5-10 years?

Practical activities

1. Select an organisation with which you are familiar and list the key stakeholders for that organisation. Discuss the relative significance and influence of each group on the strategic direction of the business.
2. Consider an organisation with which you are familiar. Does that organisation have a clearly defined strategy? Who in the organisation knows about the strategy and how is it communicated throughout the organisation?
3. Select a stock exchange listed organisation in the tourism and/or hospitality industries and search for the published accounts. Search for the mission statement or a formal statement of organisational purpose. Review this statement and comment on how meaningful it is.

References and further reading

Atrill, P. & Mclaney E. (2021) *Accounting and Finance for Non-Specialists*, 12th Edition, Pearson.

American Hotel & Lodging Educational Institute (2014) *Uniform System of Accounts for the Lodging Industry*, 11th Edition. (https://usali.hftp.org/)

Drucker, P.F. (1994). The theory of the business. *Harvard Business Review*, Sept–Oct, 95–104.

Department of Trade and Industry (DTI, 1998, p.2) *Small Firms Introduction to Franching*, London: DTI

Johnson, G., Whittington, R., Scholes K., Angwin, D. & Regner P. (2017) *Exploring Strategy (Test and Cases)*, Pearson.

OECD (2021) *Corporate Governance Factbook* Corporate-Governance-Factbook-Chapter-1.pdf (oecd.org) accessed 27/11/2023

Porter, M. E. (1996). What is a strategy? *Harvard Business Review*: Nov-Dec, 61-78.

Williamson, O.E, (1995) *Organization Theory: from Chester Barnard to the present and beyond*, Oxford University Press.

Useful websites

www.finance4hospitality.co.uk An online community with bite sized content and resources developed by experts in hospitality accounting.

www.tutor2u.net This is an excellent site which has a range of appropriate tools and aspects of strategy.

www.netmba.com This is quite a comprehensive American site covering a range of business management related topics including (amongst others) finance, accounting, economics, operations and, of course, strategy.

www.themanager.com There is a wealth of good information on this site, as well as a range of good and relevant articles, examples and Powerpoint presentations.

www.tomorrowscompany.com The Centre for Tomorrow's Company is a think-tank and catalyst, researching and stimulating the development of a new agenda for business.

www.themanager.org/Knowledgebase A range of online resources in a number of management disciplines including strategy.

www.valuebasedmanagement.net/methods_strategy_maps_strategic_communication.html Site dedicated to the development of strategy maps.

2 Introducing strategic financial management

About this chapter

This chapter will consider the tools available to the manager to assist in the strategic management process and will examine the role of management accounting systems in supporting this process. The stages within the strategic management process have been described as forming part of a continual process of analysis based on planning and control. Successful strategic decision making requires the support of an efficient management information system which should be designed to meet the needs of the individual organisation and will be required to adapt as the strategy develops. This chapter will consider in particular:

- ☐ The purpose of management accounting
- ☐ Examples of tools for strategic analysis
- ☐ Traditional management accounting versus strategic management accounting
- ☐ Strategic management accounting trends for the hospitality industry.

Learning objectives

On completion of this chapter, you should be able to:

- ☐ Distinguish between the use of management accounting and financial accounting
- ☐ Apply a range of tools and models for business analysis
- ☐ Understand how to apply a range of strategic models to determine the strategic positioning of the business
- ☐ Understand the concept of strategic management accounting.

Introduction

All business enterprises are required to monitor their financial activities and, depending on the size of the organisation, produce accurate audited accounts for external inspection. The disclosure requirements for small unlimited businesses are fairly basic, with often just the balance sheet to be submitted to the regulatory authorities based on the profit and loss and cash flow. At the other end of the spectrum, the published annual accounts of the larger listed companies are required to be somewhat more detailed. It is this information, in the form of the financial statements and the accompanying notes, which provides the potential investor and other external users with some insight into the strengths and weaknesses of the business and will affect the decision whether to engage with the business or not. Investors will be looking to understand the viability and performance of the business in terms of annual returns and investment opportunities. This activity is called financial accounting and is regulated by international and local statutory requirements such as the International Financial Reporting Standards (IFRS). The level of information required depends on the size and structure of the business as Table 2.1 illustrates.

Criteria	Reporting requirements
Micro entities	
Very small companies with any 2 of the following: ~ a turnover of £632,000 or less ~ £316,000 or less on its balance sheet ~ 10 employees or less	~ prepare simpler accounts that meet statutory minimum requirements ~ send only your balance sheet with less information to Companies House ~ benefit from the same exemptions available to small companies
Small companies	
~ a turnover of £10.2 million or less ~ £5.1 million or less on its balance sheet ~ 50 employees or less	~ use the exemption so company's accounts do not need to be audited ~ choose whether or not to send the directors' report and profit and loss account to Companies House ~ send abridged accounts to Companies House
Medium sized companies	
To be a medium-sized company, you must meet at least 2 of the following conditions: ~ the annual turnover must be no more than £36 million ~ the balance sheet total must be no more than £18 million ~ the average number of employees must be no more than 250	Medium-sized accounts must include: ~ a profit and loss account ~ a balance sheet, showing the printed name and signature of a director ~ notes to the accounts ~ group accounts (if appropriate) The accounts should be accompanied by: ~ a directors' report including a business review (or strategic report) showing the printed name of the approving secretary or director ~ an auditor's report that includes the name of the registered auditor (unless the company is exempt)

Table 2.1: Statutory requirements for reporting (sourced from www.gov.uk)

Statutory financial accounts, however, are insufficiently detailed to support the managers working within the business. Key operating information such as material and wage costs, overhead expenditure and the related percentages are not clearly visible, and individual departments within the business are hidden through the process of consolidation. The senior management team needs regular data and information, some of which will arrive on a daily basis either electronically or via team briefings, with a full detailed report available on a monthly basis. These regular internal reports are generated via the process called management accounting, where detailed reports and statistics are produced containing information tailored to meet the needs of that sector of the business.

In today's world the finance function has a critical role to play both in ensuring that financial reporting is true and accurate, to meet statutory requirements, but also in providing appropriate information for management decision making purposes as illustrated in Figure 2.1.

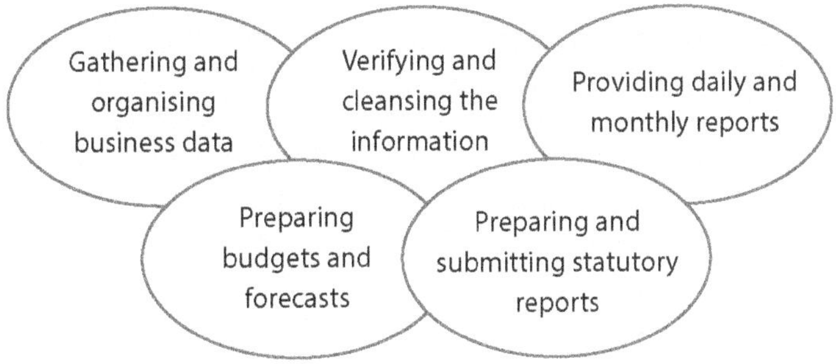

Figure 2.1: The role of the finance function in organisational decision making

It is essential that the finance function provides the central point for all data about the business and uses this to break down departmental silos. For example, with the increase in statutory requirements for sustainability reporting the finance function has a key role to play in collecting, sharing and reporting data.

In Chapter 1 a range of stakeholders were identified and each of these groups has an interest in business performance. These are summarised in Figure 2.2

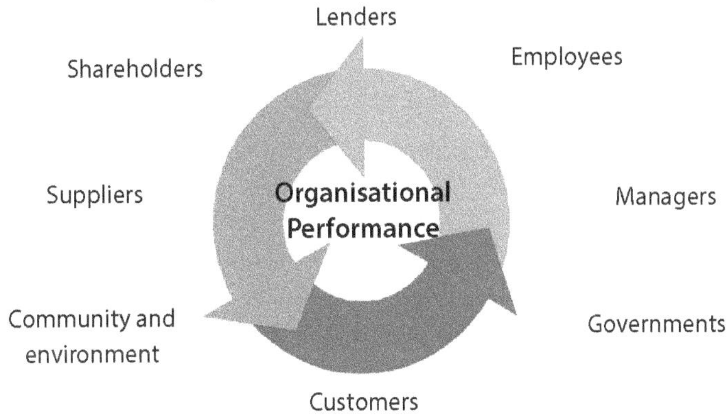

Figure 2.2: Business stakeholders

The nature of management accounting

Financial accounting involves the actual recording of every financial transaction and, therefore, operates in a historical framework. The result is a set of published statements prepared to meet the demands of a legal framework and generally accepted accounting practice. Management accounting is the process of analysing, planning and controlling the business with the purpose of supporting the financial and operational decision-making process. The emphasis, therefore, in management accounting is to provide as much information as is possible to assist the manager in controlling and developing the business. Consequently, there are several differences between financial accounting and management accounting, and these are summarised as follows in Table 2.2.

	Financial accounting	Management accounting
Legal requirements	Statutory reporting requirements	Subject to the needs of managers
Users	External stakeholders	Management team
Time dimension	Past and present	Past, present and future forecasts
Report frequency	Quarterly and annually	Daily, weekly, monthly
Scope	Summarised for the whole business	Detailed by business unit and department
Emphasis	Accuracy	Timely for decision making
Criteria	Objective and verifiable	Relevant, useful, understandable
Nature of information	Prepared to meet statutory requirements	Prepared to meet the needs of managers guidelines

Table 2.2: Financial accounting versus management accounting. Adapted from M. Allen and D. Myddelton, *Essential Management Accounting*, 1992 p.7.

The aim in management accounting is to help the management team run the business and consequently an effective management accounting system segments the business into key operating areas such as the revenue generating departments and the supporting departments, known as the overhead or undistributed operating expenses. Ideally each departmental manager receives individually tailored reports containing the appropriate level of detailed information. The way in which the business is segmented is discussed further later in the text.

Tools for strategic analysis

In Chapter 1 we identified that a key part of the strategic management process is the strategic analysis of the business to establish what is happening and why. Having established this, it is then possible to develop strategic options for moving forward. Strategic management information about the business enables these tools to be used effectively to establish where the business is currently positioned and the strategic decisions it should take in the future. There are many approaches to strategic analysis and various tools are available for analysing the internal capabilities and resources of the business. This section aims to consider those most widely discussed, including:

- ☐ SWOT analysis / PESTEL analysis
- ☐ Product life cycles
- ☐ Portfolio analysis

SWOT analysis

A simple approach for analysing the internal and external aspects of an organisation is contained in the form of a SWOT analysis. SWOT stands for strengths, weaknesses, opportunities and threats and is often displayed in 2x2 matrix as shown in Figure 2.3.

Figure 2.3: The component parts of a SWOT analysis

The *strengths* and *weaknesses* refer to the internal capabilities of the business compared to the competition and the general expectations of the marketplace. These could include both financial and non-financial factors. Strengths are special attributes or distinctive characteristics which can be identified in the organisation such as unique products, service or location. Weaknesses are issues which make the organisation less effective than other similar operations in meeting customer and investor expectations. Weaknesses could include lack of investment, poor training or out-of-date products or services. It is essential that the analysis should be performed honestly, and the results compared to the aims of the organisation as set out in the mission statement and goals. Techniques for performing the analysis, such as resource audits and performance measurement are considered in detail later in this chapter and in Part 3.

An analysis of the *opportunities* and *threats* should take account of all the external factors in the environment in which the business operates and the relationships amongst them. An opportunity is any chance to follow a new or revised strategy that could be of benefit to the organisation. Opportunities may simply exist but more usually need to be created. These could include new market opportunities or changing patterns in consumer demand. Threats are possible events or circumstances which have the potential to seriously damage the organisations ability to achieve its goals and objectives by directly impacting on revenue and profitability. The SWOT tool is often used with a tool for analysing the external environment called a PESTEL analysis. As Figure 2.4 illustrates, each letter in the acronym refers to a factor in the business environment which may present an opportunity or a threat to the organisation.

The opportunities and threats can then be structured based on the PESTLE model discussed below.

Political	How does the political environment impact the sector? Is there government support via financial incentives? Is there political stability?
Economic	What will be the impact of changes in GDP, inflation, interest rates and exchange rates?
Social	What are the trends impacting on consumer choices? What are the markets segments for your business? How are the customer demographics changing?
Technological	How will technological advances impact your business? What technologies are required for promoting your business and taking reservations? Billing and payments Data management Artificial intelligence
Environmental	ESG strategies Carbon footprint measurement Energy, Water and Waste management
Legislation	Upcoming legislation impacting on operations, construction, investment etc.

Figure 2.4: The components of a PESTEL analysis

A good SWOT analysis should highlight the critical success factors for a business and hence highlight those areas where a change in strategy is likely to have the most beneficial effect. However, a SWOT analysis is only an aid to strategic planning and the process should be carried out with considerable management judgment. There are other models which can also be used to provide a detailed analysis of the current position.

Case study: A review of business using SWOT analysis

Internal	**Strengths** • Overall financial performance • Positive cash flow • Profitability of products • Asset usage • Intellectual know how	**Weaknesses** • Reliance on loans for funding • Decreasing asset values • Declining revenues and increasing costs • Staff shortages • Aging assets
External	**Opportunities** • New markets for customers • Unutilised capacity • Cheap finance for further investment • Demand available • Changing customer expectations	**Threats** • Rising costs and inflation • World economy • Trade barriers • Heavy discounting by competitors • Increasing operational costs • Climate change

The product life cycle

It is generally believed that, from launch, products and services follow a 'life cycle', based on the current market conditions, which has significant implications for the future strategic direction of the business. The concept has faced some criticism in recent times, in that businesses can often only determine where they have *been* in relation to the life cycle rather than where they are *going*. The theory separates the economic life of the product or service into a number of life-cycle stages:

- Introduction or birth
- Growth
- Shake-out
- Maturity
- Decline

These stages are illustrated in Figure 2.5.

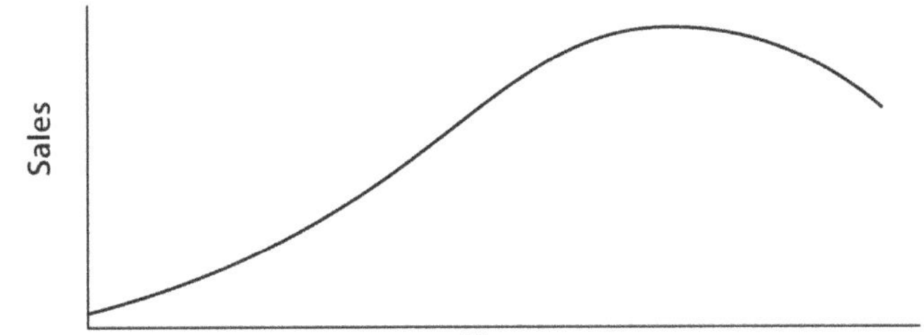

Figure 2.5: The Product Life Cycle

Stage 1 is the development and launch of the product or service and the initial sales growth will be slow. This is a period of high risk as it is quite feasible that the product or idea will fail completely. If the product is accepted by the market, there follows a period of rapid sales growth. This is **Stage 2.** Normally the potential level of sales is not infinite and eventually the rate of growth will slow. It is quite possible that other companies will enter the market at this point and will benefit from the experiences of the pioneering company who have carried the high risk through the development stage. This point is particularly true in the hospitality and catering industry where the new product is available to all by simply purchasing the product or service, and new ideas can quickly be copied without the need to go through the development stage. A number of new companies may quickly enter the market, rapidly increasing the volumes of the product available.

Stage 3 is defined as the period of shake-out which occurs when rapid growth coincides with the start of a fall in market growth. During this period there may be a period of rationalisation in the market place when several competitors leave the industry or are taken over and the total capacity is stabilised.

Once a more stable position has been established with sales demand approximately meeting product provision a period of maturity ensues. This is **Stage 4** , and it may last for several years but eventually the demand for the product will start to fall as customer tastes change and other products have been introduced.

It is possible to attempt to sustain the maturity period by making changes to the product or by seeking out new markets. **Stage 5** is defined as the decline stage when sales are falling in a declining market.

Risk and the product life cycle

Assessment of risk is a significant activity undertaken at the board level in most organisations. A range of risks need to be identified and the impact on the business assessed. Risk can be categorised into a variety of types in terms of the source and the subsequent impact.

Financial risk is derived from the nature of the financing of the project and the cost structure of the business. Financing risk occurs when the project is funded by debt capital rather than equity (share) capital, with the risk arising from the fixed interest payments and the eventual need to repay the capital.

Operating risk refers to the cost structure and the nature of the costs experienced by the business. Costs which have to be paid regardless of the level of trading are known as *fixed costs* and a high proportion of these render a business high risk, with a corresponding high breakeven point.

Business risk arises from the inherent nature of the product. A business will try to achieve a balance by rejecting those projects with both high financial risk and high business risk. However, the combination of low business risk and high financial risk could provide very favourable returns for shareholders.

A type of risk with increasing relevance is that of **climate risk**, which has the potential to impact numerous businesses in the hospitality, travel and tourism sectors. This source of risk can impact both operations through unusual weather events for example, and longer-term strategic impact such as a reduction in business value due to the shortage of key resources such as water.

The stages of the product life cycle have different intrinsic levels of risk which the business has little control over as these are created by the outside environment. The launch stage is obviously the stage carrying greatest risk but the risk is also high in the development stage when the potential size of the market is still not known. As the market matures, the risk reduces and is concentrated on the length of the maturity stage. The final stage is low risk as the demand for the product dies and the company's strategy is tailored accordingly. Risk and return are invariably linked with a positive correlation in that if risk increases so must the return. This basic economic principle is illustrated in Figure 2.6.

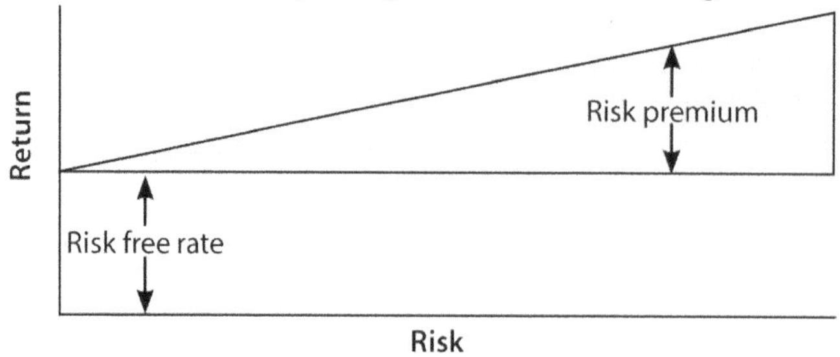

Figure 2.6: The relationship between risk and return

During the growth stage the cost per unit may be high but this can be compensated for by charging a premium for the product. The selling price is forced to stabilise or even fall in the maturity stage once the competition increases. During the maturity stage emphasis falls on improving quality to justify a premium price or where products are homogeneous, reducing operating costs whilst maintaining quality at the same level. Strategic methods for reducing costs in the maturity stage are considered in Chapter 4.

The product life cycle and management accounting

The various stages of the product life cycle raise several issues for the provision of strategic management accounting information. The type of information required for strategic decision making will vary depending on the stage at which the company is at in the product life cycle. A key part of the management accounting function should be to attempt to establish where the company is actually positioned and whether it is about to enter a new phase. The difficulty in pinpointing the current position is normally the most commonly cited criticism of the product life cycle theory, and although there will always have been an element of uncertainty, accounting information can be used to improve monitoring of the company's position. Table 2.3 illustrates the change in emphasis required at each stage of the product life cycle.

PLC Stage	*Launch*	*Growth*	*Maturity*
Product	Unsophisticated	Range widening	Proliferation
Market	Narrow segment	Wider growth	Mass market
Competition	Low	Intensifying	High cost producers exit
Price	High	Lower	Low
Profit	High/Medium	Medium	Lower
Cash	Negative	Positive	Cash rich

Table 2.3: Separate stages of the product life cycle

Each stage of the life cycle is now considered in detail in terms of

- Cash flows
- Level of operating expenses
- Performance measures.

Launch stage

A critical feature of the launch stage is that the cash flow of the business will be negative because funds are being used to develop, test and launch the new idea. If the concept is perceived to be successful more cash will be needed to invest on more non-current assets, working capital and launch marketing. Discounted cash flow (DCF) techniques are normally used with new concept launches, with the potential cash flows being projected well into the future and a discount rate used for the analysis which should reflect the perceived risk associated with the project, particularly in the early stages. However, at this stage the forecasted information cannot be sufficiently accurate to be of use for monitoring and controlling the project. Even if the initial evaluation of the project has proven to be positive, the business needs to consider how an appropriate set of financial control measures might attempt to monitor performance at this stage given the level of uncertainty. Using the DCF techniques, probabilities can be assigned to likely outcomes and the weighted average calculated. This approach is covered in more detail in Chapter 10, illustrating the advantages and disadvantages of such a technique.

Marketing expenditure will be crucial at this stage to establish the potential for the concept and above all the business should not be tempted to reduce marketing and research costs to earn short term profits as this will undermine the business's long term competitive position. It is likely at this stage that the operating costs will be fairly high and will remain so until the business is able to achieve cost reduction through improved operational techniques, the benefit of experience and sales volumes.

Traditional measures, such as return on investment, are wholly inappropriate at this stage. One of the primary objectives of a system for monitoring should be to collect information which reduces the risk associated with the project due to lack of knowledge. As a result the project should be controlled using milestones based on the achievement of overall objectives. This depends on the project being broken down into visible stages and each stage being assessed for likely expenditure. If this can be achieved, the project can be assessed at each stage to check that it is worth continuing. In order to achieve this, accounting systems need to be designed to be able to cope with an ever changing environment and as a consequence need to be flexible, informal and capable of rapid response.

Growth stage

Increasing marketing expenditure is still likely to be the key activity in order to create market growth as quickly as possible and to increase market share. At this stage it is common for the business to focus on product differentiation by emphasising the particular product attributes. At some point the law of diminishing returns set in and any further increases in marketing will not be worthwhile.

Once the product is successfully launched and the market begins to grow, financial measures become more important. Forecasting should now be considerably more accurate and the accounting measures should be able to pin point the optimum expenditure level to avoid wasted expenditure. As the market for the product expands, the business needs to grow its own sales faster than the market to increase market share. Therefore, the management accounting system should be producing information to analyse the competitors' existing marketing strategies and potential responses to changes in the organisational strategy. Sales revenues will now have increased rapidly from those produced during the launch stage but the overall cash flow of the business may still not yet be positive as extensive investment is required to sustain the growth of the business. Profits should not be the main focus stage at this stage as the company should be reinvesting in marketing and research expenditure to maximise the opportunities in the market.

Maturity stage

Once the maturity stage has been established the management style should focus on control. It is at this stage that the overall profits can be maximized, and cash flows turn positive. A typical feature of this stage is overcapacity in the market as the level of competitors increase. As a result, an extremely competitive environment is created and some operators will be forced out of business or will fall victim to takeovers and mergers. Further investment is now no longer necessary, and marketing should be aimed at maintaining market share rather than attempting to increase it. The financial control process should focus on the shorter-term performance of the business, emphasising profitability and cash flow generation. This is the most cash positive stage of the business and the business should aim to maximize the benefit of these cash returns. Consequently, the control of costs at this stage is crucial and should be principally aimed at strategically reducing unit costs in relation to the competitors. Price competition will become more important at this stage, particularly if over-capacity exists and the product is well understood by the customer. An alternative is to focus on a particular aspect, such levels of service or unique selling qualities of the product.

At this stage it is appropriate to use a profit measure to control the business and return on investment is usually considered to be the most appropriate. To ensure this ratio is used effectively, the profit margins should be monitored carefully and the manager will need information on cost structures in terms of fixed and variable costs and, where possible, similar information for the competition. The strategic thrust at this stage is to maximize cost efficiencies and achieve maximum profitability.

A business needs to carefully monitor the market in order to accurately predict when it is entering the maturity stage as a different strategic approach is required at this point. The maturity stage can be identified by reviewing the total market size and the share held by the business. Care needs to be taken to ensure that the market really has matured and that it is not simply a temporary drop in market growth. Techniques for establishing market size and share are discussed in Chapter 5.

Decline stage

The decline stage of a concept will inevitably be reached due to changing customer needs. At this stage all costs which are no longer necessary should be removed, with no further investment being necessary as the existing assets are worked on until the end of their life. Financial measures such as return on capital and profitability are no longer valid as appropriate methods of financial control. The short-term measure of free cash flow is regarded as the best measure at this stage and the preparation of short term cash flows is crucial. Cash flows may exceed profits due to declining requirements for working capital. In the hospitality industry the decline stage can be avoided by changing the nature of the business concept to match consumer needs. This is often achieved through the use of brands, which are for many organisations transferable between products and concepts, so it may be necessary to remove the branding image from a declining concept and apply it to a more growth orientated area.

Boston Consulting Group matrix

The Boston Consulting Matrix is a general strategic planning concept which can be used with the product life cycle. The simplest version of this matrix is the one produced by the Boston Consulting Group (BCG). Other more complex models have followed but the majority are based on the principles demonstrated in the BCG matrix. It should be noted that all these models require managerial judgment and common sense to make them workable in a practical situation. The matrix illustrated in Figure 2.7 enables a business to plot the position of each of its products or brands in terms of relative market share and total rate of market growth.

		Relative Market Share	
		High	Low
Market growth	High	Star	Question Mark
	Low	Cash Cow	Dog

Figure 2.7: The Boston Matrix

The rate of market growth is an attempt to measure the level of attractiveness of the industry in terms of the rate of growth of the total market available for a product. Relative market share is a guide to the competitive strength of the business in the marketplace, because companies with a dominant market share tend to produce higher financial returns. However, other factors such as service quality and operational efficiency are also influential in determining the relative financial performance. The Boston Matrix can be used as a strategic planning device if the position of the company can be identified. There may be some relationship between the stages of the BCG matrix and the product life cycle, although this is not always the case as they are based on different parameters (see Table 2.4).

Product life cycle	BCG matrix
Launch	Question marks
Growth	Star
Maturity	Cash cow
Decline	Dog

Table 2.4: Relationship between the Boston Consulting Group (BCG) matrix and the product life cycle

Like the product life cycle, it is more successfully used for charting past performance than for predicting future performance. The characteristics for each stage are illustrated in Figure 2.8

STAR Cash user Lower prices Intensifying competition Wider market Developing product	**QUESTION MARKS** Cash user High prices Low competition Narrow market Unsophisticated product
CASH COW Cash generator Low prices Mass market Intense rivalry Proliferation of product	**DOGS** Cash generator Low prices Market declining Competitors exit Withdraw product

Figure 2.8: Boston matrix characteristics

The use of the Boston Matrix leads to a focus on diversification strategies. The analysis tends to encourage the use of positive cash flows from business activities in the mature stage to fund new ventures and concepts. The positive aspect of this is that diversification reduces risk, but in practice such a policy can lead to a lack of focus and increasing corporate costs arising from managing a diverse portfolio of activities.

General Electric matrix

This model replaces market growth with market attractiveness, and competitive strength replaces market share as the dimension by which the competitive position of each SBU is assessed. Illustrated in Figure 2.9, this model is sometimes known as the directional policy matrix.

		Market attractiveness		
		High	Medium	Low
Competitive strength	High			
	Medium			
	Low			

Figure 2.9: General Electric matrix

Market attractiveness on the vertical axis is the weighted average of a range of factors including size of industry, profitability, growth rate, nature of competition, business cycle and the ability to gain economies of scale.

This is compared on the horizontal axis to competitive strength, which the weighted average of a range of factors including market share, profit levels, management ability, production capability and technological strength. The aim is to plot every aspect of the business to illustrate how each relates to the other in terms of competitiveness and attractiveness.

Designing strategic management accounting systems

The term 'strategic management accounting' was first used in the 1980s, and The Chartered Institute of Management Accountants (CIMA) defined it as *"the provision and analysis of management accounting data about a business and its competitors, for use in developing and monitoring business strategy"*, based on the work of Keith Simmonds.

In today's world, the majority of management accounting systems are designed to process large volumes of data on a routine daily basis. This approach is certainly adequate where historical information is known to be a sound basis for future decisions. However, strategic decisions which are designed to change the direction of the business cannot be supported by information which has simply been produced by extrapolating the past performance to represent the future. Traditional accounting systems tended to focus on the past, and financial planning is limited to an extension of the budgetary process. As the concept of strategic management accounting developed, Shaw (1994) highlighted the key areas for financial planning and control by identifying the differences between a traditional and a strategic approach. Table 2.5 is adapted from his recommendations.

Activity	*Strategic Approach*	*Traditional Approach*
Corporate strategy	Financial planning consistent with strategic aims based on internal capabilities and resource availability	Generally financial planning concentrates on the operational aspects of budgetary control
Capital structure	Capital structure intended to reduce cost of capital and minimise shareholder risk	Capital raised as and when it is needed leading to a possible increase in cost of capital
Dividend policy	Dividends paid only once all other possible more profitable uses of retained funds have been explored	Dividend payment level set to maximise shareholder wealth and raise share price in the short term
Investment decisions	Management only invest in projects which provide positive discounted cash flows (net present value)	Reliance on profit based capital investment appraisal methods where profit is compared to investment

Profitability	Management seek to improve the long term profitability of the business and return on capital employed	General emphasis on short profit maximisation in order to improve Earnings per Share (EPS)
Working Capital	Focus on internal cash flows	Focus on profit flows
Pricing policy	Pricing focuses on product and market considerations	Pricing based on cost and profit per unit expectations
Performance Measures	Tend to be on a historical period by period basis emphasising internal operations	To include a range of measures based on internal and external factors including financial and non financial values

Table 2.5: Differences between a traditional and strategic approach to accounting

Some strategic decisions require one-off evaluation, for example, a decision to open a new unit or revenue generating area within an existing business. The financial evaluation requires assessing the net incremental effect impact on the business. Similarly, the cost of closing a business requires an evaluation of the opportunity costs of such an action. It may be necessary to consider the cost of or benefit from continuing, closing or selling to another party. To support these types of decisions the management accounting system needs to consider future incremental cash flows. This can present a problem to traditional management accounting systems which tend to focus on historical costs based on direct costs and indirect costs which have been apportioned across the organisation. Consequently, the aims and objectives of each strategic decision need to be clearly stated, and information produced based on incremental costs only, to monitor whether the targets are in fact being met.

A range of financial performance measures should be used to assess the economic performance of the business and managerial performance. The measures should be tailored to the strategies and may need to change in focus over time.

Economic performance focuses on the performance of the business in relation to the external environment, in order to monitor the effect of all economic factors which are likely to affect the business, regardless of management performance. Managerial performance can be assessed through the use of responsibility centers, where an individual is monitored by evaluating only those revenues and costs which are controllable. The aim is to provide a system which motivates managers and clearly highlights good performance. The accounting system should produce information for internal use which is user-friendly in presentation and relevant to the needs of the user. It is essential that the information produced by accountants is understandable by the managers who need to use it. Therefore, reports should be tailored to meet the requirements of the user and this could include the use of graphs, pie charts and histograms to aid the less numerate manager.

The process of standard costing can be a useful element of a strategic management accounting system. A *standard cost* is an estimate of the cost of one unit of production, such as a bed night or a meal, and these can be used effectively for forecasting and for making comparisons to actual performance, which forms the basis of budgetary control.

There remains no consensus on a precise definition of what should be included in a system for strategic management accounting, but Drury in some of the earliest studies (2005) identified three key strands:

- ☐ The extension of traditional management accounting's internal focus to include external information about competitors.
- ☐ The relationship between the strategic position chosen by a business and the expected emphasis on management accounting.
- ☐ Gaining competitive advantage by analysing ways to decrease costs and/or enhance the differentiation of a firm's product, through exploiting linkages in the value chain and optimising cost drivers.

In more recent research published by CIMA, based on interviews with senior finance executives, it was found that the key techniques used in management accounting for supporting the strategic management process are investment appraisal, bench marking and customer profitability analysis. The following chapters of this text consider the traditional topics associated with financial and management accounting and in each case the processes described are illustrated with examples and recommendations for a strategic approach.

Summary

Many businesses use traditional management accounting systems which focus on the internal aspects of the business and the regular production of routine data. A strategic approach to management accounting includes having an external focus to monitor changes in the environment whilst providing information which enables strategic decisions to be evaluated. The power of information technology can be harnessed to produce reports which are not only timely and relevant but also enable sensitivity analysis and prediction modeling to take place. The remainder of this text will now consider some of the modern approaches available to the hospitality industry to improve the decision-making process and the subsequent monitoring and control of those decisions.

Questions

1. Many decisions in financial management in a large organisation are taken in an environment of conflicting stakeholder viewpoints. Identify the key stakeholders and give examples of possible sources of conflict.
2. Explain the difference between operational and strategic decisions in the hospitality industry.
3. Give a definition of strategic management accounting and explain how this can be used in the hospitality and tourism industries.
4. The various stages of the Product Life Cycle raise a number of issues for the provision of management accounting information. Describe each stage of the cycle and consider how each of the following differs at each stage:

a. Cash flows

b. Level of operating expenses

c. Performance Measures

References and further reading

Drury, C. (2005) *Management Accounting for Business*, Cengage Learning

Evans, N. (2024) *Strategic Management for Tourism, Hospitality and Events*, Routledge

Pitcher, G., (2018) *Management Accounting in Support of Strategy: How Management Accounting Can Aid the Strategic Management Process*, Business Expert Press

Ransley, J., Ingram, H. and Adams, D. (2022) *Developing Hospitality Properties and Facilities*. Routledge

Schmidgall, R. (2016) *Hospitality Industry Managerial Accounting*. Educational Institute of the American Hotel Motel Association

Shaw, H., (1993) *Strategic Financial Management (Managing Finance)*, Elm Publications

Simmonds, K. (1981) *The Fundamentals of Strategic Management Accounting*, Institute of Cost and Management Accountants

Ward, K. (2012) *Strategic Management Accounting*, Routledge

Useful websites

www.finance4hospitality.co.uk An online community with bite sized content and resources developed by experts in hospitality accounting.

www.businessballs.com A general management site which covers an immense array of general material.

www.tutor2u.net An excellent site which has a range of appropriate tools and aspects of strategy.

www.netmba.com A comprehensive American site covering a range of business management related topics including (amongst others) finance, accounting, economics, operations and, of course, strategy.

www.tomorrowscompany.com The Centre for Tomorrow's Company is a think-tank and catalyst, researching and stimulating the development of a new agenda for business.

www.themanager.org/Knowledgebase A range of online resources in a number of management disciplines including strategy.

www.valuebasedmanagement.net/methods_strategy_maps_strategic_communication.html A site dedicated to the development of strategy maps.

www.valuebasedmanagement.net/methods_bcgmatrix.html Information on the Boston Consulting Group Matrix

3 Understanding financial statements

About this chapter

Most business managers working in the hospitality, tourism and leisure industries will need at some point in their professional lives to be able to interpret and act upon financial information. The results of any commercial business are usually summarised in three key statements: the Income & Expenditure account (profit and loss), the Statement of Financial Position (balance sheet) and the Statement of Cash Flow, and these are prepared at a minimum at least once per year in the form of audited, publicly available statements (for public companies) and internally within the business several times per year, usually on a monthly basis (management accounts). The aim of this chapter is to provide guidance for understanding how these statements are prepared and the importance of the information contained within them. There will be no attempt in the text to illustrate and teach the principles of double entry bookkeeping as this aspect is covered in a multitude of resources on the subject. However, this chapter is very much concerned with the accounting principles and concepts which support the preparation of financial statements, which then helps the reader to understand the purpose and meaning. This includes a detailed review of each of the financial statements and an explanation of the relationship between the statements. A more detailed review of the techniques for interpreting statements, using a variety of forms of ratio analysis, is given in Chapter 8.

Learning objectives

On completion of this chapter, you should be able to:

- ☐ Appreciate the role of the regulatory framework in accounting
- ☐ Understand the fundamental concepts of accruals and prepayments
- ☐ Understand the principles for adjusting non-current asset accounts with regard to depreciation
- ☐ Appreciate the methodologies for the adjustment of the stock records to calculate cost of sales and incorporate the current valuation
- ☐ Recognise the structures for the income and expenditure account, cash flow and statement of financial position.

Introduction

Accounting is divided into separate but related branches of accounting called financial accounting, management accounting and cost accounting. The function of financial accounting is to record clearly every single financial transaction of the business in both the selling and the production of goods and services, and to classify and summarise these transactions for presentation in a series of published reports produced on an annual basis to meet statutory requirements. These reports are then used by external users who have access to very little other information other than that which is published about the business. These external users include shareholders, bank and other lenders, government, and the tax authorities and of course customers and competitors. Management accounting and cost accounting are for internal use.

Accounting principles

The statements contained in the published reports are required to give a fair and true representation of the business. To assist in the preparation of the statements to this standard, there are a series of rules and regulations to be adhered to. In the UK these are derived from:

- ☐ International Financial Reporting Standards (IFRS)
- ☐ UK Generally Accepted Accounting Practice (UKGAAP)

Non-statutory regulation is based on recommendations issued by the professional accounting bodies. The six accountancy bodies in the UK are:

- ☐ The Chartered Institute of Management Accountants (CIMA)
- ☐ The Institute of Chartered Accountants in England and Wales (ICAEW)
- ☐ The Institute of Chartered Accountants of Scotland (ICAS)
- ☐ The Institute of Chartered Accountants of Ireland (ICAI)
- ☐ The Association of Chartered Certified Accountants (ACCA)
- ☐ The Chartered Institute of Public Finance and Accountancy (CIPFA)

The preparation of financial statements is also clarified by the acceptance of accounting principles which should be uniformly applied. In practice, however, there is a considerable degree of user interpretation. The following notes provide a summary of the basic principles in statement preparation.

- ☐ **Consistency:** The accounting treatment of any items should be the same from period to period. For example, a change in the methodology for depreciating non-current assets could have a material impact on the reported profit. If this is the case, then the change made should be revealed.
- ☐ **Going concern:** An organisation is assumed to continue in operation for the foreseeable future with appropriate investment to sustain it.
- ☐ **Matching:** The costs for a period should be matched with the corresponding revenue for that period. For example, outstanding operational costs at the year end should be included if they were used to deliver the revenue.

- **Materiality:** Changes in accounting practice are only permissible if the effect is not material. The accounting techniques used should reflect the reality as closely as possible to give a true and fair view of the accounts.
- **Stated values:** Accounting records are kept for those events measured in monetary terms.
- **Prudence:** Provision should be made for all likely costs, whereas profits should not be accounted for until realised.
- **Separate entity:** A business is considered to have a separate entity to its owners, which means that personal transactions are excluded from business accounts.

The effect of the accounting policies mentioned above is effectively illustrated by comparing the cash flow and the income and expenditure account of a business. The cash flow shows simply all revenues actually received and all costs actually paid. The profit and loss account recognises both debtors and creditors. Debtors are those sales not yet received although the transaction for the sale has taken place and goods and services have been exchanged. Creditors are expenses which have been used in the accounting period but have not yet paid for. As an example, many businesses plan to pay suppliers in around 45 days from the invoice point. This means that in the monthly income and expenditure account the cost of these supplies must be accounted for although the invoice has not actually been paid.

This is called the *accruals* concept, and forms the basis of many accounting systems around the world, whereby the non-cash effects of transactions and other events should be reflected, as far as possible, in the financial statements for the accounting period in which they occur, and not, for example, in the period in which any cash involved is received or paid. Similarly, a business may pay for products and services which it has not yet used, such as annual charges for rent paid in advance. The income and expenditure account must be adjusted to include only the cost of what has been actually consumed or used and the remainder of the payment is shown as a current asset in the balance sheet, ready to be used in later periods.

Profit is calculated by considering all the sales transacted for both cash and credit and matching these with all the costs of producing and delivering the sales. As a consequence, the operating cash flow can be quite different to the operating profit over similar time periods. In the following sections we will consider the accounting treatment of specific items and activities relevant to the hospitality industry. In the preparation of accounts, a series of adjustments are required to create the Income and Expenditure Account, and these include provisions, accruals and prepayments. Depreciation is a form of provision to allow for the wearing out of the long-term assets held by the business such as buildings and equipment. Each accounting period a measure of the wearing out of the asset is set against the profit for the period. There are different methods available for calculating the depreciation charge and profits will vary depending on which method is used. The following section provides guidelines for the more common approaches.

What is depreciation?

Depreciation is a charge made to the profits of the business to write off part of the value of a non-current asset. The more common forms of non-current asset for asset intensive businesses are land and buildings, equipment and machinery and motor vehicles. In the hospitality industry the assets inside the building are known generally as Fixtures, Fittings and Equipment (FF&E). All assets must be depreciated; although in the majority of cases, land will not depreciate as this is considered to have an indefinite useful life.

Equipment and machinery can take a variety of forms but includes fixtures and furnishing, computer equipment, motor vehicles and specialist technology. Each category of item should be depreciated using an estimate of the useful life of the asset resulting in a nil value or a scrap value at the end of its life. For example, motor vehicles tend to depreciate more quickly in the early part of their life and it may be appropriate to depreciate the asset more heavily in the early years to reflect this. FRS 102 does not stipulate which assets must be subjected to which depreciation methods; however, in practice the straight-line and reducing balance methods are the most popular.

Straight line method versus reducing balance

The total depreciation to be charged over the life of the asset is calculated by measuring the difference between the original cost and the residual value, which is the value of the asset at the end of its life or period which is being considered. The straight-line method for calculating the annual depreciation charge is then to simply divide this figure by the estimated life in years. This results in an equal charge each year. An alternative approach is the 'reducing balance' method which involves depreciating the asset by a fixed percentage each year based on the year-end value of the asset. This results in higher levels of depreciation being charged in the early years of the life of the asset. The difference between the two methods is illustrated by the following example.

Example

Kitchen equipment is purchased at a value of £10,000. The estimated life of the equipment is 5 years, when it is then considered to be worth zero. In the following example the reducing balance depreciation has been calculated using a factor of 50% as illustrated in Table 3.1.

Year	Straight-line Annual charge	Year end value	Reducing balance Annual charge	Year end value
	£	£	£	£
1	2,000	8,000	5,000	5,000
2	2,000	6,000	2,500	2,500
3	2,000	4,000	1,250	1,250
4	2,000	2,000	625	625
5	2,000	zero	313	312

Table 3.1: Comparison between straight-line charges and reducing balance charges

There is some flexibility available when choosing a depreciation rate in terms of both the method and the period over which the asset is to be depreciated. This discretion can lead to the possibility where identical businesses could declare different profit levels as a result of adopting alternative depreciation methods. A business which chooses to change its depreciation method from one accounting period to the next must declare in the published accounts that this has occurred as the profits may then be materially affected.

Revaluing non-current assets

A fundamental principle that underpins financial reporting is that assets must not be stated in the balance sheet at any more than the value that would be recovered if the asset was to be sold. If asset values are overstated or understated this clearly results in the accounts becoming misleading. Assets such as land and buildings can experience both sharp rises in value during boom periods and falls in value during recession. As a result, the accounts of the company can become seriously out of line with the market value. The issue of asset revaluations is certainly a challenging one for the hotel and resort industry in particular, where there is significant asset ownership and asset value can be impacted by a range of factors such as location, profitability and the competition. The approaches for estimating asset valuations is discussed in Chapter 13.

Accounting for inflation

Inflation is the rising of prices over time and the decrease in the purchasing value of money. Low inflation levels have little impact on the balance sheet. The problem with higher levels of inflation arises when valuing long term assets as the book value will always fall short of the true value. This can distort performance measures such as return on capital employed where current profits are compared to out-of-date asset values. In periods of high inflation the current assets, in particular inventory values, can be impacted as the relationship between sales and cost of sales is also distorted as the bought in price of materials becomes out of date. For the majority of inventory purchased in the hospitality and leisure industries, such as food, beverage and consumables there is little impact as the inventory is fast moving. However, for items held for longer period times, such as a stock of high value wines or other slow-moving inventory, there can be an impact on the values in the balance sheet. This matter is now considered in detail.

Stock valuations

There are four approaches to assessing what 'cost' means when used for stock valuation purposes. This is used in the calculation:

Opening Stock + Purchases – Closing Stock = Cost of Sales

Sales – Cost of Sales = Gross Profit

The method used will affect the calculation of the cost of sales figure in the profit and loss account and also affect the stock held value in the balance sheet. The methods are:

- **First in, first out (FIFO)** where the cost of the most recently purchased items will be reflected in the valuation. During periods of inflation the earliest items with the lowest price will appear to be issued first leading to a lower cost of sales calculation.
- **Last in, First out (LIFO)** where the latest and highest prices are charged to the profit and loss account resulting in a higher cost of sales figure and lower profits, as well as a lower stock valuation.
- **Average cost** where the value of stock at any one time is the average of all items of cost.
- **Replacement cost** is the present cost to replace the asset or stock item.

The information in Table 3.2 provides a summary of the inflows and outflows of a typical commodity recording the date of receipt and the purchase price and the date of issue. This is summarized in a second table (Table 3.3) to illustrate the differences in closing stock value depending on the method used.

Date	Units received	Purchase price	Units used	Market price
		£		£
1/1	600	10.00		10.00
5/1	200	12.00		12.00
10/1			300	12.00
15/1			400	13.00
20/1	100	14.00		14.00
30/1			50	15.00

Table 3.2: Summary of the inflows and outflows of a typical commodity

		RECEIVED/ISSUED			BALANCE	
Method	Date	Quantity	Price	Value	Quantity	Value
			£	£		£
FIFO	1/1	600	10.00	6,000	600	6,000
	5/1	200	12.00	2,400	800	8,400
	10/1	(300)	10.00	(3,000)	500	5,400
	15/1	(300)	10.00	(3,000)	200	2,400
		(100)	12.00	(1,200)	100	1,200
	20/1	100	14.00	1,400	200	2,600
	30/1	(50)	12.00	600	150	**2,000**
LIFO	1/1	600	10.00	6,000	600	6,000
	5/1	200	12.00	2,400	800	8,400
	10/1	(200)	12.00	(2,400)	600	6,000
		(100)	10.00	(1,000)	500	5,000
	15/1	(400)	10.00	(4,000)	100	1,000
	20/1	100	14.00	1,400	200	2,400
	30/1	(50)	14.00	700	150	**1,700**
AVERAGE £	1/1	600	10.00	6,000	600	6,000
	5/1	200	12.00	2,400	800	8,400
	10/1	(300)	10.50	(3,150)	500	5,250
	15/1	(400)	10.50	(4,200)	100	1,050
	20/1	100	14.00	1,400	200	2,450
	30/1	(50)	12.25	612.50	150	**1,838***

*Rounded

Table 3.3: Data to summarise calculation for the closing stock valuation

The FIFO method produces the highest closing stock valuation at £2,000 and this serves to reduce the value of cost of sales and therefore increases profitability. The LIFO method produces the lowest stock valuation at £1,700 thereby increasing the cost of sales and reducing profitability. For many businesses the average value or the replacement value provides the most consistent result. The management and control of stock levels in the hospitality and leisure industries is considered in detail in Chapter 7.

International Financial Reporting Standards

The systematic recording of financial data is universally based on double-entry bookkeeping principles and accruals accounting, which have been in use by businesses since the 1400s. However, differing regional practices have in the past resulted in the presentation of results by companies with significant differences in profits reported due to the national differences in accounting procedures. As a consequence, there has been a growing movement to harmonize the accounting regulatory frameworks.

The International Financial Reporting Standard (IFRS) were developed by the International Accounting Standards Board (IASB). The IASB is an independent standard-setting body within the IFRS Foundation. IFRS Accounting Standards are, in effect, a global accounting language – companies in more than 140 jurisdictions are required to use them when reporting on their financial health.

The accounting statements explained

The financial accounting statements are produced in order to convey the performance of the business. There are three main statements supported by additional statements and notes published in the Annual Report. The aim of this chapter is to provide the reader with an understanding of the basic principles underlying each key statement. This understanding will enable the reader to interpret the financial position of any organisation. The following chapters will develop this understanding further by providing additional tools for analysis such as ratio calculations using figures drawn from the financial statements. These principles can then be applied to the management accounts of the business.

The balance sheet

The balance sheet, also known as the statement of financial position, can be described as a snapshot of the business at a particular moment in time. The statement is based on data from a single day in the business and reflects what the business owns and owes on that date. It is based on the simple equation that the total value of what the company owns will equal the financial claims on the business, that is the *total liabilities*.

$$\text{Assets} = \text{Liabilities}$$

The total liabilities comprise both the liabilities of the business and the equity and so the formula becomes:

$$\text{Assets} = \text{Liabilities} + \text{Equity}$$

IFRS Accounting Standards
IFRS 1 First-time Adoption of International Financial Reporting Standards
IFRS 2 Share-based Payment
IFRS 3 Business Combinations
IFRS 5 Non-current Assets Held for Sale and Discounted Operations
IFRS 6 Exploration for and Evaluation for Mineral Resources
IFRS 7 Financial Instruments: Disclosures
IFRS 8 Operating Segments
IFRS 9 Financial Instruments
IFRS 10 Consolidated Financial Statements
IFRS 11 Joint Arrangements
IFRS 12 Disclosure of Interests in Other Entities
IFRS 13 Fair Value Measurement
IFRS 14 Regulatory Deferral Accounts
IFRS 15 Revenue from Contracts with Customers
IFRS 16 Leases
IFRS 17 Insurance Contracts
IAS Standards
IAS 1 Presentation of Financial Statements
IAS 2 Inventories
IAS 7 Statement of Cash Flows
IAS 8 Accounting Policies, Changes in Accounting Estimates and Errors
IAS 10 Events after the Reporting Period
IAS 12 Income Taxes
IAS 16 Property, Plant and Equipment
IAS 19 Employee Benefits
IAS 20 Accounting for Government Grants and Disclosure of Government Assistance
IAS 21 The Effects of Changes in Foreign Exchange Rates
IAS 23 Borrowing Costs
IAS 24 Related Party Disclosures
IAS 26 Accounting and Reporting by Retirement Benefit Plans
IAS 27 Separate Financial Statements
IAS 28 Investments in Associated and Joint Ventures
IAS 29 Financial Reporting in Hyperinflationary Economies
IAS 32 Financial Instruments: Presentation
IAS 33 Earnings per Share
IAS 34 Interim Financial Reporting
IAS 36 Impairment of Assets
IAS 37 Provisions Contingent Liabilities and Contingent Assets
IAS 38 Intangible Assets
IAS 39 Financial Instruments: Recognition and Measurement
IAS 40 Investment Property
IAS 41 Agriculture

Table 3.4: International Financial Reporting Standards. Source: https://www.ifrs.org/issued-standards/list-of-standards/

The items that the company owns are referred to as *assets* and can be subdivided into those which are long term or fixed in nature and those that are current.

Long term assets + Short term assets = Liabilities + Equity

Long term assets are those assets to be used for longer than the period of a year and these are also known as non-current assets or fixed assets. They are typically items such as land, buildings, equipment, machinery, computers and motor vehicles. These are all assets which are normally introduced into the business with the purpose of enabling it to function in order to make profit. They are described as being *tangible* assets because they can be seen and touched. Long term assets which cannot be physically accounted for are called *intangible*, and the most common of these is called *goodwill*. This arises when a business or assets are purchased for a value which exceeds the net value of the physical assets, but includes an established customer base. Another common intangible asset is that of *brand value* which features in financial accounts in many of the major hospitality, tourism and leisure companies in recognition of the value of the brand name. The valuation of brands is more complex, and this will be discussed in more detail in Chapter 13. Purchases of long-term assets are called *capital expenditure* or *CAPEX* items, and this area will be discussed further in Chapters 10 and 11.

Current assets include stock or inventory which may be sub divided into raw materials, work in progress and finished goods. In the hospitality, tourism and leisure industries the majority of stock is held as either raw materials or finished goods. Other current assets include outstanding sales from customers, known as *debtors* or *accounts receivable*, and the business cash balances. The current assets normally have a short life and are used up in the operation of the business.

There are several types of liability classified in terms of long term and short term. Long-term liabilities include loans from external parties who have lent to the business and who receive interest in return. The owner's capital or equity is also a type of liability in that it remains the property of the owner and technically could be repaid in the event of business closure, although in practice this is unlikely to occur. Returns to equity investors are paid in the form of dividends and are related to the performance of the business. Alternatively, the annual profits made could be re-invested in the company, and these are known as retained profits or reserves. In practice most businesses will aim to pay a dividend to shareholders and keep some profits to reinvest in the business, which will show in the balance sheet as retained earnings.

Short term or current liabilities can include bank overdrafts, taxation and outstanding balances owed to trade suppliers, known as *creditors* or *accounts payable*. As a reminder the balance sheet is based on a balance between these items:

Long term assets + Current assets = Long term liabilities + Short term liabilities + Equity

The balance sheet is produced as a result of a process known as double-entry bookkeeping. This forms the basis of accounting procedures and works on the basis that for every transaction there are two equal and opposing entries. All of the business transactions are recorded during the period using this method and the balance between the equal opposing entries is checked using what is known as the Trial Balance. This approach was originally maintained using manual ledgers but, of course, today is maintained by business accounting software.

Whilst always in balance, the layout of the balance sheet can vary and the level of detail in the statement will depend on whether it is for internal or external reporting. Published balance sheets are subject to legal constraints to standardise the layout. The most usual format for UK companies is known as the vertical format where the two balancing sections lie above and below each other rather than side by side.

The vertical format is based on the equation:

$$\text{Long term assets} + \text{Current assets} - \text{Long term and current liabilities} = \text{Capital} + \text{Reserves (equity)}$$

In the example from the EasyJet accounts (Figure 3.1) the vertical format has been used.

Capital and reserves are known as the owner's equity. This may be made up of share capital which might be issued solely to the owners or to the public at large. There are various types of shares in issue, the most popular of which are ordinary shares. The types of shares available for issue are discussed in more detail in Chapter 9.

Reserves are funds accumulated from internally produced profits. Profits may be paid out as dividends, or they may be retained to fund further expansion, which is when they become known as reserves or retained profit. Reserves may stay in the form of cash, but it is much more likely that they will be used to purchase long-term assets. Other types of reserve are generated by certain activities. As an example, a *revaluation reserve* is created when long-term assets are revalued either above or below their book value. If there is a change in the long-term asset value in the balance sheet then the reserve provides the balancing entry.

The *share premium account* is a type of reserve and is created when ordinary shares are sold to the public for more than their nominal or original value when they were created. The following example illustrates how this reserve is created.

XYZ LTD is to raise additional capital through the sale of unissued ordinary shares which have a nominal value of £1.00 each, i.e. the value assigned to the shares when the business was created. The issue price is to be 10% below the market price (i.e. the price currently trading in the stock markets) of £2.20. Prior to the sale the extract from the balance sheet looked like this:

	£ million	
Assets	3	
Less Long-Term Loans	1	
	2	
Share Capital	Authorised	Issued
	£ million	£ million
Ordinary shares (£1 each)	2	1
Reserves		1
		2

Figure 3.1: EasyJet Balance Sheet. Source: www.easyjet.com

		As at 30 Sept 2023 £ million	As at 30 Sept2022 re-presented £ million
Non-current assets			
Goodwill	10	365	365
Other intangible assets	10	276	217
Property, plant and equipment	11	4,864	4,629
Derivative financial instruments	25	35	127
Equity investment	25	31	31
Restricted cash	14	2	3
Other non-current assets	12	138	91
Deferred tax assets	6	–	62
		5,711	5,525
Current assets			
Trade and other receivables	13	343	367
Intangible assets	10	676	495
Derivative financial instruments	25	186	423
Restricted cash	14	–	4
Money market deposits	14	–	126
Cash and cash equivalents	14	2,925	3,514
		4,130	4929
Current liabilities			
Trade and other payables	15	(1,764)	(1,759)
Unearned revenue	16	(1,498)	(1,042)
Borrowings	17	(433)	(437)
Lease liabilities	18	(217)	(247)
Derivative financial instruments	25	(54)	(86)
Current tax payable	6	(3)	(5)
Provisions for liabilities and charges	19	(175)	(102)
		(4,144)	(3,678)
Net current (liabilities)/assets		(14)	1,251
Non-current liabilities			
Borrowings	17	(1,462)	(2,760)
Unearned revenue 16 (3) (1)			
Lease liabilities	18	(772)	(866)
Derivative financial instruments	25	(14)	(22)
Non-current deferred income		(4)	(4)
Post-employment benefit obligation	20	(7)	(1)
Provisions for liabilities and charges	19	(626)	(589)
Deferred tax liabilities	6	(22)	–
		(2,910)	(4,243)
Net assets		2,787	2,533
Shareholders' equity			
Share capital	21	207	207
Share premium		2,166	2,166

Hedging reserve	113	170
Cost of hedging reserve	(2)	5
Translation reserve	72	(6)
Retained earnings/(accumulated losses)	231	(9)
Total equity	2,787	2,533

Figure 3.2: Profit and Loss account (easyjet). Source: easyjet.com

	2023 Headline £ million	Non-headline £ million		2022 Headline £ million	Non-headline £ million	Total £ million
Passenger revenue	5,221	–	5,221	3,816	–	3,816
Ancillary revenue						
Airline ancillary revenue	2,174	–	2,174	1,585	–	1,585
Holidays incremental revenue	776	–	776	368	–	368
Total ancillary revenue	2,950	–	2,950	1,953	–	1,953
Total revenue	8,171	–	8,171	5,769	–	5,769
Fuel	(2,033)	–	(2,033)	(1,279)	–	(1,279)
Airports and ground handling	(1,800)	–	(1,800)	(1,443)	–	(1,443)
Crew	(941)	–	(941)	(767)	–	(767)
Navigation	(422)	–	(422)	(339)	–	(339)
Maintenance	(341)	–	(341)	(301)	–	(301)
Holidays direct operating costs (excluding flights)	(582)	–	(582)	(273)	–	(273)
Selling and marketing	(232)	–	(232)	(173)	–	(173)
Other costs	(695)	(10)	(705)	(635)	(30)	(665)
Other income	5	6	11	10	–	10
EBITDAR	1,130	(4)	1,126	569	(30)	539
Aircraft dry leasing	–	–	–	(2)	–	(2)
Depreciation	(625)	(19)	(644)	(539)	–	(539)
Amortisation of intangible assets	(29)	–	(29)	(25)	–	(25)
Operating profit/(loss)	476	(23)	453	3	(30)	(27)
Interest receivable and other financing income	132	–	132	26	–	26
Interest payable and other financing charges	(180)	–	(180)	(143)	–	(143)
Foreign exchange gain/(loss)	27	–	27	(64)	–	(64)
Net finance charges	(21)	–	(21)	(181)	–	(181)
Profit/(loss) before tax	455	(23)	432	(178)	(30)	(208)
Tax (charge)/credit	(114)	6	(108)	31	8	39
Profit/(loss) for the year	341	(17)	324	(147)	(22)	(169)
Earnings/(loss) per share, pence						
Basic		43.1		(22.4)		
Diluted		42.7		(22.4)		

After the sale of the remaining shares the balance sheet will show an increase in assets due to the cash from the sale and a change in the share capital layout.

	£ million	
Assets	5	
Less Long-Term Loans	1	
	4	
Share Capital	Authorised	Issued
	£ million	£ million
Ordinary shares	2	2
Share premium	1	
Reserves		1
		4

One million shares have been sold for £2 each which represents £1 nominal value and £1 share premium per share.

Working capital

Most businesses require funds to be available on a daily basis in order to allow the business to operate. These funds may be used to purchase stock or inventory in advance of trading and to pay wages and salaries. Consequently, a business will have at any moment of time money tied up in stocks and in debtors (accounts receivable), which is those customers who have received the product or service but who have not yet paid. Too much cash tied up in these areas may deprive the business of funds for profit generating expenditure on long-term assets. Additionally, overly large volumes of stocks held and debtors outstanding may result in business failure through inefficient cashflow management. Therefore, it is essential to keep current assets as low as is viably possible without running out of inventory. The definition of working capital is:

Working capital = Current assets – current liabilities

This term provides a measure of the balance between short-term funds and short-term assets. There are various approaches to monitoring working capital ranging from those measures which focus on the total amount in relation to sales to individual measures for the components of working capital. These are considered in more detail in Chapter 7.

Investments

A company may well consider investing in activities outside the scope of the existing business. Cash surpluses may be used to invest for both the short term and the long term. A short-term investment will provide a lower return but can be converted quickly back into cash should the need arise. Long-term investments should provide the highest possible return available whilst suiting the long-term plans of the company. The business might consider making long term loans to other operations in return for interest, buying shares in other companies in return for dividends or purchasing other companies in total.

The profit and loss account

The balance sheet has already been described as a useful summary of the business position frozen at a moment in time. However, this does not reveal what the business has achieved over a period of time. The profit and loss account provides a summary of revenues and costs occurring over a given time span, typically a year and also monthly for management accounts. There is generally no single layout used for the statement and published accounts aim to produce the minimum amount of information required to meet statutory guidelines. A sample statement taken from the published accounts for EasyJet is shown in Figure 3.2.

The statement starts with the net sales (gross sales less VAT) figure for the period which includes all sales transactions for both cash and credit subdivided into Passenger Revenue and Ancillary Revenue. The revenue is then matched with the costs and charges for the period to reveal different levels of profit. The published accounts will tend to omit the detail and will illustrate (as in the case of Easy Jet) only the Earnings Before Interest, Taxation, Depreciation, Amortisation and restructuring or rent costs. (EBITDAR). In the management accounts for hospitality businesses, additional levels of profit are typically included and are now described in more detail. These definitions are based on the Uniform System of Accounts for the Lodging Industry (2014).

- ☐ **Gross profit:** The difference between net sales and the cost of the materials for producing the sales (some companies include wage costs at this point but in the hospitality and related sectors the cost of sales is the opening stock plus purchases less closing stocks, i.e. the cost of goods sold)
- ☐ **Gross operating profit**: Gross profit less all other direct and indirect costs associated with trading, such labour costs and undistributed operating expenses.
- ☐ **EBITDA**: earnings before interest, tax, depreciation and amortisation

Each of these profit levels can be useful measures of profitability depending on the users' needs. However, it should be remembered that the statement is prepared based on the interpretation of the accounting standards and therefore it is possible that the profit figure could vary for two identical companies depending on the methods used.

Internal accounts will be considerably more detailed to show departmental revenues and costs, and should be tailored to suit the needs of the business and area of responsibility. The Uniform System of Accounts provides guidelines of a format suitable for hotel operations and variations on this are widely used in the industry.

Uniform System of Accounts

The UK version of the Uniform Accounting System was developed by the Hotel and Catering Economic Development Council in 1969. However, the US system, the Uniform System for Accounts for the Lodging Industry, is more widely used and was first published by the Hotel Association of New York City in 1926. The last revision to the Uniform System of Accounts took place in 2014 and constituted a major change to the previous versions. The USALI is now owned by the Hospitality Finance and Technology Professionals (HFTP) trade association based in Texas, US, and the new revised 12th version is currently in the process of being devised for publication in 2024, with input from industry experts and practitioners, consultants and academics.

The USALI offers a standardised format for internal users in the form of departmental statements that can be applied to full-service lodging properties with food and beverage operations as well as a variety of other services and amenities. The Departmental Statement of Income is illustrated in Figure 3.3

	Actual	Budget	Last Year
Rooms available:	54327	54327	54327
Rooms sold:	40908	41565	40353
Occupancy:	75.30%	76.51%	74.28%
ADR:	£146.56	£147.29	£140.28
Rooms RevPAR:	£110.36	£112.69	£104.20
Total RevPAR:	£193.22	£199.29	£180.29

	Actual		**Budget**		**Last Year**	
	£	%	£	%	£	%
Operating revenue						
Rooms	5,995,386	57.1	6,122,275	56.5	5,660,718	57.8
Food & beverage	4,208,868	40.1	4,388,857	40.5	3,848,043	39.3
Other operating depts	99,075	0.9	114,674	1.1	111,037	1.1
Miscellaneous income	193,559	1.8	201,245	1.9	175,075	1.8
Total operating revenue	**10,496,888**	**100.0**	**10,827,051**	**100.0**	**9,794,873**	**100.0**
Departmental expenses						
Rooms	1,613,091	26.9	1,622,043	26.5	1,511,412	26.7
Food & beverage	2,546,365	60.5	2,703,536	61.6	2,370,394	61.6
Other operating depts	79,143	79.9	86,755	75.7	82,345	74.2
Total departmental expenses	**4,238,599**	**0.40**	**4,412,334**	**0.41**	**3,964,151**	**0.40**
Total departmental profit	**6,258,289**	**59.6**	**6,414,717**	**59.2**	**5,830,722**	**59.5**
Undistributed operating expenses						
Administrative & general	427,837	4.1	391,222	3.6	359,194	3.7
Information technology	51,551	0.5	58,500	0.5	56,505	0.6
Sales & marketing	240,793	2.3	238,088	2.2	209,350	2.1
Property operation & maintenance	169,829	1.6	179,197	1.7	142,316	1.5
Utilities	247,741	2.4	255,977	2.4	203,786	2.1
Total undistributed expenses	**1,137,751**	**10.8**	**1,122,984**	**10.4**	**971,151**	**9.9**
Gross operating profit	**5,120,538**	**48.8**	**5,291,733**	**48.9**	**4,859,571**	**49.6**

Management fees	180,000	1.7	180,000	1.7	162,000	1.7
Income before non-operating income & expenses	**4,940,538**	**47.1**	**5,111,733**	**47.2**	**4,697,571**	**48.0**
Non-operating income and expenses						
Income	-	0.0	-	0.0	-	0.0
Rent	-	0.0	-	0.0	-	0.0
Property and other taxes	245,087	2.3	245,463	2.3	250,024	2.6
Insurance	30,803	0.3	30,056	0.3	29,758	0.3
Other		0.0		0.0		0.0
Total non-operating income and expenses	**275,890**	**2.6**	**275,519**	**2.5**	**279,782**	**2.9**
Earnings before interest, taxes, depreciation & amortization	**4,664,648**	**44.4**	**4,836,214**	**44.7**	**4,417,789**	**45.1**
Replacement reserve						
EBITDA less replacement reserve						
Interest	585,000	5.6	585,000	5.4	540,000	5.5
Depreciation	1,200,250	11.4	1,200,250	11.1	1,200,250	12.3
Amortisation		0.0		0.0		0.0
Total interest, depreciation & amortisation	**1,785,250**	**17.0**	**1,785,250**	**16.5**	**1,740,250**	**17.8**
Income before income taxes	**2,879,397**	**27.4**	**3,050,964**	**28.2**	**2,677,538**	**27.3**
Income taxes	375,000	3.6	360,000	3.3	348,000	3.6
Net income	**2,504,397**	**23.9**	**2,690,964**	**24.9**	**2,329,538**	**23.8**

Figure 3.3: Annual Summary Statement of Income

In addition to the Departmental Statement of Income, there are altogether 30 supporting schedules. The Uniform System may be defined as a manual of instructions for preparing standard accounting statements and schedules for the various operating and productive units which make up a hotel. The purpose of the manual is to provide a simple formula for the classification of accounts which could then be adopted by any hotel regardless of size or type. The basic aim of the system is to enable users within the industry to manage their properties more effectively with the information provided, and to enable users from outside the industry to more readily understand the industry, if all the statements they are reading are similar and comparable. The benefits of using the system can be defined as follows:

- The system is simple, easy to understand and, therefore, of particular benefit to all non-accountants in the hotel industry.
- As all hotels use the same concepts and terminology the Uniform System enables the compilation of hotel statistics - nationally and internationally.

- The presentation and format is always the same. This makes the 'Statement' readily recognisable and the location of information easy.
- It is a tailor-made system for hotels and can be adopted by hotels of any size and anywhere. Time and money is saved because the design of an individual system for a hotel is unnecessary.
- The Uniform System facilitates the training of accounting and control personnel; only one generally accepted system has to be learnt.
- The system facilitates managerial mobility; there is no need to learn a new system when moving from one company to another.
- The Uniform System represents the "best practice" in the hotel industry and therefore, results in better quality of financial statements.

Many organisations adapt the principles suggested by the Uniform System of Accounts for their own purposes. The following example illustrates a monthly report layout for a contract catering business.

	Actual monthly	%	Budget monthly	%	Variance £	Variance B/w %	Budget YTD	%	Actual YTD	%	Variance £	Variance B/W %
Revenue												
Cost of sales												
Gross profit												
Labour and staff costs												
Disposables												
Cleaning												
Laundry / uniform												
Equipment												
Rentals												
Other costs												
Divisional profit												

Figure 3.4: Example of a summary monthly report layout for a contract catering business

Profit versus cash

A business may forecast to be profitable but success will ultimately depend on there being sufficient cash available to generate future sales and to survive. The difference between cash and profit is due to the timing differences incurred on the receipt of sales and on the payment of expenses, capital expenditures and loan repayments as well as depreciation. Depreciation charges will reduce profit but do not represent a cash outflow and therefore the cash flow value will always be different to the profit figure. Cash flows also include capital items such as financing and long-term asset expenditures, neither of which would appear in the profit and loss account. The cash flow is considered to represent a more factual representation of the state of the business, and it is this rather than profits which is used for appraising long-term investments. Discounted cash flow techniques, taking into account the time value of money, are discussed in detail in Chapter 10.

The cash flow statement

The principle aim of the cash flow statement is to measure the liquidity of the business. The cash-flow statement is required to be produced in the company reports and this is shown as a historical picture summarising how funds have been generated and how they have been utilised. Unlike the profit & loss account, the statement includes operating activities, sources of capital and capital expenditure items. A sample layout taken from the published accounts for EasyJet is illustrated in Figure 3.5.

	2023 £million	2022 £million	Change £million
Operating profit/(loss)	**453**	(27)	480
Net tax paid	**(12)**	(4)	(8)
Net working capital movement excluding unearned revenue	**(19)**	101	(120)
Unearned revenue movement	**458**	197	261
Depreciation and amortisation	**673**	564	109
Net capital expenditure	**(754)**	(530)	(224)
Net proceeds from sale and leaseback of aircraft	**76**	87	(11)
Increase in lease liability	**(208)**	(43)	(165)
Net funding activities	**-**	53	(53)
Purchase of own shares for employee share schemes	**(15)**	(9)	(6)
Other (including the effect of exchange rate movements)	**59**	(149)	208
Net decrease in net debt	**711**	240	471
Net debt at the beginning of the year	**(670)**	(910)	240
Net cash/(debt) at the end of the year	**41**	(670)	711

Figure 3.5: Cash flow statement (easyJet). Source: www.easyjet.com/

The statement explains the increase or decrease in the cash balances over the year in terms of the cash inflows from operating activities, sale of long-term assets and the raising of additional finance compared to the cash outflows for interest and dividend payments, taxation and the purchase of long term assets. This style of cash flow has the advantage that cash is the critical element rather than working capital changes and this can easily be reconciled with the movements in the bank account.

Preparation of the published cash flow

All the information required for the preparation of this statement can come from the business profit & loss account and the balance sheets for the opening and the close of the financial year. Consider the following example.

Example

Treetops Hotel

Balance sheet (Statement of Financial Position)	Year ended 20x2 (£000)	20x3 (£000)
Non-current assets		
Freehold premises	65	100
Equipment & furnishings	84	126
Less depreciation	22	42
Net non-current assets	127	184
Current assets		
Stocks	66	72
Debtors (Accounts Receivable)	42	48
Cash balance	14	11
Current liabilities		
Creditors (Accounts Payable)	45	56
Taxation	22	28
Dividend payable	15	20
Net current assets	40	27
Total assets	167	211
Less long term liabilities	---	20
Capital employed	167	191
Financed by		
Ordinary shares	100	100
General reserve	41	51
Retained profits	26	40
Capital employed (Total Equity)	167	191

Profit & Loss Account for the year ending 20x3		£000
Sales		250
Cost of sales		128
Gross profit		122
Operating costs		
Wages & Administration	28	
Depreciation	20	48
Operating profit		74
Interest payable		2
Net profit before tax		72
Corporation tax		28
Net profit after tax		44
Proposed dividend		20
Retained profit		24

The first step is to calculate the net cash inflow from operating activities. Companies are required to show this calculation as a note attached to the statement in the published accounts.

	£000
Operating profit	74
Add back depreciation	20
Adjust for changes in working capital by comparing the two balance sheets	
(Increase) or decrease in stocks	(6)
(Increase) or decrease in debtors	(6)
Increase or (decrease) in creditors	11
Net cash inflow from operating activities	93

An increase in current assets (stocks and debtors) represents an outflow of cash and this reduces the cash inflow value. An increase in creditors represents a cash flow inflow as creditors are being used as a source of funds. From these workings the indirect style of cash flow statement can then be prepared.

Cash flow statement for year ending 20x3		£000
Net cash inflow from operating activities		93(+)
Returns on investment and servicing of finance		
Interest paid	2	
Dividend paid (taken from previous year)	15	
		17(-)
Taxation (figure actually paid)		22(-)
Investing activities		
Freehold premises	35	
Equipment & furnishings	42	
		77(-)
Financing		
Issue of long term loan		20(+)
Decrease in cash		3

The change in the cash figure should reconcile with the cash balances shown in the two balance sheets.

Balance at 31/12/20x3	14,000
Balance at 31/12/20x4	11,000
Decrease in cash	3,000

The cash flow statement has an important role to play as an internal control statement which will be produced in the form of a forecast as regularly as is required. This is commonly on a monthly basis although weekly and even daily may be used. To illustrate the preparation of the direct style of cash flow the following information is to be used.

Example

A hotel is to start trading on July 1st. The following is the forecast trading data and expenditure for the first four months from 1st July to 30th October.

Sales:	£300,000	
Pattern of sales:	July	35%
	August	20%
	September	15%
	October	30%
Credit sales:	80% of monthly sales, payable in the following month	
Cost of sales:	50% of total sales, payable in the following month	
Labour and staff costs:	30% of total sales, payable in the month incurred	
Fixed costs		
Salaries:	£5,000 per month	
Insurance:	£10,000 for the year – £2,500 is payable in July and £7,500 payable in October	
Property tax:	£5,000 payable in September	
Depreciation:	£1,250 per month	
Interest:	£6,000 paid in October	
Other costs:	£1,250 payable on a monthly basis	

Opening balance at bank £(10,000) negative.

The forecasted cash flow is shown below:

	July	August	September	October
Cash inflows				
Sales - cash	21,000	12,000	9,000	18,000
Sales - previous month	nil	84,000	48,000	36,000
Total inflow	21,000	96,000	57,000	54,000
Cash outflows				
Cost of sales	nil	52,500	30,000	22,500
Wages and staff	31,500	18,000	13,500	27,000
Salaries	5,000	5,000	5,000	5,000
Insurance	2,500		7,500	
Property tax			5,000	
Interest				6,000
Other costs	1,250	1,250	1,250	1,250
Total outflow	40,250	76,750	54,750	69,250
Net flow	(19,250)	19,250	2,250	(15,250)
Opening balance	(10,000)	(29,250)	(10,000)	(7750)
Closing balance	(29,250)	(10,000)	(7,750)	(23,000)

The profit for the period is £9,000. This can be reconciled to the cash balance by adding back the noncash items including depreciation and cost of sales and deducting the credit sales. The difference is the opening balance value.

A review of the above figures indicates that although the business is just profitable there is cash flow difficulty leading to an increasing overdraft and the cost of this overdraft has not been included in the figures.

The above example illustrates that it is possible to be profitable but still experience difficult trading conditions due to lack of cash. As a result, for many businesses the forecasted cash flow is an essential tool for predicting the future success of the business.

Legal requirements

Most businesses are required to publish a set of financial statements. These should be presented in the standard format in order to meet the requirements of the UK Companies Act and the guidelines embodied in the International Reporting Standards. Consequently, most businesses are required to produce a profit and loss account, a balance sheet, a cash flow statement and also a director's report, auditors report and detailed notes to explain and expand upon the information presented.

The directors' report should contain information such as the level of dividends to be paid, names and interests of the directors as well as information regarding the nature of the business and details of employee policies and development. There are also a number of additions to the information disclosed, required by the Stock Exchange.

Corporate governance

The early 21st century business landscape has been dominated by the phrases 'corporate governance' and 'business accountability'. The publication of the Cadbury Report in 1992 formalised the growing interest in this area and in the following ten years the collapse of organisations such as Enron, Arthur Andersen and WorldCom ensured that interest in this topic has continued to grow.

In the UK companies are governed by the Companies Acts, case law and the additional requirements set for companies listed on the London Stock Exchange. The recommendations arising from the Turnbull Report and the original Combined Code on Corporate Governance, formed in 1999, required organisations to ensure that adequate internal control systems are in place. The Combined Code has been superseded by the UK Corporate Governance code and is now maintained by the Financial Reporting Council (FRC). The Code is separated into five sections: Board Leadership and Company Purpose; Division of Responsibilities; Composition, Succession and Evaluation; Audit, Risk and Internal Control; and Remuneration, and it operates on a 'comply or explain' basis.

The importance of adequate internal control systems has become so prominent that there is now an expectation that companies will outline their commitment to corporate governance procedures in their annual report.

Summary

This chapter serves to introduce the basic principles of accounting practice to provide the reader with an insight into the underlying principles of financial statement preparation. The balance sheet provides a historical snapshot of the business at a given in moment in time and although this is useful for analysis purposes it should be remembered that the business is never static. There are essential differences between the profit and loss account and the cash flow which must be clearly understood in order to use these statements effectively. The profit and loss account shows the profitability of the business over a given time period whereas the cash flow emphasizes liquidity. The way in which these statements are used is summarized in Table 3.5 below.

	Past	**Present**	**Future**
Profit & loss account	Published statement	Management accounts	Budgeted
Balance sheet	Published statement	Management accounts	Budgeted
Cash flow	FRS1	Management accounts	Period basis

Table 3.5: Time span of the key financial statements

Questions

1. What is depreciation and how does it affect the accounts of a business?
2. Three main methods of depreciation are used in the United Kingdom, what are they and what are the advantages of each?
3. What is the concept behind the adjustments to the balances on various expenses and revenue accounts?
4. What is the logic behind showing the prepayments and accruals in the appropriate section of the Balance Sheet?
5. What are the roles of the Balance Sheet, the Profit and Loss Account and the Cash Flow Statements?
6. Give six reasons why the accounting profit for a period will not necessarily result in an improvement in the business cash flow.
7. Give examples of balance sheet items which may change the business cash position.
8. The hotel and catering industries have developed the Uniform System of Accounts. List the advantages of the Uniform System.
9. The Marchwood Leisure Group has been operating for a number of years, and its main activity is dining clubs. The actual results for 20x3 and the comparative balance sheet figures for 20x2 are shown below:

31 May x2	Marchwood Leisure, Balance Sheet		31 May x3
(£000)	**Non current assets**		(£000)
	Fixed Assets		
800	Freehold premises		1000
200	Equipment and furnishings		300
1000			1300
	Current Assets		
60	Stock	50	
40	Debtors	60	
0	Bank	100	
100		210	
	Current Liabilities		
70	Creditors	60	
50	Bank overdraft	0	
30	Taxation	50	
35	Dividend	60	
185		170	
(85)	**Net Current Assets/(Liabilities)**		40
915	Capital employed		1340
	Financed By:		
700	Ordinary Share Capital		850
	Share Premium Account		110
200	General Reserve		215
15	Profit & Loss Account		65
	Loan Capital		
0 8%	Loan		100
915			1340

Marchwood Leisure, Profit & Loss Account for the year ending 31 May x3

	(£000)
Sales	550
Cost of Sales	200
Gross Profit	350
Wages & Admin Costs	100
Depreciation	55
Other costs (including interest)	20
Net Profit before Tax	175
Corporation Tax	50
Net Profit after Tax	125
Proposed dividend	60
Profit to Reserves	65

Notes:

a) No long term assets were sold or re-valued during the year

b) The loan was taken out on 1st Dec 20x2

You are required to:

a) Calculate cash flow from operating activities from the above information

b) Prepare the Cash Flow Statement in the published style. Use this as a guide.

	(£000)
Net cash flow from operating activities	
Returns on investments and servicing of finance	
Taxation	
Capital Expenditure	
Equity Dividends paid	
Financing	
Loans	
Capital	
Net increase/(decrease)	

c) Reconcile the cash balance shown on the 20x3 Balance Sheet with the Net increase/(decrease) shown above.

d) Summarise the aims of the cash flow statement

Practical activity

In light of recent accounting scandals, consider how these could have been prevented. What role do you think the accounting regulations could play in ensuring that the preparation of the published annual accounts is true and accurate?

References and further reading

American Hotel & Lodging Educational Institute (2014), *Uniform System of Accounts for the Lodging Industry*, 11th Edition.

Atrill, P. & Mclaney E. (2021) *Accounting and Finance for Non-Specialists*, 12th Edition, Pearson.

easyJet (n.d.) *Investors - Reports and presentations* https://corporate.easyjet.com/investors/reports-and-presentations/default.aspx

Mclaney, E. (2009) *Business Finance: Theory and Practice*, Prentice Hall.

Ransley, J., Ingram, H. and Adams, D. (2022) *Developing Hospitality Properties and Facilities*. Routledge

Schmidgall, R. (2016) *Hospitality Industry Managerial Accounting.* Educational Institute of the American Hotel Motel Association.

Useful websites

www.ifrs.org/issued-standards/list-of-standards/ IFRS Accounting Standards Navigator

www.frc.org.uk/library/standards-codes-policy/corporate-governance/uk-corporate-governance-code/ UK Corporate Governance Code:

online.hbs.edu/blog/post/how-to-read-a-balance-sheet How to Read & Understand a Balance Sheet

online.hbs.edu/blog/post/how-to-read-a-cash-flow-statement How to Read & Understand a Cash Flow Statement

Part 2: External analysis

The Chartered Institute of Management Accountants (CIMA) in the UK defines strategic management accounting as:

> *'A form of management accounting in which emphasis is placed on information which relates to factors external to the firm, as well as non-financial information and internally generated information'* (CIMA Official Terminology, 2018).

Several writers have put forward the notion that management accounting should be more outward-looking, enabling a business to evaluate its competitive position relative to the rest of the industry sector by analysing sales volumes and cost structures for its competitors. In the strategic management process, an informed view of environmental influences and competitive forces is an essential part of the strategic planning process. Typically, there are a number of techniques which can be used to assist in the process of environmental analysis including:

- PESTLE analysis
- Portfolio models
- Competition analysis

It is well established that an understanding of the environment enables a business to develop a strategy to meet the demands of the future. The first stage of a formal analysis is to examine the global macro environment using a framework such as a PESTLE analysis. The aspects to be reviewed with this analysis are:

- *Political*: assessing the impact of political systems, laws and regulations, political stability and risk
- *Economic*: the rate of growth, pattern of consumption, rate of exchange, monetary and fiscal policy, interest rates, inflation, taxation levels and labour skills
- *Social*: Factors such as demographics, culture, social factors, education and nationalism
- *Technological:* The impact of emerging technologies
- *Legislation:* The impact of national and world legislation.
- *Environmental:* The impact of local, national and environmental issues

The chapters in this section consider how accounting information can be used to develop strategies to create sustainable competitive advantage. In order to do this a range of portfolio models, based on the work of Porter, is described to provide a range of tools for evaluating the competitive environment.

The accounting role is critical for producing information on competitors to help the business select its own strategy. The comparison of competitors' relative costs and investments will provide valuable information which can be used in the setting of pricing strategies. A business needs to establish whether competitors are setting prices at levels which are sustainable in the long term. It may be that competitors are setting prices below their true cost levels in order to dominate the market and drive out local competition before increasing selling prices to improve profitability. The competitive situation is far more serious if competitors have already achieved long-term cost reductions and are able to offer lower prices for similar products or services, without eroding the profit level per unit.

Consequently, there is most certainly potential for the management accounting information system to provide information to assist in the development of strategies with the intent of pursuing competitive advantage, although evidence suggests that this is not widely understood in practice.

The following chapters consider the importance of cost control and revenue maximisation in the context of maintaining competitive advantage.

4 Managing costs

About this chapter

The effective management of operational business costs is a major challenge for any organisation. In the hospitality, tourism and leisure industries it is particularly crucial as margins are often low for each sale, with the business dependent on achieving high volumes of transactions. The benefits are obvious in that a reduction in operational costs will lead to an increase in the profits and the profit to sales ratio (profit margins), and an improved return on capital employed. Yet for many organisations the need for cost controls is only highlighted when costs have already started spiraling out of control, or when revenue levels are falling during periods of intense competition or recession. This chapter considers first how routine performance can be monitored and controlled and then provides suggestions for a longer-term approach to strategic cost reduction with the purpose of improving a business's opportunity for competitive advantage. The specific aspects to be covered are:

- ☐ The nature of costs
- ☐ Costs for decision making
- ☐ Monitoring routine performance
- ☐ Investigating the cost base
- ☐ Cost leadership
- ☐ Competitive analysis
- ☐ Porter's approach to competitive advantage.

Learning objectives

On completion of this chapter, you should be able to:

- ☐ Understand the meaning of different classifications of cost
- ☐ Understand how to classify costs into different categories and apply techniques for determining the nature of costs
- ☐ Construct break-even, contribution and profit volume graphs
- ☐ Apply cost-volume-profit analysis to varying sales mix situations
- ☐ Understand how a knowledge of cost structure facilitates competitive advantage.

Introduction

Costs can be classified in different ways depending on the source of the information and also on how the cost information is to be used (Table 4.1). Essentially all cost information can be used for control and planning purposes as follows:

- ☐ **Control purposes** where costs are being matched to revenue to establish profitability for an area, product or market
- ☐ **Planning purposes** where information about costs is used to set pricing strategies, monitor profit margin and manage sales-mix profitability.

Basic cost elements	Direct and indirect	Fixed and variable
Materials Including food and beverage costs	*Direct* Materials Salaries and wages Expenses	*Variable costs* Costs which vary linearly with the volume of products and services sold
Salaries and wages Costs associated with the employment of the permanent and contracted staff	*Indirect* Materials Salaries and wages Expenses	*Semi-variable* Costs which contain a variable element and a fixed element
Expenses Operating and overhead		*Fixed costs* Costs which remain constant regardless of the level of business activity over a 'relevant range' of activity

Table 4.1: Alternative approaches for the classification of costs

The basic cost element approach represents the simplest methodology for classifying costs, based on an analysis of the resources required to produce the product or service. There are three types of costs found in operations:

1. **Materials** represent the cost of the components that make up the product – for example a restaurant meal or drinks cocktail.
2. **Labour** includes all the wage, salary and related costs associated with rewarding the workforce for their efforts, including uniforms and pensions as well as salary costs.
3. **Expenses** includes all other operating and overhead costs

This approach forms the basis of the sequence of the basic profit and loss account.

A second approach is to divide costs into those which can be assigned to products, services, departments or particular activities, i.e. *direct* costs, and those which cannot be assigned, i.e. *indirect or overhead* costs. The hospitality industry overhead costs are often known as '*undistributed operating expenses*'. Examples of direct costs include the basic cost elements, but this time these costs are directly attributable to a specific area of the business:

- ☐ **Materials**: cost of sales, e.g. ingredients
- ☐ **Labour**: restaurant manager's salary
- ☐ **Expenses**: laundry of table linen.

In this example all these costs are clearly directly attributable to the restaurant within a larger operation such as a hotel.

Examples of indirect costs include all indirect material costs, labour costs and expenses included in the operation such as:

- ☐ Sales and marketing
- ☐ General administration
- ☐ Utility costs

Some businesses have tried to allocate indirect costs to products and services; however, this is often problematic, as it is usually difficult to arrive at a basis of apportionment which is truly representative of how the cost has been accumulated.

The third category of cost classification considers cost behaviours in relation to revenue or volume. This is done by defining two basic cost types:

- ☐ Fixed costs
- ☐ Variable costs.

Fixed costs are those that remain unchanged in total over a given period or volume of activity, whereas *variable* costs change proportionately with a change in the level of activity. Fixed costs remain constant over a period of activity or sales volume known as the 'relevant range'. Beyond the relevant range the fixed costs will start to increase. This means that the cost *per unit* falls for fixed costs as volume increases, whereas the variable cost per unit remains the same regardless of volume of units. This can be demonstrated graphically (Figures 4.1 and 4.2).

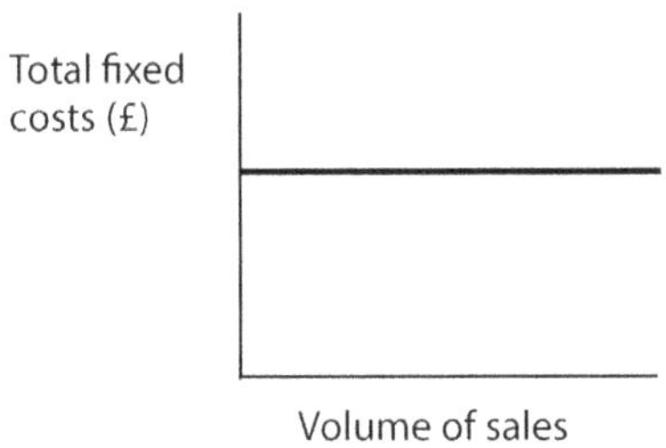

Figure 4.1: Fixed costs

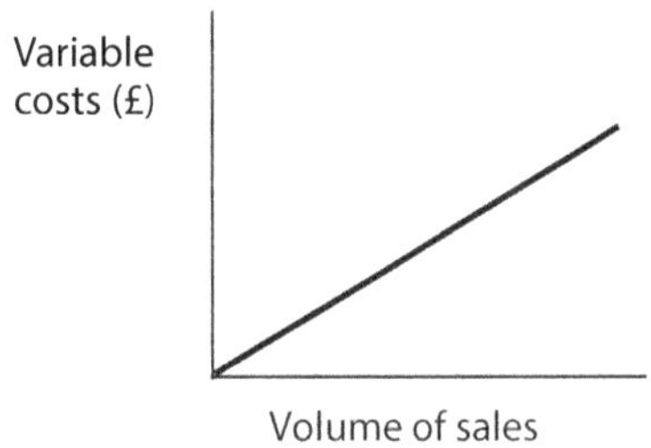

Figure 4.2: Variable costs

Many costs have both a fixed and a variable element. Energy consumption for example can clearly be partly fixed and partly variable. This cost is illustrated in Figure 4.3.

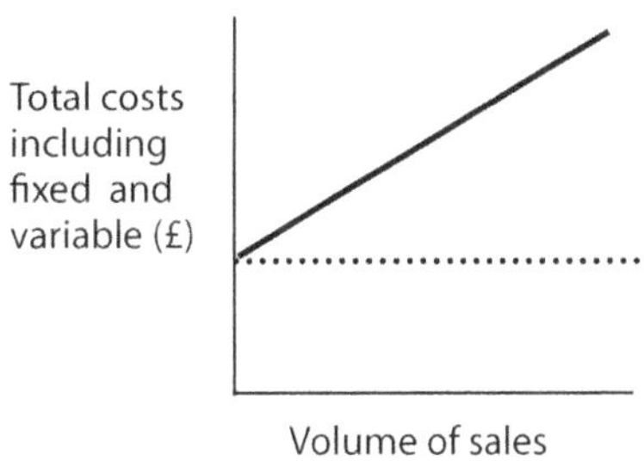

Figure 4.3: Semi variable costs

Classifying costs in this way provides a powerful tool in analysis terms in the *contribution*, which is the interim profit before fixed costs are deducted, and can be used for a series of decision-making activities, as well as being the essential determinant of breakeven point. The key relationships are:

Sales revenue - Variable costs = Contribution

and

Contribution - Fixed costs = Profit

Breakeven point

In order to cover all fixed costs there needs to be a sufficient contribution generated from each unit of sale, which when combined with volume will exceed the level of fixed costs. This can then be used with the relationship: fixed costs divided by the contribution per unit to establish a breakeven point in units, that is, the level of trading where neither a profit nor a loss is made. For example, given the following information for a specific time period:

	Per unit
	£
Sales	10
Variable costs	4
Contribution	6
Fixed costs	£60,000 in total

We can see that the breakeven point must be 10,000 units because each unit provides a contribution of £6 towards the total fixed costs. The proof being:

Sales	10,000 x £10	100,000
Variable costs	10,000 x £4	40,000
Contribution	10,000 x £6	60,000
Fixed costs		60,000
Profit/(loss)		NIL

The breakeven point can be illustrated graphically as demonstrated in Figure 4.4. When creating the graph it is important to ensure that:

- The horizontal axis is used to plot sales (£) or volume of business
- The vertical axis is used to plot sales and costs in monetary terms
- The graph scales start from zero at the origin
- The graduation of the scales is equally spaced.

This sequence of instructions will help you to complete an accurate graph:

1. Insert the fixed cost line which represents the fixed costs over the relevant range of activity.
2. Insert the variable cost line from the origin to the maximum level of sales volume.
3. Insert the sales line from the origin to the maximum level of sales volume.
4. Insert the total cost line from the point on the vertical axis where fixed costs occur and add the variable costs.

Figure 4.4 illustrates how the breakeven or cost-volume-chart should appear.

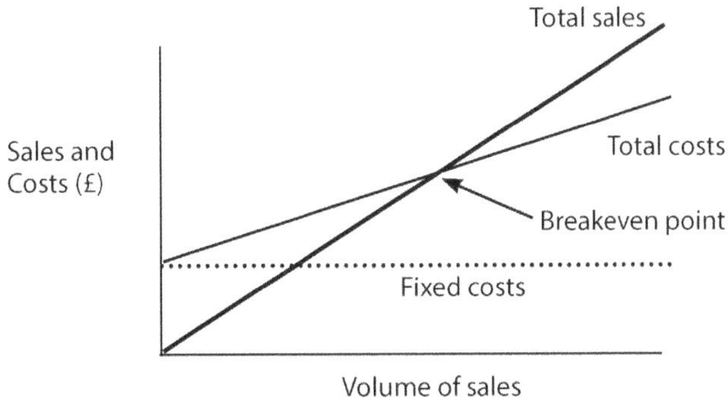

Figure 4.4: Breakeven chart

Forecasting required profit

A certain level of required profit can also be built into the equation. Using the previous example, if an operation requires a level of profit of say, £20,000 possibly to meet a return on equity consideration then this figure can be used with the cost information to establish the required level of sales as the following workings demonstrate.

$$\frac{\text{Required profit + fixed costs}}{\text{Contribution per unit}} = \text{Required volume of sales}$$

Using the previous data

$$\frac{20{,}000 + 60{,}000}{£6} = 13{,}333 \text{ units}$$

Margin of safety

The margin of safety illustrates how much sales activity can fall by before a loss will occur. Using the previous example if the breakeven volume of sales is 10,000 units and the forecasted level of sales is 15,000 units the percentage margin of safety is calculated as:

$$\frac{\text{Expected sales – breakeven sales}}{\text{Expected sales}} = \frac{15{,}000 - 10{,}000}{15{,}000} = 33\%$$

The following examples illustrate breakeven calculations in practice.

Yellow Hammer Tours sells adventure holidays direct to the public via the internet and has the capacity to organise and sell 3,000 tours per year. The average unit cost and selling price per tour is as follows:

	£
Selling Price	1,500
Variable costs:	
Accommodation & Meals	500
Flight and Transfers	250
Other Costs	200

Fixed overhead costs are £350,000 per annum for up to 3,000 tours (the relevant range) and the forecasted sales for the year are 2,000 tours.

The starting point is to calculate the breakeven point arithmetically. The contribution that is the selling price minus variable costs per tour is £550. The total fixed costs are £950,000 and so the breakeven point in number of tours is:

$$\frac{950{,}000}{550} = 1{,}727 \text{ tours}$$

The margin of safety represents the margin between the breakeven sales and the expected sales and is calculated as follows:

$$\frac{\text{Expected sales} - \text{breakeven sales}}{\text{Expected sales}} = \frac{2{,}000 - 1{,}727}{,000} = 13.65\%$$

In this example we have calculated the breakeven point using the contribution per unit. However, when we sell a range of products or services the use of contribution per unit is not always possible. This is particularly true in the hospitality industry where a business may well sell thousands of different products.

Breakeven and sales mix

The reality for many hotels and restaurant businesses, is that a combination of products and services is sold, each with their own cost structure and resulting contribution per unit. The overall contribution and resulting breakeven point then become dependent on the actual sales mix achieved as the following example demonstrates.

The Regent Hotel has prepared this budget for the forthcoming month:

Total sales:	£400,000		
Sales mix:	Rooms	50%	
	Food	30%	
	Beverage	20%	
	Total sales	*100%*	
Cost of sales:	Food	40%	
	Beverage	35%	
(Note: Rooms has zero cost of sales)			
Other Variable Costs:			
	Rooms	£40,000	
	Food	£45,000	
	Beverage	£35,000	
Fixed costs for the total business			£170,000

In this situation it is not possible to calculate the contribution per unit because each department will be selling numerous products, each with their own selling price and resulting contribution. Instead, the relationship between total sales and total contribution which is known as the C/S ratio is used. To calculate the overall C/S ratio and the resulting breakeven point from the above data the following workings are required.

	Rooms	Food	Beverage	Total
Sales	200,000	120,000	80,000	400,000
Cost of sales	----------	48,000	28,000	76,000
Gross profit	200,000	72,000	52,000	324,000
Variable costs	40,000	45,000	35,000	120,000
Contribution	160,000	27,000	17,000	204,000
Fixed costs				170,000
Net profit				34,000
C/S ratio	80%	22.5%	21.25%	51%

The resulting breakeven point is calculated using the fixed costs as follows:

$$\frac{170{,}000}{51\%} = £333{,}333 \text{ in sales}$$

If the sales mix were to change to say

Rooms	40%
Food	40%
Beverage	20%

Then the resulting C/S ratio would change and a new breakeven point would need to be calculated. A simple approach to calculating the new weighted C/S ratio is by using the percentage points as follows:

	C/S ratio	Sales mix	Percentage points
Rooms	80%	40%	32 (80 x 40%)
Food	22.5%	40%	9 (22.5 x 40%)
Beverage	21.25%	20%	4.25 (21.25 x 20%)

The new weighted C/S ratio is the sum of the percentage points, 45.25%.

The resulting breakeven point is:

170,000 / 45.25% = £375,690.60 in sales

Breakeven analysis is an essential tool for assessing the viability of a new business and most feasibility studies for a new investment will include a review of the breakeven point as the following example illustrates:

Example

A small company operating a number of restaurants is searching for a location to open another. A possible opportunity has been identified and the following forecasts made:

1. This operation requires an investment of £5,500,000 to purchase the site, furniture and equipment and the balance for working capital.
2. The shareholders of the company have £3,000,000 of their own to invest and will borrow the remainder at 10%.
3. Estimates for the first year of trading are that food cost will be 30%, variable labour costs will be 15% and other variables will be 5% of total sales.

4. Other cost estimates are:

Management salaries	£950,000
Depreciation	£350,000
Insurance	£100,000
Other costs (excluding interest on loan)	£50,000

5. The company requires a return of 20% on its own initial investment.

Based on the figures given, the forecasted profit and loss statement for the first year of trading will appear like this:

	£	%
Revenue	4,600,000	100.0
Cost of sales	1,380,000	30.0
Gross profit	3,220,000	70.0
Labour costs	690,000	15.0
Variable expenses	230,000	5.0
Contribution	2,300,000	50.0
Fixed costs excluding interest	1,450,000	31.5
Profit before interest	850,000	18.5
Interest	250,000	5.4
Net profit	600,000	13.0

To calculate the revenue figures a bottom-up approach is required. The profit required by the shareholders is 20% of the shareholder investment. The interest payable will be based on the loan of £2,500,000 borrowed at a rate of 10%.

The breakeven point is calculated from the total fixed costs divided by the C/S (contribution to sales) ratio.

$$\frac{1{,}700{,}000}{50\%} = £3{,}400{,}000 \text{ revenues}$$

We can prove this as follows:

	£	%
Revenue	3,400,000	100.0
Cost of sales	1,020,000	30.0
Gross profit	2,380,000	70.0
Labour costs	510,000	15.0
Variable expenses	170,000	5.0
Contribution	1,700,000	50.0
Fixed costs excluding interest	1,450,000	42.6
Profit before interest	250,000	7.3
Interest	250,000	7.3
Net profit	NIL	0.0

CVP assumptions

This approach is known as Cost-Volume-Profit (CVP) analysis and provides a powerful tool for assessing the viability of a business. There are, however, a number of assumptions associated with the CVP analysis which it is important to be familiar with.

1. Variable costs increase linearly with revenue.
2. Fixed costs remain constant.
3. The analysis applies to a relevant range of fixed costs only.
4. The analysis applies only to a short-term horizon.
5. Costs can be accurately divided into their fixed and variable elements.

We are now going to consider this final point which highlights that the difficulty in using CVP analysis often falls not in the analysis but in the initial classification of costs into those which are fixed and those which are variable in nature. However, there are a number of simple, as well as more sophisticated, statistical techniques available to assist in this exercise.

The following example demonstrates a methodology known as the High - Low approach to cost analysis.

The following sample of costs and activity levels were recorded for a food servery for increasing levels of customer numbers (covers):

	Covers	
	1,800	2,400
	£	£
Labour	9,000	11,400
Food Costs	12,600	16,800
Administration Costs	6,000	6,000

Labour costs are analysed by taking the difference between the costs and dividing by the additional covers the assumption being that the additional cost must be a variable cost as fixed costs remain constant:

$$\frac{11{,}400 - 9{,}000}{2{,}400 - 1{,}800} = £4$$

This procedure isolates the variable cost per unit. From this we can deduce the variable costs as being:

2,400 x £4 = £9,600

and so the fixed costs must be:

11,400 - 9,600 = £1,800

Food costs are proven to be totally variable because, by dividing the cost by the covers, we find that the food costs remain constant at £7 per cover:

$$\frac{16{,}800 - 12{,}600}{2{,}400 - 1{,}800} = £7 \text{ per unit}$$

Administration costs are purely fixed costs as the same level of cost is recorded for differing levels of volume.

Another approach using a wider range of data is demonstrated as follows:

A department has the following breakdown of its revenue and employment costs for the past year:

	Revenue (£)	Salaries (£)
January	49,100	22,800
February	49,000	22,600
March	52,300	23,900
April	48,800	22,500
May	69,200	29,800
June	93,500	38,400
July	107,600	43,800
August	89,100	37,200
September	69,100	30,500
October	60,900	26,800
November	57,500	25,600
December	55,200	24,600

With these data the fixed and variable costs can be estimated by applying the high and low method to the July and February figures as follows:

By using the highest set of data, that is revenues of £107,600, and corresponding cost of £43,800 along with revenues of £48,800 and costs of £22,500, the additional variable costs arising from the additional sales can be calculated.

$$\frac{43{,}800 - 22{,}500}{107{,}600 - 48{,}800} = \frac{21{,}300}{58{,}800}$$

The variable costs are 36.2 % of sales. This means that the fixed costs can be calculated approximately:

Revenue	Total cost	Variable cost	Fixed cost
49,100	22,800	17,774	5,026
49,000	22,600	17,738	4,862
52,300	23,900	18,933	4,967
48,800	22,500	17,666	4,834
69,200	29,800	25,050	4,750
93,500	38,400	33,847	4,553
107,600	43,800	38,951	4,849
89,100	37,200	32,254	4,946
69,100	30,500	25,014	5,486
60,900	26,800	22,046	4,754
57,500	25,600	20,815	4,785
55,200	24,600	19,982	4,618

An alternative approach would be to plot the values on a graph with revenue on the horizontal axis and costs on the vertical axis. To ensure accuracy it is essential to ensure that:

- ☐ The graph scales start from zero at the origin
- ☐ The graduation of the scales is equally spaced
- ☐ The pairs of figures are accurately plotted

In practice it is highly unlikely that the points will form a perfectly straight line but if there is a relationship between revenue and costs the points plotted will approximate to straight line. From this it is possible to determine the fixed costs and the variable cost as illustrated by Figure 4.5.

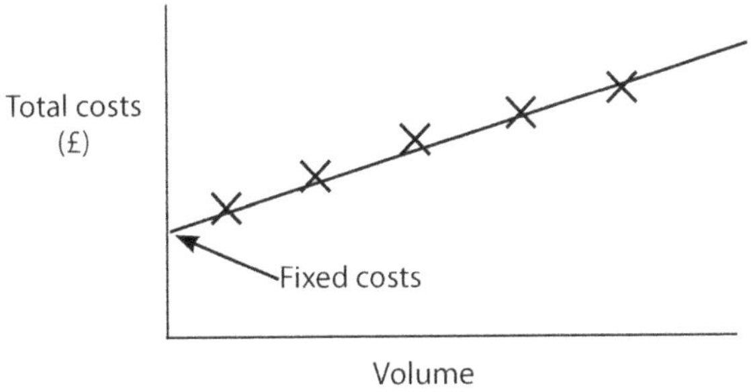

Figure 4.5: Relationship between costs and volume

The CVP approach can also be used to help explain why some businesses are more risky in nature than others. Consider the following CVP graphs in Figure 4.6

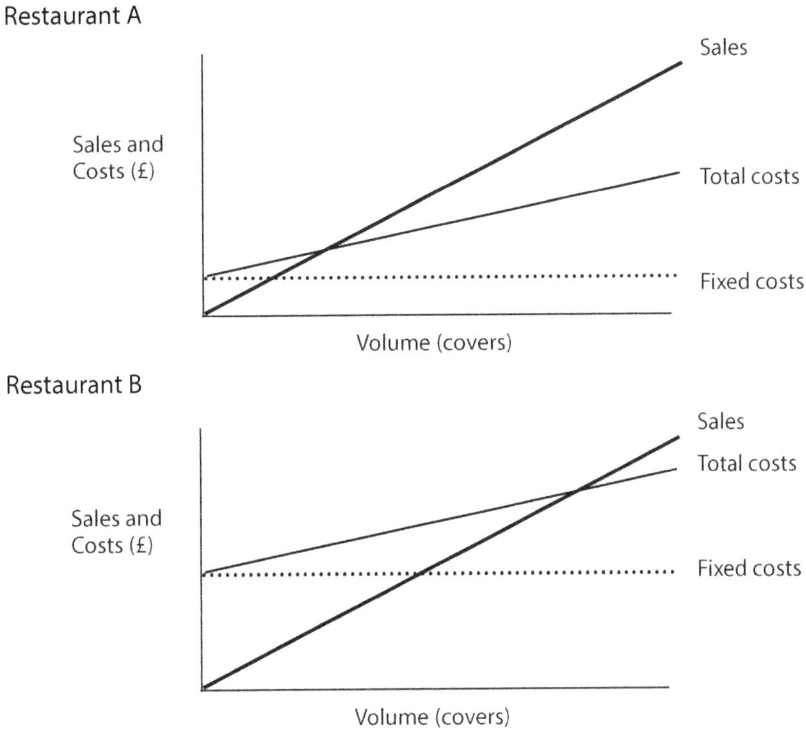

Figure 4.6: Represents two businesses with varying cost structures

Restaurant A illustrates an operation with lower fixed costs and hence a lower breakeven point. This means that lower sales are required to achieve a profit and if sales revenue falls the loss will be relatively small. Restaurant B illustrates a high fixed cost operation where the breakeven point is much higher, but once this has been achieved the resulting profitability will be much higher. The traditional approach to investment in the hospitality industry, that is direct equity investment, means that many operations have substantial fixed costs in terms of salary costs, property operation and maintenance costs and the servicing of finance. The high-risk nature of this type of investment has led to the growth of other forms of expansion using techniques which serve to reduce risk, and these are discussed in further detail in Chapter 10.

Costs for decision making

For the purposes of operational decision making, it is often useful to consider what are known as the *relevant costs* associated with a particular project. These are costs which will be incurred as the result of taking the decision which could be to switch supplier or change to a different style of service or to focus on specific products and services. In many cases the relevant costs are in fact the variable costs and these may be used in the decision making process. The variable costs may only be used in the short term and in situations where spare capacity exists. In the long term it is likely that both fixed and variable costs will need to be considered as relevant costs.

In most decisions it is also necessary to consider the nature of the *opportunity cost*. This can be defined as the benefit foregone as a consequence of taking an alternative course of action. No cash exchanges hands, the cost results from foregoing an alternative which requires no transaction. These costs are often not clearly understood and are then left out of the decision-making process. An example of an opportunity cost could be the business revenues lost when a restaurant closes for refurbishment. The lost revenue should be regarded as part of the total cost of the renovation.

Finally, a *sunk* cost is defined as one which has already been incurred and cannot be recovered. It is considered to be not relevant in the decision making process and should be left out. In the following example the different types of costs are identified.

Example

XYZ is a food manufacturer specialising in cook chill meals. An unexpected order has been received for which labour and production line capacity is available. The two main ingredients required are:

- Ingredient A which is used regularly in the existing process and 1,000 kgs are required for this order. The existing stock holding is 1,500 kgs purchased at 85p per kg. The current replacement cost is 90p per kg.
- Ingredient B is currently in stock with a stock holding of 500kg purchased at 60p per kg. This order requires 300 kg to be used. Without the order the entire stock would be either wasted or sold off as waste products at 30p per kg.

	Ingredient A	Ingredient B
Relevant cost	90p/kg	30p/kg
Sunk cost	85p/kg	60p/kg
Opportunity cost		30p/kg

Monitoring routine performance

This is most usually carried out as part of the budgetary control process where variances are used to compare actual performance with budgeted values, and this is most likely to be reported in the monthly profit and loss account circulated to departmental managers and heads of department. This area is covered in some detail in Chapter 6. The essential requirement for effective budgetary control procedures is a system for analysing revenues and costs incurred in the organisation. This normally means breaking the organisation down into areas of responsibility known as budget centres or cost centres. Responsibility is then assigned to individuals for the management of the sales and costs in those areas. The three types of responsibility centre typically are:

- ☐ Cost centre
- ☐ Profit centre
- ☐ Investment centre.

Typically, an organisation will comprise of cost centres, where only servicing activities take place, such as marketing, personnel and training and administration, and profit centres where trading activities take place. The performance of a profit centre is based on a comparison of revenues and costs. An investment centre is often the complete operation, where overall profitability can be compared to the investment. Variances are normally considered in terms of cost types such as materials, labour and expenses, and the comparison to budget is normally made on the basis of the cost of the resource (price per unit) and the volume used in the process. A typical layout for a regular report comparing budget to actual performance is illustrated in Figure 4.7.

	Yearly budget (£)	% to sales	Budget to date (£)	% to sales	Actual to date (£)	% to sales	Variance budget to actual (£)	Variance (% B/W)	Projected end of year (£)	Projected variance to full year budget £	Projected variance to budget % B/W
Sales											
Cost of sales											
Gross profit											
Salaries and wages											
Operating expenses											
Net income											

Figure 4.7: Report comparing budget to actual performance

The budgeted figures are based on standard costing procedures to forecast the spend at a given volume and the actual results are then compared to this. It may then be useful to prepare a flexible budget statement which reflects actual volumes at standard or target cost, to provide a means of effective comparability with the actual results. This is illustrated in Chapter 6.

The system of flexing is certainly useful for monitoring performance but often the data required to produce the flexed statements is not available and variances in practice are often calculated simply by comparing original forecasts with the actual performance.

Investigating the cost base

In periods of high inflation, it is essential to continue to monitor costs to ensure value for money is being achieved and that the cost is adding value to the business activity. In many hospitality, tourism and leisure businesses a large proportion of the total operational cost is payroll and related costs. These may be largely fixed with the majority of the teams employed on a permanent basis.

Therefore, it is essential to ensure that the resource is used effectively to maximise revenue, as well as monitoring overtime hours and the hours worked by casual or agency workers. Ratios can be used to monitor the cost by comparing the total payroll and related cost to the revenues, and also by comparing the revenues to the head count or numbers of full-time equivalents (FTE).

Costs which provide the greatest scope for improvement are often the indirect or overhead costs, which are most often fixed in nature. These are often the greater proportion of costs in any case and deserve further attention. It is often assumed that because they are fixed in nature they cannot be effectively controlled or reduced. In practice other costs which are directly attributable to revenue levels are much harder to reduce without reducing the quality of the product or service, although considerable management time is spent in tracking them.

Planning to reduce costs can be supported using techniques such as Zero-Based Budgeting (ZBB) during the planning phase, a technique which has its origins in the public sector. This technique requires the relevance of all operational costs to be questioned during the budgeting process rather than relying on an incremental approach where last year's performance is the starting point for setting this year's budget. This technique is described in more detail in Chapter 5, with its relevance to the hospitality and tourism industries. ZBB can produce substantial benefits, but it is a time-consuming activity and requires considerable expertise on the part of the operational manager to be used effectively.

An approach which has attracted considerable attention in recent years, particularly in the manufacturing sector, is that of Activity Based Costing (ABC).

Activity Based Costing

This approach focuses on indirect costs and attempts to establish links between expenditure and the activities carried out by the organisation. This contrasts with the traditional approach of allocating overheads arbitrarily to departments on the basis of revenue, floor space, head count or any other base deemed to be appropriate. ABC has its origins in the manufacturing sector but is now being more widely applied in many different types of organisation. The process requires the identification of the key activities which take place in the organisation and establishing a cost centre for each of those activities. The next step is to determine what is known as the *cost driver* for that activity. That is the event which can be described as the significant determinant of the cost of the activity. Finally, a unit cost should be derived for each activity, and these are assigned to each product on the basis of the demand for the activity.

This is probably better understood if it can be applied to a practical situation. In the case of a hotel, major activities performed include receiving reservations, checking in, room servicing, billing and checking out. Examples of cost drivers that might be appropriate to these activities include:

- Number of reservations received
- Number of guests arriving at the front desk
- Number of guests in house and the number of point of sale transactions.

The next stage is to divide the cost by the total number of driver units to calculate the cost per unit of activity. Finally, the cost of activities is traced to products according to the product demand for activities, by multiplying unit activity costs by the quantity of each activity that a product consumes. Hence the process attempts to measure as accurately as possible the *total* actual cost of each activity in the organisation rather than focusing specifically on direct or variable costs.

Cost leadership

In the hospitality, tourism and leisure industries competing on price is often a key element of sustaining competitive advantage. Cost leadership is vitally important to achieve as it enables the operation to gain increased market share by providing the best value for money to the customer at an attractive price. It also enables the operation to strengthen its position of competitive advantage by utilising the higher financial returns to improve quality, customer service and product innovation for the future. Cost leadership means that a business seeks to achieve the status of being the lowest cost supplier to the market for comparable products. This does not mean that the business is the lowest priced supplier but there is the potential to reduce prices during periods of intense competition or earn additional profits which can be reinvested in the business. The management guru Michael Porter has written extensively on this theme and says that:

> *"Its cost position gives the firm a defence against rivalry from competitors, because it can still earn returns after its competitors have competed away their profits through rivalry"*. (Porter, 1980)

Porter has argued that there are only two alternative routes to competitive advantage, these being cost leadership or differentiation, with little advantage in being the industry average competitor pursuing a '*stuck in the middle position*'. The alternative competitive positions are illustrated clearly in Figure 4.8.

Lowest cost competitor	Industry average competitor	Highest price competitor
Cost leadership	Stuck in the middle	Differentiator

Figure 4.8: Alternative competitive positions

Other writers argue that such a polarised approach is a dangerous strategy to pursue, and that practice suggests that it is possible to be both cheaper and better. Certainly, customers in the hospitality and tourism sectors are demanding evidence of constantly improving levels of value, quality, consistency and innovation.

Achieving long-term cost leadership requires a strategic approach in that the long-term nature of costs needs to be considered, with investment in alternative methodologies for delivering the product or service. Short-term measures for cost reduction, such as cuts in operational staffing levels, material costs and operating costs normally cannot be sustained and inevitably lead to a drop in product and service quality. Instead, a long-term approach with a *'spend to save'* policy is required. Lynch (2000) described the main routes to strategic cost reduction as:

- *Designing in cost reduction*: this is based on designing the product or service carefully during inception so that it is cheaper to deliver.
- *Supplier relationships*: using relationships with suppliers to achieve long term cost reductions – this approach has been popular with some of the UK large scale catering operators who have been able to drive down unit costs through changing specifications and centralised purchasing to take advantage of bulk buying.
- *Economies of scale and scope*: unit costs can fall as the business increases in size and processes are streamlined to take advantage of bulk buying
- *The experience curve*: The learning organisation will be able to achieve cost reduction as it becomes more experienced in the preparation and delivery of products and services.
- *Capacity utilisation*: the hotel industry in particular has significant high fixed costs and achieving the best utilization of space, for example, can achieve cost reductions per unit.

Conventional approaches to cost analysis tend to be based on an historical analysis of costs focusing on a single accounting period at a time. The approach tends to be introspective, operations based and reactive to short term crisis. A strategic approach has a wider focus, looking forward, analysing costs as they change throughout the product life cycle. The aim should be to consider the external environment, which is the competition, in addition to internal factors, and to be proactive in analysing information.

A limited approach to cost management often occurs because the responsibility for cost cutting usually lies solely with operating managers rather than being part of the strategic planning process. Frequently costs are only managed during crisis situations and many important costs are ignored. All too often employees hold negative perceptions of the cost cutting activity and personal relationships and emotions stand in the way of objective action. As a consequence, exercises in cost reduction are neither followed up nor maintained whilst the wrong costs are often cut first because they are the easiest to eliminate.

Profit planning

The profile of business costs is a critical element in profit planning. The cost structure, also called *operating leverage,* is measured in terms of the proportions of fixed costs and variable costs present in the business structure. An understanding of the influence cost structure has on profits is a crucial element in management decision making.

The hospitality and tourism sector is characterised by a wide range of different cost structures found in different types of business. In Chapter 1 the profile of the sector was considered, and the following list of operations typify the sector:

- Hotels
- Restaurants
- Pubs, bars and nightclubs
- Contract food service providers
- Membership clubs
- Events
- Gambling
- Travel services
- Tourist services
- Visitor attractions
- Youth hostels
- Holiday parks
- Self catering accommodation
- Hospitality services

Each of these elements of the sector will experience a differing cost structure. Typically, owned hotels, for example, have high fixed costs whereas the contract catering sector is typified by a low fixed cost structure but higher variable costs per unit of sale.

Sensitivity analysis

The term sensitivity analysis is used to describe a technique employed to measure the effect of cost structure on profitability. The technique enables the manager to establish which factors are critical to a decision, with the critical factors including unit volume, selling price, variable costs and fixed costs. Profit multipliers are used in sensitivity analysis to determine the effect of a percentage change in critical factor on the level of profit.

$$\text{A profit multiplier} = \frac{\%\ \text{Change in net profit}}{\%\ \text{Change in critical factor}}$$

In general terms, the profits generated by a business with a high fixed cost structures are relatively more sensitive to changes in critical factors. This suggests that the profits are potentially more at risk than for businesses with low fixed cost structures. Cost structure has implications for management decision making.

Competitive analysis

The process of competitive analysis covers a number of key characteristics of a business. These include:

- The external attractiveness of the different products and/or market opportunities measured;
- Using the growth in the market in total;
- Competitive position of the individual business in terms of current market share and relative cost levels.

These characteristics are often hard to measure in practice, although a profiling approach, which is based on matrix analysis, is often used.

Market development

The nature of competitive strategy is very much influenced by the stage of development of the product in the market place. The stages are defined as being:

Stage 1: Product launch

Stage 2: Sales growth

Stage 3: Competitive shakeout

Stage 4: Maturity

Stage 5: Decline

Techniques for analysing how each stage might be identified were discussed in Chapter 2.

During the launch stage competitive advantage is established by virtue of the fact that a new product has been launched in the marketplace ahead of the potential competition. The focus for competitor analysis at this stage will be on the relative levels of development and launch costs. However, this type of information is often difficult to obtain.

As the industry moves into the rapid growth stage, the key factor is the growth in market share and the focus switches to monitoring marketing expenditure. This information is more readily available in that the level of marketing activity is easily visible and it is therefore simpler to evaluate.

Once the product can be determined as being in the mature stage the basis of competition is frequently selling price, and the key success factor to obtaining competitive advantage is in the effective management of costs to ensure that in a highly price sensitive market profit levels are maintained. This exercise is obviously vitally important to many business operations in order to sustain competitive advantage throughout the maturity stage, which in practice is proportionately considerably longer than the other stages of the product life cycle.

The competitor analysis should not be simply limited to relative cost comparisons however. Relative selling prices and customer perceptions should also be monitored. Products which are perceived to have a higher value in the eyes of the customer do not need a lower cost base because the premium selling price compensates the resulting profit levels. Therefore, relative cost comparison exercises should start from an appreciation of the strategic product positioning that the competitor is seeking to achieve.

Sources of competitive information

The problem with achieving effective competitor analysis lies in obtaining good, reliable and meaningful information. It is not always necessary to obtain absolute values as quite often relative financial data that is data, relative to one's own business is sufficient. The management accountants within the business should be sufficiently experienced to be able to apply their own knowledge of cost structures to develop data drawn from the competition. The overall aim is to build up a comprehensive database about the competition which is continually being updated. The information contained within this can be drawn from a number of sources without in any way resorting to unethical forms of industrial espionage. A varied range of sources are listed in Table 4.2

Online research	Annual reports and press announcements
	Investment analysts reports
	Government reports
	Published market intelligence
	Company website
	Competitor advertising
Interviews	Journalists
	Academics
	Others with specialist knowledge
Direct contact	Visits to other establishments
	Physical observation
	Physical analysis of product
Conferences	Industry associations
Soft information	Own staff and management
	Mutual suppliers
	Mutual customers

Table 4.2: Sources of competitor information

Porter's approach to achieving competitive advantage

Michael Porter (1995) offers a three-step approach to achieving competitive advantage. These are:

1. Analysis of industry structure
2. Choosing a competitive strategy
3. Implementation of strategy.

Analysis of the industry structure enables firms to gain a good understanding of the cost structure of competitors and assess where advantages can be gained. This is discussed in more detail using Porter's five forces model.

Analysis of industry structure

The structure of the industry is determined by the pressure from five competing forces acting upon the business. These are the:

- ☐ Threat from new entrants;
- ☐ Bargaining power of suppliers;
- ☐ Bargaining power of suppliers;
- ☐ Bargaining power of buyers
- ☐ Threat of substitutes and rivalry between existing competitors.

This often illustrated diagrammatically as shown in Figure 4.9.

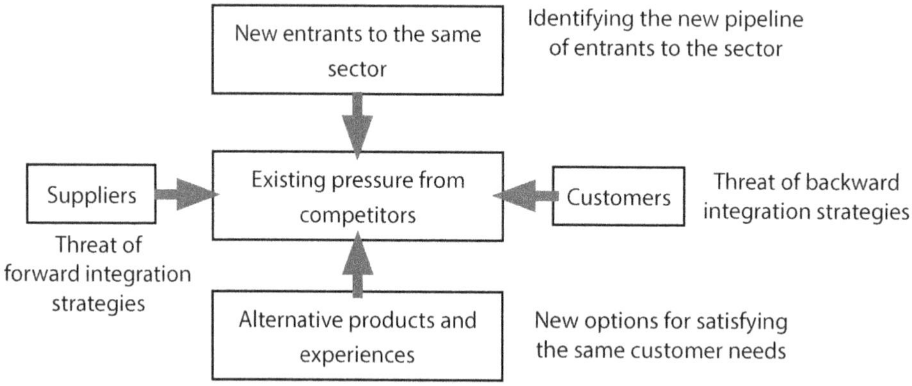

Figure 4.9: Current and potential competitor analysis (Using the Porter model as a basis), Adapted from Ward (1992) Strategic Management Accounting

Barriers to entry

The threat of entry by new competitors is often influenced by the economies of scale, brand loyalty and cost advantages already being achieved by the existing players, in the market, along with the capital required for entry. This can have significant effect in the hospitality industry where all of these conditions can apply.

An entry barrier is anything which represents a significant economic disincentive to a business to invest in a particular industry. In the hospitality industry it is often the size of the investment required to set up the business which acts as a significant barrier to possible new entrants. The cost structure may also serve as a barrier, particularly when fixed costs are high and higher volumes are required to achieve profitability. Finally, another common barrier is through the use of heavily marketed brands to try to create customer loyalty.

Power of suppliers

The power of the suppliers is derived from the availability of resources and may have more significant effect for operations setting up in developing economies. The conditions which make suppliers more powerful include those situations where there are no substitute products available for the buyer to switch to or the cost of switching supplier is too high to be viable.

Power of buyers

The power of buyers is derived from the level of supply and demand and the homogeneity between product suppliers. The power buyers can exert is increased when a number of buyers unite or when a number of suppliers exist and few costs are incurred in switching supplier. The threat from buyers is also increased when there is a real risk that the buyer will consider backward integration, that is expanding by buying out a supplier in an attempt to achieve satisfactory prices and quality.

Substitute products

To identify the level of threat from substitute products it is necessary to identify those products and services which perform the same function. Often these products are situated in industries which seem quite remote from the industry in question. For example, within the leisure industry there is a whole range of leisure activities, each vying for a limited customer leisure time and spends.

Existing firms

Rivalry amongst existing firms can occur in a number of ways, which can include price competition, new products and increased levels of customer service. The degree of rivalry depends on a number of features related to industry structure. Numerous or equally competitive competitors may cause instability by attempting to make strategic moves whilst hoping to remain unnoticed. Where there is low market growth the level of competition can intensify as firms attempt to expand by capturing market share from other firms. This intensifies still further where there is little opportunity for product differentiation. High levels of competition often means that profitability is eroded but high exit barriers can prevent firms from moving into other more profitable areas.

Exit barriers arise when the business is supported by high cost dedicated assets which have limited alternative uses, such as hotels. Exit costs might also include redundancy settlements and wasted material costs.

The level of rivalry is also dependent on the market position and is most intense during the mature stage of the product life cycle, and results in a condition called *shakeout* when the less profitable operations are forced to retire. Consequently, the higher the pressure from the five forces the less attractive the industry, as profit levels are constantly being reduced and it is increasingly difficult to maintain market position.

Competitive strategy

The next stage in Porter's approach is to decide upon a competitive strategy. Porter suggests there are only two generic competitive positions, these being either cost leadership or product differentiation.

- **Cost leadership** involves achieving competitive advantage through overall lowest cost compared to competing firms.

- **Differentiation** involves identifying the product or service characteristics which customers perceive as valuable and meeting those needs better than any of the competition, and as a result a premium charge can be made.

Strategy implementation

The final stage is implementation of the strategy and Porter has produced what is known as the '*value chain*' model to illustrate how this final stage can be achieved. The value chain comprises of a grouping of the primary and secondary activities of the organisation by which the product or service, or both, are provided to the customer. This is illustrated in Figure 4.11.

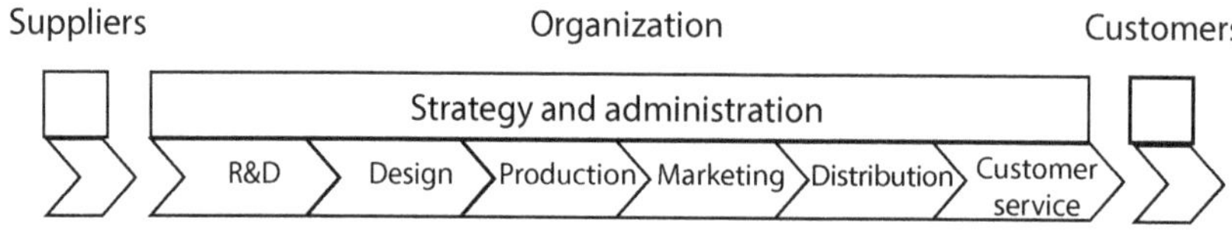

Figure 4.11: Porter's value chain model.

A business can be described as having a collection of activities that are performed to design, produce, market, deliver and support its product. The way in which an organisation does this is a reflection of the organisation's history, structure, past strategies and the nature of the activities themselves. It may be useful at this stage to illustrate how this chain might apply to a hotel operation.

- **Inbound logistics:** the activities concerned with receiving, storing, and distributing the input resources in the system. Practical examples include bookings received from customers using a variety of reservation capture methods.
- **Operations:** this stage converts the inputs into the final products and or services of the organisation, that is the management of the whole experience which converts needy customers into satisfied customers.
- **Outbound logistics:** this stage is concerned with the collection, storage and distribution of products and services to the customers, i.e. the service distribution points such as room service, restaurants etc.
- **Marketing and sales**: these are activities designed to attract further purchases during the period of the customer stay.
- **Service:** these activities ensure that customers enjoy their purchased goods and services ,and are associated with customer care and after sales service.

Porter's approach has been designed with the intention of providing a framework for classifying the various areas of the organisation in order to understand how the activities interrelate and contribute to the firm's competitive position. The aim is to understand what resources exist in the organisation and how they might be used more effectively.

Summary

The management of costs is an essential part of any business and should be carried out throughout the life of the business and not just in times of crisis. The routine control of costs can effectively be achieved using budgetary control systems based on assigning areas of responsibility to individuals and monitoring the variances which occur between expected and actual performance. In the long term a strategic view of cost management is required, which may mean moving away from the traditional approaches to cost monitoring. A strategic view means that all levels of managers in the organisation should be reviewing the cost base and be seeking ways of achieving long-term cost savings which are sustainable. This may mean incurring expenditure to save in the long term but thereby ensuring that the organisation can achieve competitive advantage through control of the cost base. Monitoring the competition can provide a wealth of information to assist an organisation in establishing its position in the marketplace.

Questions

1. Define the meaning of fixed and variable cost.

2. Give examples of the following for a hotel and resort operation:

a) Direct materials
b) Direct labour
c) Indirect materials
d) Indirect labour
e) Direct expenses

3. Explain the meaning of each of the following and give 3 examples of each for a travel operator:

a) Variable cost
b) Fixed cost
c) Semi variable cost

4. Contribution for decision making.

The Westgate Hotel operates at an average of 85% capacity and offers three types of bedroom. The information on the rooms is shown below:

	Family	Twin / Double	Single
Number of rooms available per night	100	150	100
Average tariff per room per day	£120	£95	£85
Cleaning time per room	120 mins	90 mins	70 mins
Daily cost of consumables per room	£10	£8	£6

Due to a staff shortage on one particular day the number of available cleaning hours is only 300. The fixed costs of the hotel including the salaries of the cleaning staff are £15,000 per day.

You are required to:

a) Calculate the contribution per room.

b) Calculate the most profitable combination of rooms to be made available given the staff shortage.

c) Calculate the profit if all the rooms are available and the revised profit given the staff shortage.

d) The hotel can use agency staff to fill the shortfall but the cost per labour hour is 20% higher than the usual staff. Comment on the viability of using the agency staff and illustrate your answer with workings. Give your conclusions as to whether the agency staff should be used.

5. Breakeven analysis and sales mix

The following figures relate to the Zena Restaurant for the monthly accounts for June:

	Starters	Main Course	Sweets and Coffee	Total
Sales mix	30%	60%	10%	100%
Variable costs	30%	40%	20%	
Fixed costs				£120,000

You are required to:

a) Calculate the breakeven sales revenue per period, based on the sales mix assumed above.

b) Prepare a contribution break-even chart illustrating the above figures.

c) Calculate the impact on the breakeven point of a change of sales mix to:

Starters	20%
Main course	65%
Sweets and coffee	15%

d) Explain the assumptions underlying the cost-volume-profit-analysis technique.

e) Explain how a business with multiple products can use cost-volume-profit analysis.

6. Breakeven and sales mix

The Foxglove Restaurant has prepared the following budget for the forthcoming quarter:

Total sales:		£750,000
Sales mix:		
Food	70%	
Beverage	20%	
Other	10%	
Cost of sales:		
Food	30%	
Beverage	25%	
Other	80%	

Labour:		
Fixed	£95,000	
Variable	20% of sales	
Other Fixed Costs:		£175,000

a) Calculate the contribution and the Contribution to Sales Ratio for each area and the total net profit for the year.

b) Compute the effect of the following changes in sales mix and cost of sales percentage on the contribution and the total net profit.

Sales Mix		Cost of Sales	
Food	65%	Food	30%
Beverage	25%	Beverage	28%
Other	10%	Other	85%

c) Discuss the effect of these changes on the breakeven point and the margin of safety.

7. Breakeven and selling price

A proposed restaurant operation is scheduled to open in a few months. The owner seeks your advice on pricing and gives you the following information:

Total capital investment	£500,000
Target return on investment	15%
Annual fixed costs other than depreciation	£100,000
Depreciation	£60,000
Operating costs	£750,000
Cost of food and beverage	30% of sales

The restaurant will have 150 seats and an average seat turnover per day of 2.5. The restaurant will be open for 320 days per year.

a) Calculate the average spend per meal.

b) Calculate the breakeven point for the operation

c) Calculate the margin of safety.

8. Feasibility study

A small company operating a number of restaurants is searching for a location to open one other. Two possible opportunities have been identified and the following forecasts made regarding each one:

Option 1

This operation is to be leased under the terms of a management contract with present revenues of £600,000 a year, operating variable costs of £450,000 and fixed costs of £75,000. In addition to these costs the lease contract calls for the company to pay an annual rental of 5% of sales plus a fixed amount of £10,000 per year.

Option 2

This operation requires an investment of £550,000 to purchase the site, furniture and equipment and the balance for working capital. The company has £300,000 to invest and will borrow the remainder at 10%. Estimates for the first year of trading are that food cost will be 30%, variable wage costs will be 15% and other variables will be 5% of total sales. Other cost estimates are:

Management and salaries:	£55,000
Depreciation	£35,000
Insurance	£10,000
Other costs (excluding interest on loan)	£50,000

The company requires a return of 20% on its initial investment.

Ignore taxation.

You are required to:

a) Prepare a trading statement for each option to meet the criteria specified.

b) Calculate the breakeven point for each option in terms of sales

c) Evaluate each option in terms of risk and profitability and make appropriate recommendations for the selection of one of the options.

9. Using variable and fixed costs

Preparing a Profit and Loss Statement

Adele manages the Oak Inn, a 100-bedroom limited service hotel. She provides you with the following details for preparing the May 2024 operating budget as follows:

Expected paid occupancy percentage	80%
Average room rate	£120
Day's trading	31 days
Average spend Food & Beverage	£13
Total covers expected	700
Room operating expenses:	
Fixed	£60,000
Variable	£18 per room sold
Food and Beverage operating expenses:	
Fixed	£1,000
Variable	50% of food and beverage revenue

Other undistributed operating expenses (not included above):

	Fixed £	Variable as % of total revenue
Administration & general	4,000	5%
Sales & marketing	2,500	4%
Property operation & maintenance	2,000	2%
Information and Telecommunications	4,000	nil

Based on the above data, prepare the Operating Budget for May 2024 to Gross Operating Profit level.

	£	%
Revenue		
Rooms		
Food and Beverage		
Total revenue		
Rooms operating expenses		
Fixed		
Variable		
Rooms Departmental operating profit		
Food and Beverage operating expenses		
Fixed		
Variable		
Food and Beverage operating profit		
Total Departmental Profit		
Undistributed Operating costs		
A&G		
Sales and marketing		
Property operation and maintenance		
Information and Telecommunications		
Total Undistributed operating costs		
Gross operating profit		

10. Example to calculate COS and GP

The Ensbury Cafe has the following figures for the week:

Sales	40,840
Opening Inventory	14,135
Closing inventory	6,018
Purchases	4,135
Employee meals	1,475

a) Calculate the cost of food sales.

b) Calculate the food cost percentage.

c) Calculate the gross profit percentage.

If employee meals served cost £475 what are the adjusted figures for a) to c)?

11. Example – to calculate the target selling price

The following ingredients, together with their cost prices, are required for a particular menu item (Chicken pie) that yields eight portions.

Ingredients	Quantity	Cost (£)	Total cost
Chicken	3 kilos	£2.40 per kilo	7.20
Mushrooms	0.25 kilos	£1.80 per kilo	
Four medium onions	0.2 kilos	£1.90 per kilo	
Chicken stocks	0.5 litres	20p per litre	
Streaky bacon	0.5 kilos	£2.62 per kilo	
Egg	2	£1.32 per dozen	
Salt, pepper, parsley	To taste	2p in total	
Puff pastry	0.45 kilos	£1.60 per kilo	
		Total cost	
		Cost per portion	
		Plus Vegetable portion	
		Total cost of food on the plate	
		Net selling price	
		Gross selling price	

a) Calculate the cost per portion for this menu item.

b) Calculate the selling price for the meal assuming accompanying vegetables will cost 80p, a Gross Profit Margin of 70% and that VAT at 20.0% needs to be included.

References and further reading

Atrill, P. & Mclaney E. (2021) *Accounting and Finance for Non-Specialists*, 12th Edition, Pearson.

Lynch, R. (2000) *Strategic Management*, Sage Publications

Porter, M., (1980) *Competitive Strategy: Techniques for Analysing Industries and Competitors*. New York, The Free Press.

Porter, M., (1985) *Competitive Advantage: Creating and Sustaining Superior Performance*. New York, The Free Press.

Ransley, J., Ingram, H. and Adams, D. (2022) *Developing Hospitality Properties and Facilities*. Routledge

Useful websites

hbr.org/2010/05/when-youve-got-to-cut-costs-now When You've Got to Cut Costs—Now

5 Managing pricing strategies

About this chapter

This chapter reviews the various pricing methodologies available to the hospitality and tourism industries for the pricing of accommodation, food, beverages and other activities. The review of accommodation pricing techniques considers formulistic approaches to pricing such as the rule of thumb method and the Hubbart formula which are based on cost plus calculations, as well as market demand approaches such as yield management. Food and beverage pricing is considered with specific reference to sales mix and approaches to menu analysis for maximising gross profit in percentage and cash terms. In theory, price setting appears to be a simple task, but in reality, the pricing process is complicated by market, economic and psychological influences and, as a result, the pricing decision requires input from financial, marketing and operational managers in order to ensure that the resulting pricing policy is based on the correct information.

Learning objectives

On completion of this chapter, you should be able to:

- ☐ Describe how the optimum sales volume and selling price is determined using economic theory
- ☐ Understand the principles of cost-based approaches to pricing
- ☐ Apply cost-based pricing techniques to commodities such as accommodation, food and beverage and other tourism services
- ☐ Make pricing decisions based on market conditions.

Introduction

The principle aim of any pricing policy should be to increase revenue without sacrificing the required level of volume, while increasing profitability and ensuring long-term business value. It should also aim to impact customer buying behaviour by responding to influences arising from the competitive environment. A good starting point is a knowledge of economic theory that provides a suitable basis for introducing the concepts required for pricing decisions.

Economic theory

Economic theory describes the relationship between changing prices and the impact on customer demand as the *price elasticity of demand*. Demand is described as being elastic when a change in price results in a change in the buying behaviour of customers. This relationship is illustrated in Figure 5.1.

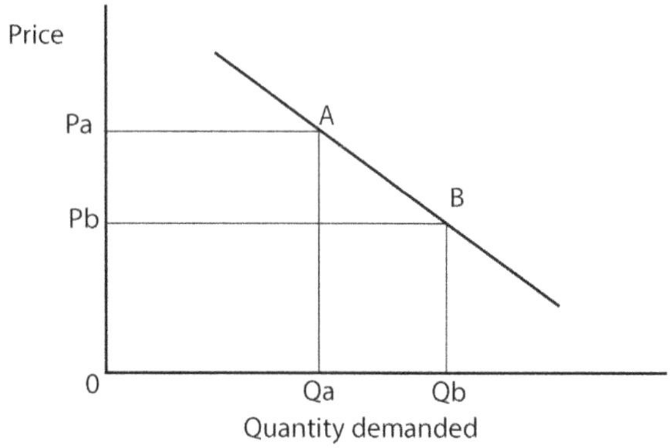

Figure 5.1: The demand curve

The points marked A and B represent two of the many possible price/quantity combinations. As the price falls the quantity demanded increases. Inelastic demand arises where the customer buying decision is unaffected by price changes. Figure 5.2 illustrates the price elasticity of demand where there is elastic demand and inelastic demand. When demand is inelastic an increase in price has only a minimal effect on quantity purchased, whereas with elastic demand a change in price results in a significant change in quantity demanded.

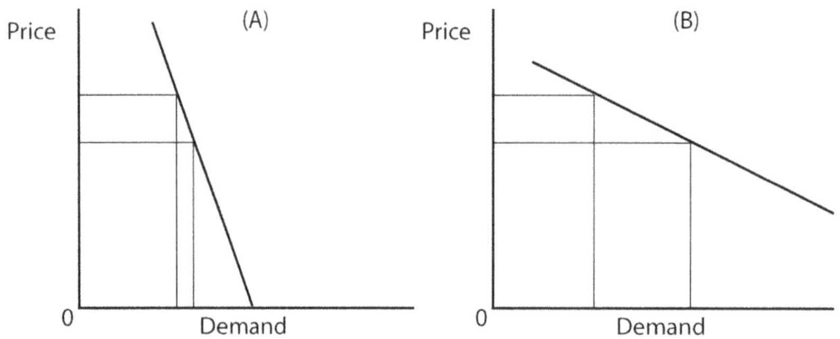

Figure 5.2: Price elasticity of demand: (a) inelastic demand; (b) elastic demand

Price and the product life cycle

The concept of the product life cycle was introduced in Chapter 2. The development of pricing strategies should be considered in the light of the positioning of the product or service on the product life cycle. Figure 5.3 illustrates the relationship between product life cycle and price. At each stage on the product life cycle the pricing strategy needs to adapt, to respond the levels of demand.

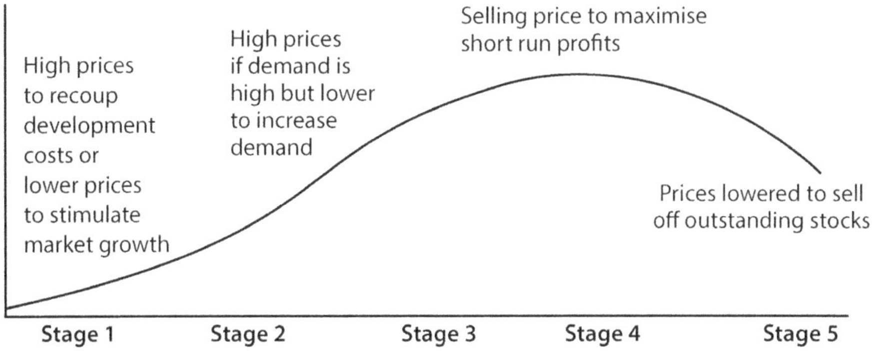

Figure 5. 3: Relationship between the product life cycle and pricing strategy

Cost based approach to pricing

The overall aim of an effective pricing policy is to ensure that the profit per product is maximised while maintaining a perception of value for money in the eyes of the customer. Despite this aim, the traditional approach to pricing tends to be based on cost plus techniques where a mark-up is added to the cost of producing the product to arrive at the selling price. The cost of the product can range from simply calculating the food or material cost, in the case of menu pricing, through to attempting to calculate a total cost per product, including materials, wages, expenses and overhead. However, this level of detail is reliant on adequate information being available to enable fixed or indirect costs to be allocated to individual products in a satisfactory manner, particularly where there are several products or services available.

When the pricing policy is based solely on direct costs or on material costs, the difference between the selling price and those costs must be sufficient to cover all other costs and provide an adequate level of profit. The following example illustrates a mark up policy of 33.33% food cost of sales.

Example:

A restaurant produces a dish which costs £3.00 in terms of the food portion cost. The aim is for the food to cost a third of the resulting net selling price. The restaurant has forecasted to sell 10,000 of these dishes over a set period with other variable cost expected to be 25% of net sales and fixed costs of £12,000.

Net Selling price	=	£3.00 x 3
	=	£9.00

Therefore

Net Sales	=	£90,000
Food cost	=	£30,000
Gross profit	=	£60,000
Variable costs	=	£22,500
Fixed costs	=	£12,000
Net profit	=	£25,500

The profit required to meet investors' target returns is often used as the basis for establishing the total revenue for an operation where costs can clearly be predicted. The required profit is added to the estimated cost figures to produce a value for total sales. This figure is used with volume forecasts and sales mix predictions to arrive at selling prices for individual products and services. For food and beverage operations the material costs are used as the basis for determining the net selling price, assuming that the resulting gross profit will be sufficient to cover the other operational and overhead costs.

Price setting

The economic theory of supply and demand argues that as an item becomes scarcer its price should increase and that there is a direct relationship between price and demand. In the hospitality industry this simple relationship is complicated by the seasonality of the business, giving rise to differing demand patterns and the multiple numbers of products available in a restaurant, for example, where sales are interrelated.

The hospitality industry also differs from the manufacturing industry in terms of the product. Although products may be very similar, no two establishments offer the exact same product and service. There will always be some difference in terms of the product itself and the nature and quality of service. This factor means that for operators, the competition prices should only be used as a guideline. However, this does give the operator far greater scope for achieving product and therefore price differentiation.

One approach might be to deliberately charge more than the competitors and use product differentiation to justify the higher price. However, the cost of raising the quality of the product should be considered in relation to the increase in selling price and continual monitoring is required to ensure the customer still perceives the product to be good value.

Alternatively, an operation may choose to price the product at a level below the competition. This tactic can be dangerous in that unless real cost savings can be made without undermining quality, the profit per product will drop without a sufficient corresponding increase in sales volume. This in turn may lead to a price war situation with a downward spiral of price cutting which leads to profit reduction for all operators, with even the possibility of bankruptcy.

The accepted pricing practice is to set the published prices at the maximum the market will bear and then, particularly in the case of rooms, to discount or use tactical promotions to maximize utilisation during the weaker trading periods.

Accommodation pricing

Managing the room resource in hotel operations requires achieving a careful balance between maintaining room rate and achieving maximum occupancy, where a relatively small increase in room rate may be worth a drop in occupancy in terms of profitability as each extra room sold will need to be cleaned. Traditionally, room occupancy percentage was the critical determinant of success for many operators, particularly where substantial sales can be generated in other trading areas within the hotel, such as food and beverage with the larger number of customers in house. However, the measure which encapsulates both occupancy and the average room rate is REVPAR – the room revenue per available room. This measure can be calculated on a daily basis and is used to monitor the success achieved against budget, forecast, prior year and also the competition.

Hotel occupancy levels are commonly viewed to be directly related to the size of the hotel, average room rates, conference facilities, hotel ownership and location. Severe discounting may serve to maintain volumes in a period of recession but the effect of this can have a dramatic downward effect on profitability and the cash flow levels of the operation.

There are various approaches to setting the room rate, ranging from those which are simply formulistic to an extensive analysis of target profit levels and costs, and these will be discussed in detail. However, a successful approach to rooms pricing requires an accurate knowledge of the markets to which the product is attractive and a clear knowledge of price elasticity patterns. The *yield management* (YM) approach to pricing, also known as *revenue management,* does just this, and with widespread usage of computerised reservation systems, is now used extensively. As a result, a detailed discussion of this approach will follow later in the chapter.

Rule of thumb method for price setting

In an operation where the majority of revenue is derived from room letting, one approach is to base the average room rate calculation on the capital cost for building one room. It should be reasonable to assume that there should be a fairly direct relationship between the cost of the building and the room rate to be charged. The rule of thumb states that £1 of room rate should be charged for each £1000 invested in building the room. If a room costs £100,000 to build, the average net room rate is calculated to be £100. This relationship is based on the assumptions that the hotel is fairly large (several hundred bedrooms), with other departments such food and beverage, and that the operation will achieve 65 - 70% average room occupancy.

This approach is used as a very general guide only and can lead to incorrect pricing strategies where the emphasis is purely on historical costs.

Profit based pricing techniques

This approach is sometimes referred to as the 'bottom-up' approach to pricing or the *Hubbart formula,* and was originally developed for the American Hotel and Motel Association. This method is based on accurate forecasts for operating costs and for room occupancy. The sales figure is calculated by summing the target profit with the fixed and variable costs. This total figure is then subdivided to arrive at different rates for different room types. The following example demonstrates the method in practice.

Example

Forecasted projections for a 100-bedroom hotel operation are given below.

Investment details

	£
Long term assets	2,500,000
Working capital	150,000
Total net assets	2,650,000
Financed by:	
Owners equity	2,000,000
10% mortgage debenture payable 20x1	650,000
	2,650,000

Trading forecasts

- average of 70% occupancy
- annual forecasted profits from other departments £400,000
- owners require a 20% return on equity invested.

	£
Net profit required (based on after-tax target percentage return on equity)	400,000
Corporation tax (at 25% of profit before tax)	133,333
Profit before tax	533,333
Interest (relating to mortgage debenture)	65,000
Depreciation (10% straight line method on fixed assets)	250,000
Insurance and licence (forecasted)	20,000
Property operation (forecasted)	520,000
Administration (forecasted)	55,000
Management salaries (forecasted)	400,000
Less profit from other departments (forecasted)	(400,000)
Operating expenses for accommodation (forecasted at 26% of revenue)	274,920
Annual accommodation revenue required	1,718,254

The room occupancy percentage should be an accurate forecast for the likely number of rooms sold based on current achievable levels in similar operations. An accurate forecast will improve the reliability of the rate setting calculation.

100 rooms x 365 nights x 70% occupancy = 25,550

$$\text{Average room rate required} = \frac{1{,}718{,}254}{25{,}550} = £67.25$$

The rate calculated from this approach is simply the average room rate before VAT. From this, rates for room types and market segments will need to be calculated.

Setting the room rate

Single and double rates can be calculated by considering historical double and single occupancy rates. Using the data generated in the example given above if twin occupancy is 60% of room sold and single occupancy is then 40% and a 20% difference is required between twin and single rates the calculation would be:

$$(60\% \times 60\% \times 100 \text{ rooms} \times 365 \times 1.2R) + (40\% \times 60\% \times 100 \times 365 \times R) = £558,558$$

where R represents the single rate. This solves to:

$$15,768R + 8,760R = £558,558$$

$$R = \frac{558,558}{24,528}$$

$$= £22.77$$

The double rate will be £27.32.

This type of algebraic formula could be expanded to include other room type and market segments as long as the occupancies for each type could be forecasted.

Room pricing options

The simplest approach would be to offer all rooms at one rate. The advantage of this approach is that it is easy to administer and to communicate to customers. However, the approach fails to respond to peaks and troughs in demand by recognising customer price sensitivity and as a result fails to maximize revenue.

Alternatively, room rates can be set by room type depending on the room characteristics. This approach is also fairly simple to administer but is useless where all rooms are uniform. Even if the hotel has different room types it is still limited by the stock of each of those room types and consequently the approach becomes product led rather than market led.

Another approach is to use price segmentation; that is to introduce logical restrictions on the booking in return for a discounted rate. This allows customers to have access to lower rates in return for reduced flexibility and differentiates those who are willing and able to pay higher prices from those who are willing to change their behaviour in exchange for a lower price. Such an approach enables the hotel to penetrate new markets without encouraging existing business to trade down.

Accommodation markets

Traditionally the transient hotel market excluding groups may be crudely classified into two market segments, business and leisure and each market has had its own booking pattern characteristics.

Leisure travellers	**Business travellers**
Advance bookings	Short booking lead times
Quality required varies	Tend to require high quality
Destination flexible	Destination predetermined
Highly price sensitive	Relatively less price sensitive
Stays longer	Short-term stay avoiding weekends.

In more recent times the booking patterns have become blurred with a growth in travellers combining business with leisure known as *bleisure* markets. The impact of this is to increase the traditional short business trip of a couple of nights away into a longer trip. Hotel pricing strategies should take advantage of these differing market characteristics by attempting to expand the price elastic markets whilst ensuring that inelastic business revenues are maintained. Practically this means managing capacity to ensure that an appropriate number of rooms are left available at high rates to accommodate the late booking business market. The industry has long been at ease with charging different rates to different markets and the key is to ensure that any rate charged should exceed the variable cost of providing the product to ensure a contribution towards fixed costs.

The following example illustrates the typical range of variable costs incurred when a hotel room is occupied by the guest.

Variable costs per occupied room	£
Labour - include National Insurance contributions and benefits	15.00
Cleaning supplies – cost to clean the room	5.00
Laundry cost - Linen	5.00
Utilities - hot water, lighting, air con, etc	10.00
Guest amenities – bathroom products	5.00
Reservation commission (cost of acquisition)	60.00
Total variable costs	**100.00**

Note that the largest cost is the reservation commission which is incurred when a guest books through a third party such as an online travel agent. The difference between the net average room rate and the variable cost is called the contribution. With this example, if the room sells for £300.00 per night the contribution will be £200.00 per night.

A similar calculation takes place when pricing an airline seat in the tourism industry. The net ticket price should be more than all the variable costs including the taxes to ensure a contribution towards the fixed costs of running the airline is created.

The strategy of matching rates to customer behavior needs to be carefully managed, particularly where customers who pay one rate later realise that they could have negotiated a cheaper rate. However, these techniques, known as dynamic pricing, have become widespread in the airline, hotel and tourism industries.

A note of caution with regard to room rate discounting

Discounting is a widespread practice in the hotel tourism industry and is particularly suited to a product based on minimal variable costs and substantial fixed costs. Providing that a room is sold at a price in excess of variable costs some contribution to fixed costs will be made. This knowledge has led to an almost unchecked approach to room rate discounting by some operators. Rate cutting can generate more revenues, if occupancy increases but this is not always transferred to the bottom line. Hotel profitability is measured using Gross Operating Profit (GOP) which is calculated in the Profit and Loss as:

Total profit from revenue generating departments – Undistributed operating expenses.

To achieve target GOP levels, it is essential to control both the revenue generating department costs and the costs from the supporting departments such as sales and marketing and utilities.

Yield (Revenue) Management

The process of YM, commonly known as revenue management, is used widely in the hotel and tourism industry and is used predominantly to control airline seat and hotel room inventory. This involves controlling inventory to maximise sales by adjusting rates in response to the level of bookings already received. The commonly accepted definition of revenue management is to sell the right product to the right customer at the right time for the right price.

The airline industry introduced the technique in the 1970s, following deregulation, enabling more flexibility in the pricing of different routes. When airlines cannot fill all of the seats on an aircraft with full fare customers, they then try to fill them with customers paying discounted rates. An empty seat represents an opportunity lost owing to the perishable nature of the product. The airline must decide how many fares to discount while making sure they have enough seats left to sell to late booking full fare paying customers in order to maximise the possible revenue. This requires a good understanding of what is known as booking pace – the rate at which customers book as the date for departure grows closer.

Comparisons can easily be drawn between the management of airline seats and hotel rooms, where fixed capacity exists and the products are sold in easily segmented markets with variable levels of demand often well in advance of the consumption date. The cost structures of the two industries are also similar, both being capital intensive with high fixed costs, whilst the marginal cost of selling one more airline seat is minimal and the same is true for the selling of a hotel room. Revenue Management uses the basic principles of supply and demand economics in a tactical way to generate incremental revenues. There are three essential conditions for Revenue Management to be applicable:

- There is a fixed amount of products or services available for sale
- The product or service is perishable
- Customers are willing to pay a different price for the same product or service

Calculating room yield

The two main factors management uses to measure performance in room revenues are occupancy and average room rate. Both of these should be maximised to ensure that the full potential room's revenue is achieved. The yield is an integrated statistic based on actual potential revenue and is calculated using the following example.

Hotel A has 100 rooms and a rack rate of £100. The following sales mix represents the pattern of business for one night.

Rack rate	25% at £100
Corporate rate	15% at £80
Walk in trade	3% at £50
Travel agency	3% at £45
Groups	10% at £30

This results in total revenue of £4,285, occupancy of 56 rooms or 56% and rate per available room of £42.85

The 'yield statistic' is expressed as follows:

$$\text{Yield} = \frac{\text{Realised revenue}}{\text{Potential revenue}}$$

Potential revenue being the maximum sales that could be obtained if all the available rooms are sold at full rack rate and realised revenue is the actual sales generated. The yield statistic for the previous example would be:

$$\frac{£4,285}{100 \text{ rooms} \times £100} = 42.85\%$$

In terms of room sales many combinations of of occupancy and achieved room rates could generate equal revenue and yield percentages as the following figures for Hotel A illustrate.

Average room rate	Occupancy %	Realised Revenue £	Yield %
100	42.85	4285	42.85
90	47.61	4285	42.85
80	53.56	4285	42.85
70	61.21	4285	42.85
60	71.42	4285	42.85
50	85.70	4285	42.85

The yield statistic can also be expressed as a combination of occupancy percentage and average room rate. It can be calculated by multiplying the average rate ratio by the actual room occupancy percentage where the average rate ratio is calculated by expressing the average rate as a percentage of the average maximum potential rate. Given the data in the example above,

$$56\% \text{ occupancy} \times \frac{76.52}{100} = 42.85\% \text{ yield}$$

This simple statistic provides a single value for measuring a hotel's performance and forms the basis of YM. Another popular measure is the REVPAR calculated from the Rooms revenue achieved divided by the rooms available. From the previous example the REVPAR would be:

$$\frac{£4,285}{100} = £42.85$$

The purpose of the approach is to maximise room yield and REVPAR by managing both the room rate and the occupancy percentage so that when demand exceeds supply the customer pays more and when demand is low the price is discounted whilst ensuring each customer pays the maximum possible price.

Critics of this approach have identified the fact that not all these combinations of occupancy and rate as illustrated in the above example produce the same level of profitability. By introducing the marginal cost of servicing a room, of say £10 per room, the hotel contribution to fixed costs can be calculated.

Occupancy %	Realised Revenue £	Servicing cost £	Contribution £
42.85	4,285	429	3,856
47.61	4,285	476	3,809
53.56	4,285	536	3,749
61.21	4,285	612	3,673
71.42	4,285	714	3,571
85.70	4,285	857	3,428

The room's contribution can be seen falling as occupancy increases and rates fall. However, the effect of the fall in room's contribution arising from discounted room prices may well be outweighed by the resulting increase in food and beverage revenue derived from increased volumes of customers present in the hotel.

Increasingly RM techniques are used in other revenue generating areas such as restaurants and meetings and events.

Revenue management requirements

In order to effectively use revenue management techniques, it is essential to have a clear understanding of the markets in which the business operates. This will be achieved by analysing historical data in terms of the patterns of demand, the market segments and price elasticity. Demand analysis is essentially based on clearly defining the product and differentiating the main market segments to identify the levels of demand from each market segment at different times of the year, thereby predicting the level of inventory needed to meet each segment's needs.

Specifically, it is essential to capture information relating to customer booking patterns and behaviour and the timing of demand in each market segment. This will need to be supported with data relating to the policy and volumes of overbooking, and a clear knowledge of the impact of price changes on demand patterns and occupancy. Producing this level of information is a task of some complexity but the process can be assisted with the use of expert system packages. These are software packages containing a 'knowledge base' which allows the system to approach and solve problems by interpreting the 'facts' based on decision rules written into the software.

Problems specific to hotels

In certain circumstances revenue management practices translated directly from the airline industry may fail to adjust to the complexities offered by the hospitality industry. The key problem arises when a guest who has stayed one night then decides to extend the stay for one or more nights. If the first night stay is determined to be a low-demand, low-rate reservation, problems will arise if the ensuing nights of stay are during high-demand periods. Similar problems arise where a customer wishes to stay through a period of both low and high demand. The solution in this case might be to offer an average of the high and low rates generated.

Customer perceptions

The issue of fairness from the customer's perspective can affect the maximisation of profits. Generally, customers feel that price rises are fair when costs are increasing, and the price rise has been incurred in order to simply maintain profits and not to increase them. To convince customers of the fairness of the pricing strategies whilst maximising price, one approach is to increase the reference price, that is the rack rate, in the knowledge that virtually all customers will pay less than this.

Research drawn from surveys on hotel guests has established that customers express satisfaction with revenue management practices when information on the different pricing options is available, when a substantial discount is given in return for cancellation restrictions and finally different prices are charged for products which are perceived to be different. This would indicate that improved communication with the customer is necessary to ensure complete acceptance of the approach. Finally, research has indicated that customers perceive unacceptable practices to include:

- Offering insufficient benefit in return for booking restrictions
- Imposing severe booking restrictions such as nonrefundable, non changeable restrictions on discounted rooms
- Not informing customers of the availability of discounted rates.

Food & beverage pricing

Restaurant management has traditionally been based on unsophisticated techniques for establishing menu item prices and the most commonly used approach has been to simply to multiply the food cost by a factor of three or even four to produce a target gross profit percentage. This approach ignores the labour cost incurred to prepare the product and assumes that the labour cost will be covered sufficiently by the target gross profit percentage. Alternatively, the average spend per customer can be determined in the same way as average room rates by using a bottom up, profit based approach. Again, the problem with a cost-based approach lies in the accurate forecasting of costs and volumes and ignores the market perception of price and value.

Pricing menu items

A common approach to menu pricing is to calculate the standard cost to produce one of each menu item. This cost is then multiplied by a factor to achieve the target gross profit as the following example demonstrates.

Standard food cost to prepare dish	£1.00
Multiplication factor	3
Net selling price	£3.00
Gross selling price with VAT	£3.60
Gross profit %	67%
Gross profit	£2.00

Naturally, this is a mechanistic approach and in reality, the price should be set to reflect what the market will pay. As a result, some items will have a higher gross profit percentage than others and the combination of products sold then becomes important otherwise known as sales mix.

It is also important not to solely rely on gross profit percentages, often it is the cash gross profit figure which is important as the following figures in Table 5.1 demonstrate.

Menu item	Cost of sales	Net selling price	GP %	GP £
1	£5.00	£10.00	50%	£5.00
2	£2.00	£6.00	67%	£4.00

Table 5.1: Illustrating the relationship between net selling price, cost of sales and gross profit (GP)

It would be preferable to sell more of Menu item 1 than Menu item 2 despite the lower GP percentage.

Sales mix

This is defined as the combination of menu items sold from the menu. The sales mix will influence the average spend per cover and the resulting achieved gross profit percentage as the following figures in Table 5.2 demonstrate.

Menu item	Quantity sold	Net selling price £	Total sales £	Cost of sales £	Total costof sales £	GP%
1	10	4.00	40.00	2.00	20.00	50%
2	15	3.00	45.00	1.00	5.00	67%
3	20	2.00	40.00	1.50	30.00	25%
4	10	1.00	10.00	0.20	2.00	80%
5	5	1.00	5.00	0.30	1.50	70%
Total	60		140.00		68.50	51%

Table 5.2: Calculating the average gross profit using the sales mix and cost of sales

This combination of menu items produces an average spend of £2.33, a gross profit percentage of 51% and gross profit in cash terms of £71.50. If the sales mix were to change the effect would be that shown in Table 5.3.

Menu item	Quantity sold	Net selling price	Total sales	Cost of sales	Total costof sales	GP%
		£	£	£	£	
1	15	4.00	60.00	2.00	30.00	50%
2	15	3.00	45.00	1.00	15.00	67%
3	15	2.00	30.00	1.50	22.50	25%
4	5	1.00	5.00	0.20	1.00	80%
5	10	1.00	10.00	0.30	3.00	70%
Total	60		150.00		71.50	52%

Table 5.3: The impact of a change of sales mix on the average gross profit

These variables make the setting of food menu selling prices particularly complex and the problems are equally valid for establishing beverage prices. This in turn makes the process of controlling gross profit percentage a time-consuming exercise in practice, and for many operations the exercise can never be accurately completed due to the range of information required.

Demand based menu pricing

Increasing profits can either be achieved by reducing expenses, the usual targets being material and labour costs, or by raising the selling price. In recessionary times this latter option may appear to be out of the question. However, the reality is that for a high fixed cost operation a 1% increase in price will have a considerably more substantial effect on profitability as the following example illustrates.

Assume: Selling price £10
Variable cost £2
Volume of 2,000 units
Fixed costs £10,000

	Original data	Increase selling price (10%)	Reduce costs by 10%
Sales	20,000	22,000	20,000
Variable costs	4,000	4,000	3,600
Fixed costs	10,000	10,000	9,000
Net profit	6,000	8,000	7,400

These figures clearly illustrate that, where possible, the selling price should be maximised by considering the most that a customer is likely to spend on that item before the value/price relationship is lost. For food and beverage businesses, this approach can be developed further using techniques known as menu analysis.

Approaches to menu analysis

An approach to menu analysis called *menu engineering* was proposed in 1982 by hospitality industry gurus Michael Kasavana and Donald Smith. This is a portfolio approach whereby menu items are classified in terms of those with highest contribution margin and highest sales volume. Contribution margin is defined in this case as the difference between selling price and direct costs. Menu items could then be plotted in terms of a grid as shown in Figure 5.4 and managers seek to choose those menu items with the lowest direct costs and the highest profitability.

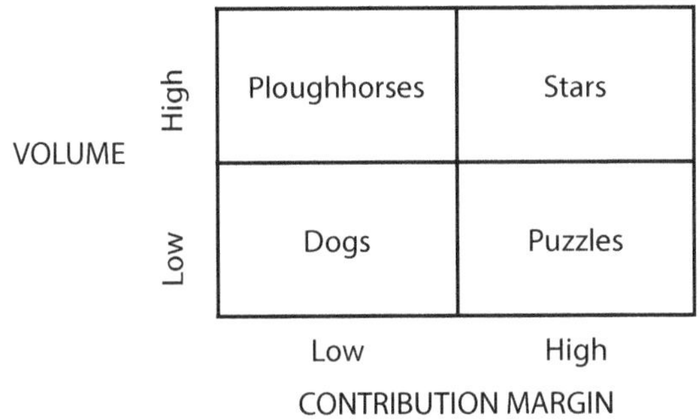

Figure 5.4: Kasavana and Smith's approach to menu analysis

The bias in this approach may result in favouring high price items which maximise contribution resulting in a strategy which eventually decreases demand and profitability. The target is to achieve a sales mix which optimises the cash contribution margin, defined as sales less food costs, and total sales revenue whilst achieving the lowest food cost percentage. The menu items are classified into the groups:

- ☐ *Standards*: High contribution margins, high food cost %;
- ☐ *Primes*: High contribution margins, low food cost %
- ☐ *Sleepers*: Low contribution margins, low food cost %;
- ☐ *Problems*: Low contribution margin, high food cost.

Primes are often the specialty dishes which can be priced at what ever the market will bear, whilst *standards* are often popular items which are offered on most menus and need to be priced keenly. The *sleeper* category includes new items being test marketed to see how the clientele responds to them. The final group is made up of the '*problem*' items and these should be eliminated from the menu. The maximum contribution will be achieved when the predominant sales mix is made up from primes and standards whilst sleepers are used to diversify the menu and attract new clientele to the establishment.

Profitability analyses can be performed at several levels ranging from a) the entire restaurant; b) individual business operations such as breakfast lunch dinner and banqueting; c) product groups and d) individual menu items.

Prices based on contribution margin are useful for short term decisions such as bidding for a banquet where knowledge of contribution levels can suggest the lowest bidding strategy. Any selling price in excess of variable costs will provide a contribution towards fixed costs. Completion of the analysis may indicate that a segment is not profitable. However, it may be decided that pricing to achieve a loss in one segment is acceptable when that segment draws custom to the restaurant.

Summary

This chapter introduces the reader to the various pricing methodologies that are available to the hospitality, leisure and tourism industry. All pricing strategies need to consider both internal factors such as cost and target returns as well as external factors such as competition and market demand.

Questions

1. What does the price elasticity of demand measure?
2. What are the limitations of cost-plus pricing?
3. Describe the different types of pricing policy which can be applied in the hospitality and tourism sectors.
4. Pricing accommodation

The Lexus International Hotel has 100 rooms and is expected to achieve an average occupancy of 80%. The owners of the hotel expect a net profit after tax of 20% of the investment.

The following data is available for the hotel:

Owners investment	£2.5 million
Loans (10%)	£1.0 million
Selling and distribution costs	£225,000
Administration expenses	£355,000
Bar and restaurant staff costs	£165,000
Target food and beverage cost of sales %	30%
Target annual profit for the restaurant is	£40,000
Accommodation staff costs and expenses	£355,000

The taxation on profits is 25%.

a) Calculate the total accommodation revenue required per annum to meet the targeted returns and forecasted costs.

b) Calculate the average room rate.

c) Discuss the advantages and disadvantages to the above approach to pricing.

5. Pricing food items

Clarendon Caterers Ltd has been researching its pricing policy for the operation of a new restaurant in London TV which will operate for 50 weeks of the year. The capital cost of the venture will be £900,000 and the company requires an annual net profit of 15% of this figure. The restaurant is expected to have a maximum turnover of 1,000 covers per week. Labour costs, rental, maintenance and other fixed costs will total £2,875 per week when open.

The company proposes the following menu structure together with anticipated food cost and sales mix percentages.

	Cost % of Selling Price	**Sales Mix %**
Appetisers	30	23
Main Course	40	56
Sweets	35	12
Beverages	40	9
		100

(a) Calculate the annual net profit required.

(b) Calculate the overall gross profit percentage required.

(c) Set the selling price for a complete meal, and the individual courses based upon the anticipated number of covers and required net profit - ignore VAT.

(d) Calculate the break even point per week in sales revenue, number of covers, and occupancy percentage.

(e) Write a short report to the Managing Director indicating the actions that could be taken to achieve the net profit required if the actual number of covers sold fell below expectations.

6. Pricing accommodation

The Raven Hotel is a 40-bedroom hotel being built for and owned by Raven Group (Europe) PLC.

For this venture the following forecasts are available: -

i)	Investment	£000
	Land and buildings	2,110
	Furniture and Equipment and Working Capital	382
	Total Investment	2,492
ii)	Financing of the Investment	
	Debt - long-term loan at 18% p.a. gross	1,492
	Owners have invested some of their own money and expect an after-tax return of 15% on	1,000
	Total Finance	2,492

iii) Projected occupancy is 80% of available room accommodation for a 52 week accounting period open 7 days per week

iv) Corporation tax is calculated at 25%

v) Debt and equity rates of return are to be calculated on a calendar year basis

vi) Rooms department operating expenses (wages, supplies, laundry, etc.) are 27% of the required room sales.

vii)	**a)**	Fixed Charges	£
		Depreciation, Insurance etc.	183,000
	b)	Undistributed Operating Expenses	
		Administrative and general	38,300
		Marketing	28,900
		Energy Costs	35,100
		Repairs and maintenance	28,800
		Total	131,100

viii) Departmental Information

	Food and Beverage
Sales	£575,000
Direct Wages	15% of Sales
Direct Expenses	10% of Sales
Cost of Sales	35% of sales

i) Prepare a financial statement from the above information to include:
   a) required room sales for the year
   b) average room rate

ii) What would the hotel's average rate per guest be if 60% of rooms sold were for double occupancy, with the remaining rooms for single occupancy?

iii) If the hotel did operate with 60% of rooms sold being for double occupancy and management wanted a £15 spread between single and double room rates, what would these rates be?

Practical activities

1. Research the terms 'Yield Management' and 'Revenue Management'. List the range of applications of these techniques to the hospitality, leisure and tourism industries.
2. Prepare a report to explain how selling prices are set in a hospitality, leisure or tourism organisation. The report should include:
   a) A description of the products and services being offered
   b) A review of each of the following techniques:
      Cost based pricing
      Market led pricing
      Value based pricing

   Give your recommendations as to how the pricing strategy should develop in the future.

References and further reading

Atrill, P. & Mclaney E. (2021) *Accounting and Finance for Non-Specialists*, 12th Edition, Pearson.

Hayes, D. K. & Miller, A. (2011) *Revenue Management for the Hospitality Industry*, USA: John Willey & Sons

Cooper, C. & Whittington, L. (2010) *Hotel Success Handbook*. London: MX Publishing.

Kasavana, M. & Smith, D., (1992) *Menu Engineering*, Michigan: Hospitality Publishers

Legoherel, P., Poutier, E. and Fyall, A. (2013) *Revenue Management for Hospitality & Tourism* Oxford: Goodfellow

Pavesic, D. (1983) Cost/margin analysis: a third approach to menu pricing and design. *International Journal of Hospitality Management* 3(3), 127-134

Ransley, J., Ingram, H. and Adams, D. (2022) *Developing Hospitality Properties and Facilities*. Routledge

Useful websites

www.hospitalityupgrade.com

www.eyefortravel.com/revenue-and-data-management

www.finance4hospitality.co.uk

Part 3: Internal appraisal

An essential part of the strategy process is to compile a position audit or capability profile to gain a better understanding of where the business fits in relation to the external environment, and also the internal strengths and weaknesses. The prime objective of internal appraisal is to establish a clear picture of the organisation in terms of its capabilities, which requires identifying and tabulating resources and evaluating the management utilisation of those resources. Internal appraisal involves reviewing the main functional areas of the business, accounting and finance, marketing, operations, technology, talent management and research and development. The financial area is an important aspect of internal appraisal in that a review of the key financial data usually provides an immediate insight into the health of the company.

Generally, the first area for inspection is the historical financial results of the company which are analyzed through ratio analysis. Although the results are retrospective, they are important in that they are reflective of the effectiveness of past management decisions and may also give some indication of the future potential for the business. The internal analysis should also encompass a review of current resources and existing accounting procedures for budget setting, forecasting and control and performance measurement. The following three chapters focus on these important aspects of internal appraisal, providing tools and techniques for implementing effective budgeting and forecasting procedures, cash management and performance measuring mechanisms.

6 Making budgets work

About this chapter

This chapter considers the role of the budgeting process as a key factor in implementing the strategy of an organisation. Budgeting has an essential role to play in converting the objectives of the strategic plan into financial statements' projections to provide a standard for performance for the short to medium term future (usually up to 18 months ahead). If used correctly, the budgeting process ensures that organisational resources, such as capital and labour, are allocated efficiently and effectively, and provides a vehicle for departmental coordination and communication. This chapter considers the role of budgeting and forecasting with reference to the following:

- ☐ Budgetary planning process
- ☐ Using a forecast update
- ☐ Behavioural issues
- ☐ Budgetary control
- ☐ Improving the effectiveness of the budgeting and forecasting process.

Learning objectives

On completion of this chapter you should be able to:

- ☐ Prepare a SWOT analysis to support the planning process
- ☐ Prepare a budgeted trading account, cash flow and balance sheet
- ☐ Update a forecast
- ☐ Understand how to analyse the actual performance with variances
- ☐ Understand the behavioural aspects of budgeting.

Introduction

Technology has enabled budgeting and forecasting to become embedded at an operational level in the hospitality and tourism industries. Departmental managers can expect to work to weekly and monthly budgets for revenues and costs, and be required to reforecast revenues and costs on a regular basis. Achievement against budget is usually a critical element in departmental performance. However, successful budgetary planning and control systems require certain conditions to be in place. Best practice in budgetary planning and control depends on:

- **Frequency and timeliness** of management reports, and the hospitality and tourism industries this means daily business reports, weekly trading reports and monthly reporting packs.
- **Flexibility** in preparing budgets by introducing rolling budgets rather than relying solely on an annual fixed budget.
- **Accountability and ownership** to ensure that departmental managers feel motivated to raise actual performance to meet budget expectations.
- **Transparency and access** to financial data and measures ensures that managers can lead teams to achieve maximum performance.
- **Accuracy** in reporting ensures that managers are working with comparable figures and have confidence in the information for decision making.

Budgeting and the strategic planning process

The budget provides a short-term plan for the organisation and is normally prepared in advance of the financial year with a detailed plan for the year ahead. This plan should be drawn from the long-term plans of the organisation providing a scheme for the implementation of the organisational goals and objectives. The budget should be more than just an extension of last year's actual results with incremental increases for revenues and costs. However, for many organisations the budgeting process is reduced to this basic exercise, which ensures that each year more and more slack and inefficiency is built into the budgeted values. Instead, the budget setting exercise should reflect the current and planned activities of the business allowing for a distinction between two types of activities:

- **Maintenance activities,** these are a continuation of existing activities.
- **Development activities,** which can be considered to be new opportunities in terms of products or markets or both.

A maintenance budget reflects an organisation pursuing well-established activities, whereas a development budget should reflect changes in strategic direction, such as investment to expand or changes in product or market base. A budget for a business planning to launch a new product or concept will require a capital budget for capital expenditure and in the operational budgets, high levels of marketing costs. A business in the mature stage or entering the decline stage of the product life cycle will need to budget for substantially reduced marketing and investment costs and will focus on the cutting of critical costs.

The purpose of budgets

The successful implementation of the budgeting process should achieve a number of aims. These include enabling the organisation to:

- **Quantify future plans:** the budgeting process compels operational managers to look ahead and set short-term targets. This enables shortfalls in sales and resources to be identified and provides the opportunity for measures to be implemented to overcome these difficulties.

- ☐ **Set performance objectives and targets:** the budgeting process provides the opportunity to set targets to raise operational performance by increasing management motivation levels.
- ☐ **Co-ordinate departmental activities:** the preparation of the sales budget for each trading department forces the different departments to co-ordinate with each other. This is particularly true in a hotel where the restaurant sales budget is dependent on the forecasted room occupancy levels.
- ☐ **Communicate plans and objectives:** the budgeting process provides a formal opportunity for higher level managers at divisional regional levels to set targets based on the long-term objectives of the organisation.
- ☐ **Control business performance:** the process provides a standard based on expected revenues and costs to which actual performance can be compared. Variances between actual and planned performance can then be identified and inefficiencies targeted and eliminated.

The whole budgeting process can be time-consuming and costly in terms of management resources. Critics of the process argue that the cost and time involved is not justifiable because the end result is based on many unknown factors and the actual performance will almost certainly be different. This needs to be considered in the light of the overriding benefit of the process, which is that it forces managers to consider all relevant factors likely to affect their business and plan for the effective use of resources, and this requires both an internal and an external analysis.

Finally, it can be argued that the budgeting process encourages managers to spend up to budget. Certainly, it is true that this can occur towards the year end when responsibility centre managers note that they have not utilised the full value of their expenses budget and are tempted to spend more than is required. This can be minimized through effective communication and participation in the budgeting process. Many businesses in the hospitality, tourism and leisure industries use participative budgeting techniques, engaging their management teams and supervisors. This contrasts with a top-down approach where budgets are set at a senior level and imposed on the teams who will be working to the targets set.

Determination of goals and objectives

The budget is the translation of the organisational business and financial goals into monetary values. The nature of organisational objectives has already been discussed in detail in Chapter 1 and there it was concluded that goals may range from profit or revenue maximization through to just pure survival tactics. The short-term planning in the organisation should aim to achieve long-term objectives but invariably conflict can arise. For example, maximising return on capital employed in the short term may mean that the long-term future of the business is compromised. Emphasising the maximisation of this ratio means that there is a temptation to artificially increase profits by cutting expenditure in areas such as maintenance, training and marketing, whilst plans for further investment in assets are curbed. Therefore, it is far better to use more than one criteria for setting targets and assessing performance.

The planning process is based on three types of objectives all of which are closely related. These are known as business, operational and financial objectives and may be described as follows:

- **Business objectives** relate to markets, economic and business conditions, organisational style and personnel policies.
- **Operational objectives** are based on realistic levels of activity given the supply of resources available. A limiting factor is a scarce resource which impedes the operation or growth of business activities.
- **Financial objectives** are incorporated into the budget and used to evaluate performance. They directly relate to the budget setting process and may be expressed in a variety of forms which might have targets set as follows:
  - **Absolute terms** e.g. sales to reach £2 million
  - **Relative terms** e.g. sales to increase by 10% on the previous year
  - **A range** e.g. salary and payroll costs to be between 30 – 35% of revenue
  - **A ratio or percentage** e.g. food cost of sales to be 30%
  - **A maximum** e.g. debt to equity ratios not to exceed 50%
  - **A minimum** e.g. the return on investment to be at least 10%.

Planning to achieve organisational goals

Most organisations aim to produce a series of budgets for all departments in the operation. In a hotel for example each department will require a budget with sales and associated costs for the revenue generating areas and costs for those departments providing support services such as sales and marketing, utilities and property operation. Each of these areas is required to produce a budget from which a consolidated master budget can be prepared. If an organisation is comprised of several locations each is assumed to be a business unit or budget centre and a consolidated master budget can then be prepared for the region or division.

Each of these budget centres is defined as an area in the organisation where responsibility has been devolved to a manager and their team. Budget centre types can be categorised into investment, profit and cost centers. These are defined as:

- **Investment centre** is an area where the manager and the team are responsible for revenues, costs and assets employed for example, a hotel or leisure centre within a larger group of outlets or for an individual location. The traditional measures of performance for this group include return on capital employed, asset turnover and profitability to sales as well as the usual operational ratios as discussed in Chapter 8.
- **Profit centre** is an area where the manager and the team is responsible for both revenues and costs, for example the restaurant within a hotel operation or a retail outlet in a leisure centre. Performance measures focus on the relationship between revenues and operational costs.
- **Cost centre** is where managers and the team are responsible for costs only, such as sales and marketing, or property operation and maintenance. Performance measures focus on cost, using standard costs and calculations such as the cost per occupied room or the cost per customer.

Figure 6.1: Monthly Management accounts sample layout for the F&B department

	Current Period						Year-To-Date					
	Actual		Budget		Last Year		Actual		Budget		Last Year	
	£	%	£	%	£	%	£	%	£	%	£	%
Revenue												
Restaurant Food	487,412	53.4%	457,221	58.0%	284,154	60.5%	2,751,412	52.9%	2,647,725	55.4%	1,925,427	70.5%
Bar Food	185,410	20.3%	165,881	21.0%	142,500	30.3%	1,145,210	22.0%	997,245	20.9%	721,542	26.4%
C & B Food	225,144	24.7%	151,442	19.2%	35,140	7.5%	1,225,540	23.6%	1,054,258	22.1%	81,541	3.0%
T& C	14,775	1.6%	14,340	1.8%	7,800	1.7%	74,352	1.4%	75,988	1.6%	1,500	0.1%
Total Food Revenue	912,741	46.3%	788,884	46.2%	469,594	46.2%	5,196,514	48.2%	4,775,216	48.0%	2,730,010	63.8%
Restaurant Beverage	289,252	30.0%	254,210	29.7%	191,420	35%	1,745,422	35.4%	1,554,152	35.2%	784,425	51.4%
Bar Beverage	482,514	50.0%	425,411	49.8%	321,540	59%	2,410,444	49.0%	2,214,547	50.1%	625,548	41.0%
C & B Beverage	192,540	20.0%	175,414	20.5%	28,455	5%	768,255	15.6%	652,425	14.8%	115,424	7.6%
Total Beverage Revenue	964,306	48.9%	855,035	50.1%	541,415	53.3%	4,924,121	45.6%	4,421,124	44.4%	1,525,397	35.6%
Room Hire Revenue	95,524	4.8%	63,685	3.7%	5,241	0.5%	670,040	6.2%	758,325	7.6%	25,144	0.6%
Total F & B Revenue	1,972,571	100%	1,707,604	100%	1,016,250	100%	10,790,675	100%	9,954,665	100%	4,280,551	100%
Cost of Sales												
Food	319,459	35.0%	252,443	32.0%	164,358	35.0%	1,636,902	31.5%	1,528,069	32.0%	982,804	36.0%
Beverage	221,790	23.0%	188,108	22.0%	131,564	24.3%	1,083,307	22.0%	972,647	22.0%	366,095	24.0%
Total Cost of Sales	541,250	27.4%	440,551	25.8%	295,922	29.1%	2,720,209	25.2%	2,500,716	25.1%	1,348,899	31.5%

F & B Expenses												
Commission	35,451	60.6%	33,225	62.7%	4,254	13.3%	234,225	63.9%	325,541	72.7%	95,541	53.3%
Cleaning Materials	2,214	3.8%	1,584	3.0%	476	1.5%	10,142	2.8%	9,526	2.1%	5,373	3.0%
Contract Cleaning	625	1.1%	625	1.2%	235	0.7%	3,750	1.0%	3,750	0.8%	1,954	1.1%
Laundry	5,454	9.3%	4,525	8.5%	1,373	4.3%	32,582	8.9%	28,441	6.3%	11,667	6.5%
Restaurant Other Supplies	3,378	5.8%	1,993	3.8%	686	2.1%	20,239	5.5%	14,138	3.2%	8,258	4.6%
Kitchen Other Supplies	541	0.9%	200	0.4%	54	0.2%	1,874	0.5%	1,200	0.3%	524	0.3%
Printing & Stationery	291	0.5%	100	0.2%	25	0.1%	448	0.1%	900	0.2%	189	0.1%
Christmas Costs	-	0.0%	-	0.0%	-	0.0%	-	0.0%	-	0.0%	-	0.0%
Flowers & Decorations	9,802	16.8%	10,000	18.9%	24,483	76.4%	58,525	16.0%	60,000	13.4%	53,002	29.6%
External Stocktaker	750	1.3%	750	1.4%	480	1.5%	4,500	1.2%	4,500	1.0%	2,800	1.6%
F & B Expenses	58,506	100%	53,002	100%	32,066	100%	366,286	100%	447,996	100%	179,309	100%
Payroll	512,868	26.0%	443,977	26.0%	264,225	26.0%	2,805,576	26.0%	2,588,213	26.0%	1,112,943	26.0%
Total F & B Expenses	1,112,624	56.4%	937,529	54.9%	592,213	58.3%	5,892,070	54.6%	5,536,926	55.6%	2,641,151	61.7%
F & B Gross Operating Income	859,947	43.6%	770,075	45.1%	424,037	41.7%	4,898,605	45.4%	4,417,739	44.4%	1,639,400	38.3%
F & B GOI %	44%		45%		42%		45%		44%		38%	
Food Gross Profit %	65%		68%		65%		69%		68%		64%	
Beverage Gross Profit %	77%		78%		76%		78%		78%		76%	

Figure 6.1 (cont.): Monthly Management accounts sample layout for the F&B department

Normally the responsibility for a department is assigned to a manager who oversees the team efforts and must accept financial responsibility for that area. Regular reports will be produced on a daily, weekly and monthly basis in the management accounts, containing absolute figures but also ratios and percentages. An example of a layout for such a report is illustrated in Figure 6.1.

Successful implementation of this process for responsibility accounting can lead to much higher actual performance, particularly where participation and communication are encouraged. Traditionally multi-unit organisations tend to assign profit centre responsibilities to individual unit managers with investment responsibilities being held at area or divisional management level. However, with the large volume of managed and franchised businesses in the hospitality industry in particular, many hotel general managers are managing an investment centre on behalf of the owners.

Responsibility accounting will not be successful where managers are held responsible for costs over which they exert no, or only partial, control. This situation can occur in organisations where costs are allocated or apportioned to departments from the centre or where a system for transfer pricing exists.

Administration of the budgeting process

Having established areas of responsibility within the organisation, the administrative control of the budgetary process should be considered. This requires a specific person in the organisation, usually the financial or management accountant, taking responsibility for coordinating the budgeting process throughout the period of preparation. This involves setting guidelines to ensure that the budget is prepared to a standard format in the appropriate timescales. A typical sequence of activities is shown in Figure 6.2.

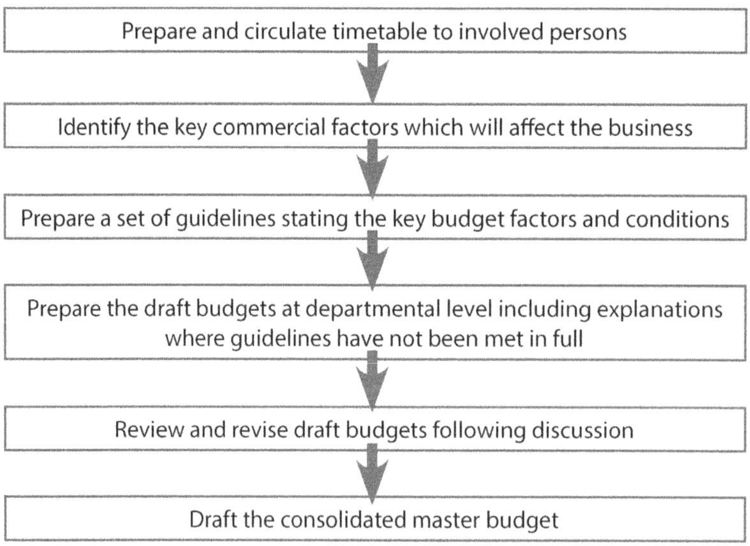

Figure 6.2: Sequence of activities in the budgeting process

It is generally considered desirable for managers and their teams to participate in the budgeting process. In some organisations the budget is imposed from the top without participation from or consultation with those managers who will execute it. This is considered to be a less effective approach for raising performance levels compared to an environment where managers can participate.

The budget period

This may vary between organisations, but for the preparation of a fixed budget it is usually one year in length and is often dependent on the natural business year. In the hospitality and tourism industries, the seasonal nature of trading means that the control periods within the budget need to be accurately determined. Traditionally, the budget period is split into twelve periods coinciding with the calendar months. The disadvantage with this is that the periods are of different lengths and will straddle the weeks, with one period often ending mid week. An alternative approach is to use thirteen budget periods, each of four weeks, but this is now rarely used. A business which is reliant on virtually all seasonal trade would then need to split the budget month down further into a week-by-week budget to take account of factors such as Bank Holidays. Traditionally, one year is planned in detail and this is worked through almost to completion before the next budget is considered. This results first in an intensive period each year when the budget is being prepared, and then a period at the latter end of the year when the manager is working without a short-term plan. The use of a rolling budget provides the solution, where a month or quarter is being prepared to add to the budget year whilst the current month or quarter drops out of the time frame.

The process of communication

Each responsibility centre is required to prepare its own budget of what it hopes to achieve and the resources it intends to employ. In order to harmonize the budgets of the various locations and to avoid interdepartmental conflict, a budget committee should be constituted. The various heads of department form the membership and the accountant assumes the role of budget officer or budget co-coordinator. This process ensures that individual budgets complement each other and that the lines of communication between departmental heads are open. During the budgeting process in the preparation of a fixed budget it is important to communicate the following points to those involved in the process.

- ☐ A statement of the objectives of budgetary planning and control and the procedures to be used to ensure uniformity of approach
- ☐ A definition of responsibilities for each person involved
- ☐ A timetable for the preparation of the budget
- ☐ The budget and control period
- ☐ The responsibility centre for the preparation of each budget
- ☐ The cost codes to be used for cost collection and classification
- ☐ The standardised report layouts to be used by each unit to assist in consolidation.

Information technology has a vital role to play in providing a medium for the distribution of standardised forms for data entry. Most organisations are using technology which enables managers to enter budgeted figures onto computerised management accounting packages which allow for the manipulation of data and the consolidation of information at head office level.

Preparation of the budget statements

There are potentially three forms of budgeted statements to be prepared. These are the:

- Profit and loss account or operating budget
- Cash flow
- Balance sheet.

However, it is not always necessary for all responsibility centres to prepare all three statements. Centres termed as profit centres may only need the operating budget whilst the investment centre, of which the profit centre forms a part, will find all three statements of value. In the larger multi-unit organisation, it is often the case that individual units prepare the operating budget and the other statements are only prepared at a higher level in the organisational structure. This may well be appropriate in an organisation where much of the accounting activity takes place centrally, such as the payment of suppliers and the receiving of outstanding monies from customers. However, self-accounting units should also prepare forecasted cash flow and balance sheets. The operating budget may well be divided down into further areas of responsibility with key personnel being responsible for achieving specific targets such as average room rate, revpar and cost of sales percentages.

Predicting revenue

The starting point for the preparation of a budget is normally to estimate the sales revenue for the period. There are numerous factors to taken into account, both internal and external to the organisation. These include:

- **Past actual figures** based on customer volumes, selling prices and sales mix.
- **Current anticipated trends** with the most up to date information to be used.
- **Economic factors** such as trading conditions, inflation rates and unemployment levels in addition to details regarding planned local activities and events.
- **The competition,** including general information and projections as well as current advance bookings.
- **Capacity restraints,** which will limit the sales budget by the level of capacity and resources available (known as limiting factors). It is important that these factors are clearly identified, and their effect reduced or

eliminated entirely if possible. For a hotel the number of rooms available per day is a limiting factor as is the number of seats on an aircraft.

These physical constraints might be coupled with constraints relating to labour such as shortages of skilled staff and limited management skills, as well as equipment capacity restraints and limited capital available for expansion. In order to capture the impact of these factors it could be useful to prepare a SWOT analysis for the business based on a review of the above factors. The SWOT analysis technique was discussed in detail in Chapter 2. This analysis can then be used to inform the preparation of the budget.

Sales trend analysis

This approach to forecasting future sales is based on the use of product demand curves or the product life cycle to analyse past levels of sales with the assumption that these will be an indicator for the future potential. A description of the principles of the product life cycle is included in Chapter 2. To predict the trend in past data to inform future sales, past sales figures are collected and are plotted on to a graph against time. This shows the sales trend and indicates the stage in the product life cycle that has been reached. This methodology is much improved upon with the use of time series analysis which attempts to eliminate the seasonal nature of past data and seeks to establish the underlying trend through averaging. This technique is demonstrated with the following example.

Example

The Ferdinand Hotel has had the following occupancy percentage levels during the past 3 weeks.

Day	Week 1	Week 2	Week 3
Monday	68	67	67
Tuesday	75	80	77
Wednesday	85	95	90
Thursday	82	84	87
Friday	62	49	48
Saturday	65	60	58
Sunday	53	48	46

This technique is based on averaging historical data to calculate the underlying trend. To calculate this trend data (Column 4) it is necessary to calculate a seven-day average. The adjusted trend values (column 5) represent the deviation between the average trend values and the actual (Column 1 – Column 4).

1	2	3	4	5
Day	Occ %	7 day total	Trend value	Trend adjusted
Mon	68			
Tues	75			
Wed	85			
Thur	82	490	70	12
Fri	62	489	70	-8

Sat	65	494	71	-6
Sun	53	504	72	-19
Mon	67	506	72	-5
Tues	80	493	70	10
Wed	95	488	70	25
Thur	84	483	69	15
Fri	49	483	69	-20
Sat	60	480	69	-9
Sun	48	475	68	-20
Mon	67	478	68	-1
Tue	77	477	68	9
Wed	90	475	68	22
Thur	87	473	68	19
Fri	48			
Sat	58			
Sun	46			

The following table illustrates the average of the trend deviations for each day of the week.

	Mon	Tues	Wed	Thurs	Fri	Sat	Sun
				12	-8	-6	-19
	-5	10	25	15	-20	-9	-20
	-1	9	22	19			
Total	-6	19	47	46	-28	-15	-39
Average	-3	9.5	23.5	23	-14	-7.5	-19.5
Adjusted average	-1.29	7.79	22.33	21.29	-12.29	-5.79	-17.79

The variations around the basic trend line are almost complete, but there is one more step to take. The average weekly variations need to be corrected so that they add up to zero and so we spread the total of the variations across the seven days so that the final total of the variations goes to zero.

In order to achieve this all the averages are summed and divided by seven as follows:

Sum of the averages = -3 + 9.5 + 23.5 + 23 + -14 + -7.5 + -19.5 = 12

This is then divided by the number of days in the week = 1.71

This adjustment is then added to each of the averages to calculate the adjusted average as the following table illustrates.

	Mon	Tues	Wed	Thurs	Fri	Sat	Sun
Forecasted trend line	68	68	68	68	68	68	68
Adjusted average	-1.29	7.79	22.33	21.29	-12.29	-5.79	-17.79
F/Cast	66.71	75.79	90.33	89.29	55.71	62.21	50.21

The forecasted trend line is estimated by plotting the trend line and extending this line into the future to read off the future trend values.

Sales mix and average spend

Trend analysis and moving averages provide an approach for forecasting future sales levels based on historical data. In order to calculate sales from a zero base it is necessary to determine the predicted sales volumes, average spends and sales mix. This can require some research to determine what the sales volumes and business mix will be. It is possible to access statistics for a specific sector on sales patterns, occupancy levels and average room rates, for example, and these are available from some of the large accounting firms specializing in hospitality and tourism. It is important to note that historical data is not always an indication of the future volumes of business and whilst the analysis is useful it is only part of the process of predicting the future revenues.

Preparation of the operating budget

Having determined the likely level of sales for the budget period the next step is to determine the level of resources required to service those sales. An important requirement in predicting costs is an understanding of cost behaviour. Once this has been established the problem of predicting the future level of the costs is considerably easier. An inspection of past records will clearly highlight those costs which are variable and those which are fixed, but the difficulty arises when attempting to classify semi-variable costs, i.e. those with both a fixed and a variable element. A range of methods are available for assisting in this process ranging from the simple high low method to the more complex techniques such as multiple regression analysis. The first of these methods is illustrated in Chapter 4.

Predicting variable costs is based on using the standard cost as a metric for different levels of volume. The standard cost could be a cost per unit in monetary terms such as cost per occupied room (CPOR) or a percentage to sales as in cost of sales. The key in budget preparation is to combine an appropriate level of challenge with realism based on the resources of the organization and the opportunities identified in the external market.

In a recent article based on research with leading hotel companies, the consulting firm, HOTSTATS concluded that budgets need to adapt to changing market conditions especially during times of high uncertainty. An update to the budget on a regular basis becomes a forecast and this is often done on a monthly basis.

Preparing a forecast

A financial forecast is an update to the budget based on a review of the latest trading conditions and will include revised values for revenue and costs. Typically, forecasts are prepared every month to update the expected number of customers, average spends and the associated costs with variable costs expected to increase as the number of customers increases.

Another form of forecast is known as the demand forecast which is used by revenue managers to monitor the current level of bookings and the expected levels of demand. A demand forecast is usually calculated by taking the actual number of reservations on hand (i.e. actual number of rooms booked = Business on the Books, or *BOB*) and adding the predicted number of rooms that will be booked (this is sometimes known as *pickup*).

BOB + **Pickup** = **Forecast**

This type of forecasting is prepared on a daily basis and will inform the decision to open or close different price points for that particular day. If the demand forecast suggests that the demand is lower than usual, it may be appropriate to open a lower price point/band to stimulate demand.

The cash budget

Knowledge of the company's cash cycle is essential to the success of any business. The cash flow statement assists in the management of the company's finance by disclosing the peaks and troughs in cash levels within the budget period, indicating where extra funds will be needed. Short term needs may be met from short term sources such as overdrafts, but normally long-term funding is preferable, even for supporting the working capital needs of a seasonal business.

The majority of cash flows will contain all or many of the following transactions:

- Net cash generated from trading operations
- Sales and purchases of long term assets
- Issue and redemption of equity, i.e. shares
- Long term borrowings and redemption of debt
- Changes in working capital requirements.

It is essential to regularly monitor the cash flow budget and update this with a regular forecast to highlight both potential cash shortfalls and surpluses.

Balance sheet

The asset budgets serve several purposes by ensuring that all assets, both long term and current, are planned for in the budget. Charges are made to the operating budget in respect of depreciation for existing assets and new assets acquired or coming on stream during the budget year, and when new facilities start to trade the related income and costs are to be incorporated into the operating and cash budgets. The relationship between the components of the budgeted balance sheet can then be monitored using ratio analysis. Working capital ratios and asset management ratios can be used futuristically when applied to the budgeted values to ensure that the financial targets being forecast are both realistic and efficient.

Example

Blue Tulip Restaurants ltd

Balance Sheet as at 31 December 20x3

NON CURRENT Assets	**Cost**	**Depreciation**	**Net**
Tangible Assets	**£**	**£**	**£**
Freehold Premises	3,355,000	80,000	3,275,000
Furniture and Fittings	575,000	125,000	450,000
Kitchen Equipment	720,000	150,000	570,000
		355,000	**4,295,000**

CURRENT ASSETS			
Stock		6,500	
Debtors		43,500	
		50,000	
Less: CREDITORS - Amounts due for payment within one year			
Trade Creditors	68,000		
Bank Overdraft	10,000		
		78,000	
NET CURRENT (LIABILITIES)			(28,000)
			£4,267,000

Financed by:

CAPITAL AND RESERVES

Share Capital	**Authorized**	**Issued**
	£	£
Ordinary Shares of £1 each fully paid	**5,000,000**	3,000,000
Reserve		
Retained Profit		1,267,000
		£4,267,000

The restaurant group is a private company and the Directors work in the business. In discussions with lenders to the business it has been suggested that in future budgetary planning techniques should be used. As a result, you are required to prepare an Operating Budget and a Cash budget for each of the months of January and February 20x4, and a Budgeted Balance Sheet as at 28 February 20x4.

The following information has been forecast:

a) Sales - January £150,000, February £160,000. Three quarters of the sales are for cash, the other quarter is on one month's credit.

b) The Gross Profit on Sales has been calculated at 70%.

c) Direct Wages are payable in the month incurred - January £30,000, February £32,000.

d) The level of stock remains at £5,000 throughout the period. All purchases are on one month's credit.

e) Direct Expenses are payable the month incurred. January £15,000, February £16,000.

f) Creditors are paid in the following month less a 5% Cash Discount.

g) Depreciation is calculated on the Straight Line Method at the following rates:-

Land & buildings	5% per annum
Furniture and Fittings	10% per annum
Kitchen Equipment	20% per annum

Where new assets are purchased, depreciation is calculated on a monthly basis.

h) Selling Promotion Expenses are allocated - January £10,000, February £12,000. However, these are not payable until March.

i) Establishment Expenses are allocated - January £20,000, February £20,000. All are payable in the month incurred.

j) Additional Kitchen Equipment to cost £120,000 is planned to be purchased in February. Allow depreciation for the whole of the month.

k) Administrative Expenses (which include Directors' Salaries) are forecast to be January £15,000, February £16,000. All are payable in the month incurred.

Budgeted Profit and Loss Account

	January	%	February	%
Sales	150,000		160,000	
Cost Of Sales	45,000		48,000	
Gross Profit	105,000		112,000	
Labour costs	30,000		32,000	
Direct Expenses	15,000		16,000	
Depreciation:				
Land & buildings	13,979		13,979	
Fixtures & Fittings	4,792		4,792	
Kitchen Equipment	6,000		7,000	
Selling & Promotion	10,000		12,000	
Establish Expenses	20,000		20,000	
Admin Expenses	15,000		16,000	
Add back: Discount On Creditors	(3,400)		(2,250)	
Profit / (Loss)	(6,371)		(7,251)	

Budgeted Cash Flow

	January	February
CASH INFLOWS		
Cash Sales	112,500	120,000
Sales from Debtors	43,500	37,500
	156,000	157,500
Creditors paid	64,600	42,750
Labour	30,000	32,000
Direct Expenses	15,000	16,000
Selling & Promotion	-	-
Establish Expenses	20,000	20,000
Administrative Expenses	15,000	16,000
Kitchen Equipment		120,000
Net Flow	11,400	-89,250
Opening Balance	(10,000)	1,400
Closing	1,400	-87,500

Balance Sheet as at 28th February 20x4

Capital budget	Cost	Depreciation	Net
Long term Assets:			
Freehold Premises	3,355,000	107,958	3,247,042
Furniture & Fittings	575,000	134,584	440,416
Kitchen Equipment	840,000	163,000	677,000
	4,770,000	405,542	4,364,458
Current Assets:			
Stock		6,500	
Debtors		40,000	
Less Creditors:			46,500
Trade Creditors		48,000	
Bank Overdraft		87,850	
S & P Expenses		22,000	
			(113,350)
Financed By:			4,253,108
Share Capital			3,000,000
			1,253,108
Reserves:			
Retained Profit			4,253,108

The budgetary control process

Having prepared and agreed the budget for the forthcoming financial year a key factor in the success of the budgeting process is the level of monitoring which then takes place in order to compare actual results to those that were planned. This level of control is supported by what is known as a system for variance accounting where the planned activities of the organisation are compared to the actual results and the differences analysed. Table 6.1 illustrates an example.

Table 6.1

	Actual	Budget	Variance to Budget	Last Year	Variance to LY
Rooms Available	6600	6600	0	6600	0
Rooms Sold	4439	4062	377	3545	894
OCC %	67.3%	61.5%	5.7%	53.7%	13.5%
ARR	£ 989.40	£ 944.12	£ 45.28	£ 1,083.99	-£ 94.59
REVPAR	£ 665.45	£ 581.06	£ 84.38	£ 582.23	£ 83.21
Total REVPAR	£ 1,007.27	£ 876.07	£ 131.20	£ 744.09	£ 263.18
Sleepers	7990	7312	679	6381	1609
Sleeper Density	1.8	1.8	0	1.8	0
Revenue	£6,647,973	£5,782,057	£865,916	£4,910,982	£1,736,991
Rooms Gross Operating Income	79.09%	77.49%	1.60%	78.47%	0.63%
F & B Gross Operating Income	43.60%	45.10%	-1.50%	41.73%	1.87%
Other Gross Operating Income	10.05%	14.62%	-4.57%	-53.65%	63.71%
Food Gross Profit %	65%	68%	-3%	65%	0%
Beverage Gross Profit %	77%	78%	-1%	76%	1%
Payroll %	20.8%	22.2%	-1.4%	21.1%	-0.3%
Gross Operating Profit %	57.3%	55.7%	1.6%	62.5%	-5.1%
Linen cost per room sold	£ 4.53	£ 4.32	£ 0.21	£ 3.91	£ 0.62
Commission cost per room sold	£ 46.91	£ 43.96	£ 2.95	£ 45.77	£ 1.15
Utilities cost per room sold	£ 14.74	£ 14.58	£ 0.15	£ 12.76	£ 1.98

Broadly speaking there can be many potential causes for variance. These range from those which have occurred due to external factors such as economic, social, legal and political changes, changes in competition and changes in supply conditions, to those which have arisen due to changes and inefficiencies in the operating systems. Effective variance accounting is based on establishing individual unit selling prices and costs, in a process known as *standard costing*. This enables performance to be monitored in terms of both price and volume changes.

Standard costing in food cost management

This approach provides a method for identifying the causes of the variation between actual and budgeted results and can exist only where standard costs are set. A fast-food outlet is a good example of an operation where standardised products are sold and where it is then possible to establish standard ingredient costs designed to hold constant over a set period. The process of standard costing requires the setting of five standards for:

- ☐ **Purchase prices** where each unit has a set selling price
- ☐ **Purchase specifications** where each ingredient is clearly specified
- ☐ **Portion sizes** where each dish is specified in term of size
- ☐ **Yields** where weight changes in the cooking process are identified
- ☐ **Recipes for production** to ensure a uniform procedure is followed

The standard cost of the final recipe represents what the cost should have been if there is minimal waste, maximum efficiency and the supporting standards are followed. The use of such an approach has distinct advantages in that presetting the standard means that the best methods and materials for the product are determined and variances may be produced which indicate where the actual costs have varied against the standard. It may also mean that targets are set against which employee performance may be measured, and assisting in the training of staff. Such activity focuses management attention on the shortfalls, which is known as *"management by exception"*. Finally, the process can improve the quality of pricing decisions because the business has accurate information about costs.

However, standard costing can be a difficult system to administer in practice to ensure all records are maintained, and time consuming to set up in the first instance as all dishes need to be costed. Computer technology can certainly assist where purchasing and inventory control packages can be linked to menu costing options to provide up-to-date dishes.

Flexible budgeting

A budget prepared in advance of the trading period set at an assumed level of activity is called a fixed budget. This original budget can then be used in comparison with the actual data. However, this comparison is less meaningful when actual activity is significantly different to the budgeted activity. Where standard unit costs are available or where the proportions of fixed and variable costs have been calculated, it is possible to calculate a revised budget based on the actual level of sales using the budgeted levels of costs. This revised budget is called a *flexible* budget. This approach can be used to monitor variances caused by changes in volume, changes in sales mix and operating cost inefficiencies.

The following example illustrates the use of a flexible budget.

Example

The following figures have been extracted from the fixed budget for the Bay Restaurant for Budget Period 5.

Budgeted covers	3,200
Average spend	£12.00
Gross profit %	60%
Labour & expenses	30%
Fixed costs	£2,500

The actual results were:

Covers	4,500
Average spend	£10.00
Gross profit	£27,900
Labour & expenses	£13,000
Fixed costs	£2,900

The following table illustrates how the results might be analysed.

	Fixed budget	Flexed budget	Actual	Variance
Covers	3,200	4,500	4,500	
Average spend	£12.00	£12.00	£10.00	
Sales	38,400	54,000	45,000	9,000A
Gross profit	23,040	32,400	27,900	4,500F
Labour & expenses	11,520	16,200	13,000	3,200F
Fixed costs	2,500	2,500	2,900	400A
Net profit	1,340	2,900	1,200	1,700A

The variances can be summarised as follows:

Variance due to volume	2,900 - 1,340	1,560F
Variance due to operations	2,900 - 1,200	1,700A
Variance overall	1,340 - 1,200	140A

Using budgets to motivate

The budgeting process is often used, not only to plan ahead, but also for target setting and for raising individual performance. Traditional theories of motivation focus on the identification of specific factors such as pay systems, working conditions and self fulfillment as being associated with producing increased levels of motivation. There have been various industrial studies conducted on the theme of employee motivation and performance with relation to budgets, across a range of industries. Generally, these have concluded that difficult goals produce either very good or very bad results compared with goals of normal difficulty and that difficult goals lead to reduced effort on the part of those managers who are less mature and experienced and who have less self confidence. Results from a various sources of research including Hofstede (1968) indicate that:

- ☐ Budgets have no motivational effect unless they are accepted by the managers involved as their own personal target.
- ☐ Up to the point where the budget target is no longer accepted, the more demanding the budget target the better the results achieved.
- ☐ Demanding budgets are seen as more relevant than less difficult targets, but negative attitudes result if they are seen as too difficult.
- ☐ Acceptance of budgets is facilitated when good upward communication exists. The use of departmental meetings was found helpful in encouraging managers to accept budget targets.
- ☐ Manager reactions to budget targets were affected both by their own personality and by more general cultural and organisational norms.

The relationship between budget difficulty and the ensuing level of performance can be shown graphically and is illustrated in Figure 6.3

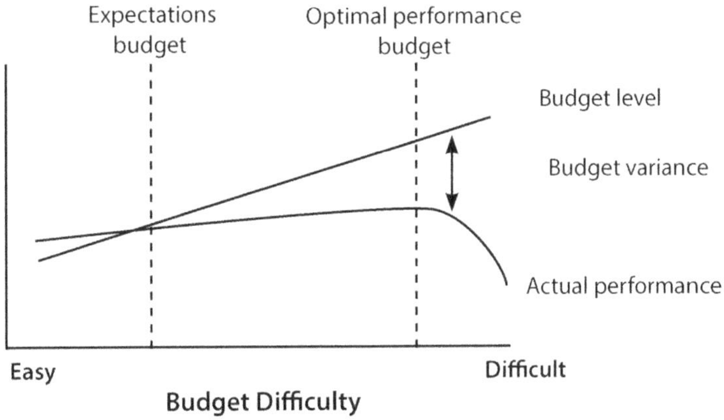

Figure 6.3: The relationship between budget difficulty and the ensuing level of performance (Based on the work of Otley, 1987)

This shows that a budget level which is perceived as being more likely to be achieved will motivate a lower level of performance. Consequently, in order to improve performance the budget level should be set in excess of the average performance likely to be attained.

Improving the effectiveness of budgeting

The effectiveness of budgeting relies on reducing slack or bias by ensuring that forecasts are accurate during the budget preparation stage, and by ensuring the timeliness of the reporting of the actual results. Bias in budgeting is a major problem and detection in the budget setting process can sometimes be impossible. Bias occurs when a manager incorporates a certain amount of slack into the budgeted figures. There are various reasons for doing this, but it occurs mainly when the manager's performance is being assessed against the budgeted targets. Slack may be built into sales by understating what is possible or into costs thereby masking potential overspends. Alternatively in tough environments managers may set unachievable budgets to divert attention away from current poor performance. Delays in reporting the actual results against budget delays the taking of corrective action which may in the long term reduce management motivation. Consequently, a system of 'flash' reports may be useful which report rough numbers relating to sales and key costs, such as materials and wages, within a few days of the end of the budget period, with the complete results coming no more than a week later.

The incremental approach to budget setting is widely used and is based on the assumption that a budget will grow each year as a result of inflation or with the provision for 'natural growth'. As a result gradual changes in the business may be overlooked. These may be basic changes such as differences in the cost structure or the customer base. Even without such changes occurring the traditional approach ensures that previous overspends and inaccuracies are compounded with each budget period.

An alternative is Zero Based Budgeting which is an approach which challenges the existence of all items in the budget.

Zero Based Budgeting

The concept of Zero-Based Budgeting (ZBB) relies on the assumption that levels of expenditure in previous periods do not justify continuation of that spending in future periods. Instead, all spending must be justified each year and this approach is most useful in control of indirect, overhead costs such as marketing, maintenance and training. Each activity in the organisation is scrutinized and the expected outcome determined. These activities are then ranked based on the following criteria:

- The activities' objectives in relation to the organisation's overall objectives.
- The required budget for the activity
- Justification for the outcomes of the activity against cost

One of the key elements in successful implementation of ZBB is the decision unit. A decision unit represents an activity carried out in a particular area of an operation. The number of units required varies depending on the size of the organisation and a large organisation would expect to have several units for each type of overhead expense. Each unit should contain just one or two employees and the associated costs. Once the decision units have been established the department head must prepare an analysis for each separate unit in his or her responsibility.

For each decision unit the following will need to be documented:

- The unit's objective
- The unit's present activities
- Justification for continuation of the unit's activities
- A list of alternative ways of carrying out the activities
- Selection of recommended alternatives
- Budget required.

Ranking

In order to determine how money will be spent in the organisation it is necessary to rank all activities in order of importance to the organisation. This maybe achieved using committees who may approve automatically the first 50 to 60 per cent of all activities and the remainder is ranked by mid and top management. The completed ranking process and approved expenditures constitute the new budgets for those areas or departments.

Advantages of ZBB

The details required to complete zero based budgeting successfully is obviously extensive and therefore, time consuming, requiring a management team who know the whole business very well. This may present difficulties in an industry where staff and management turnover is traditionally very high. However, the advantages of ZBB are that the process:

- ☐ Concentrates on the cash value of each department's activities and budget and not on percentage increases
- ☐ Can reallocate funds to the department or activity providing the greatest benefit to the organisation
- ☐ Provides a quality of information about the organisation that would otherwise not be available
- ☐ Involves all levels of management and supervision in the budgeting process
- ☐ Obliges managers to identify inefficient or obsolete functions within their areas of responsibility.

Summary

The preparation of a detailed budget will be of value to most operations by helping to quantify the short to medium-term objectives and plans. This will then provide a benchmark against which actual performance can be compared and action taken to improve future results. A checklist for effective budgeting will include:

- ☐ Establish attainable goals or objectives
- ☐ Planning to achieve these goals or objectives
- ☐ Comparing actual results with those planned and analyzing the differences
- ☐ Taking corrective action if required
- ☐ Improving the effectiveness of budgeting.

Questions

1. Preparing a budgeted trading account

Produce a budgeted trading account for three different annual sales levels - £800,000, £900,000, and £1,000,000 using the following information.

Food cost	40% of sales
Variable labour expense	25% per cent of sales
Fixed labour cost	£60,000
Other variable costs	12% of sales
Other fixed costs	£120,000
Taxation rate	30%

2. Preparing a cash flow budget.

The budget year for a catering business starts in July.

The following is the forecast trading data and expenditure for that year from 1st July 20x4 to 30th June 20x4.

Sales:	£1,500,000
Sales mix:	Food - 60%
	Beverage - 40%
Pattern of Sales:	July - September 35%
	October - December 20%
	January - March 15%
	April - June 30%
Credit Sales:	20% of each quarter's sales, payable in the following quarter.
	Outstanding debtors from the previous year are £300,000
Cost of sales	Food - 40%
	Beverage - 35%
	(stocks remain constant throughout)
	Cost of sales follows the pattern of sales and are payable in the month incurred.
Fixed costs	
Salaries:	£300,000 a year, payable monthly
Insurance:	£100,000 a year, of which £25,000 is payable in January and £17,000 in October
Property charges	£25,000 payable in September
Depreciation:	£15,000 for the year.
Interest:	£26,000 a year, half of which is payable in September, and half in March.
Other costs:	£25,000 a year payable on an equal monthly basis
Capital expenditure:	Purchase of equipment for £215,000 in January
Finance:	
Opening Balance	at Bank £ (10,000) negative

You are required to:

a. Prepare a cash budget on a quarterly basis.

b. Prepare an operating budget for the year in total and reconcile the budgeted profit figure to the closing cash balance.

3. Preparing a budget

A new hotel is to open for business on August 1st. It is expected that the preceding month will be devoted to staff training and other start-up requirements.

The following is the forecast trading data and expenditure for the first month from 1st July 20x4 to 30th June, 20x5.

Sales	£6,600,000	
Pattern of Sales:	July – September	20%
	October – December	20%
	January – March	15%
	April – June	45%
Credit Sales:	20% of each quarter's sales, payable in the following quarter	
Variable Costs:	35% of total sales, payable within the quarter in which they were incurred	
Fixed Costs		
Salaries:	£1,650,000 a year, payable monthly	
Insurance:	£28,000 a year, of which £16,000 is payable in January and £12,000 in October	
Property tax	£250,000 payable in September	
Maintenance etc.	£27,000 payable in December, and £23,000 payable in January	
Depreciation:	£300,000 for the year	
Vehicle Running Costs	Road tax £1,200; insurance £3,200; petrol, oil and maintenance £10,200; depreciation £6,000 The tax and insurance are payable in July, and the petrol etc. are payable equally each month	
Interest:	£160,000 a year, half of which is payable in December, and half in June	
Other costs:	£124,000 a year payable on an equal monthly basis	

You are required to:

a) Prepare a cash budget on a quarterly basis.

b) The budgeted net profit for the year is different to the cash flow balance. Explain why this differs from the closing cash balance.

c) Does the cash budget reveal any problems? How would you overcome this?

4. Flexible budgeting

Elite Holidays is a holiday resort open 365 days per year. The manager of the restaurant in the holiday resort is required to work with a budget and reviews performance weekly and monthly. The period accounts for June monitors revenue and costs against the period budget highlighting any variances.

	Actual (£000)	Budget (£000)	Variance (£000)
Covers	38,666	41,700	-79
Revenue			
Food	254	333	-79
Beverage	155	230	-75
Other	55	63	-8
Total revenue	464	626	-162
COS			
Food	64	73	10
Beverage	36	46	10
Other	28	30	3
Total Cost of sales	127	150	23
Direct Wages	138	184	46
Direct Expenses	44	50	6
Admin Expenses	25	32	7
Sales & Marketing Expenses	10	12	2
Utility costs	3	4	1
Property Operation & Maintenance	10	8	-2
Gross Operating Profit	107	187	-79

You are required to:

a) Explain what is meant by the terms 'fixed budget' and 'flexible budget', and state the main objective of preparing flexible budgets.

b) Prepare a revised performance statement using flexible budgeting. Your statement should show both the revised budget and the revised variances. You should assume that:

1. Direct wages are £100,000 fixed costs
2. Direct expenses are £35,000 fixed costs
3. Administration, sales and marketing, energy and maintenance are fixed costs.

c) Comment on the performance of the restaurant using the table above and your workings from b).

d) *'Budgets are set to help managers achieve objectives'.* Comment on this statement and discuss how effective you believe budgets are for motivating the performance of a department.

5. Moving averages

The Allen Hotel has had the following occupancy levels during the past 3 weeks.

Day	Week 1	Week 2	Week 3
Monday	68	67	67
Tuesday	75	80	77
Wednesday	85	95	90

Thursday	82	84	87
Friday	62	49	48
Saturday	65	60	58
Sunday	53	48	46

You are required to:

(a) Forecast the daily occupancy level for week 4 by using the 7-day moving average method to establish the 'trend line' and then adjusting for seasonal variations.

(b) Briefly describe the main reasons for preparing sales forecasts and the limitations of the method used above.

6. Standard costing

The following information relates to a contract catering company providing employee meals at a pharmaceutical company.

Budget

Number of covers sold	50,000
Average spend per head	£1.60
Food cost as percentage of sales	50%
Variable labour cost (% of sales)	20%
Fixed labour cost	£10,000
Fixed overhead	£10,000

At the end of the year the total results were:

Actual

Number of covers sold	55,000
Sales revenue	£97,000
Food cost	£48,000
Variable labour	£20,000
Fixed labour	£9,000
Fixed overhead	£10,000

You are required to:

i) Prepare a statement for the year showing the fixed budget, the flexed budget, actual results and variances

ii) Evaluate the results you have prepared and suggest possible causes for the variances

iii) Briefly explain the following terms:
- Standard cost
- Standard price
- Food price variance
- Food usage variance

iv) Describe the limitations of fixed budgets and comment on the practical value of flexible budgeting for a particular sector of the hotel and catering industry.

7. The Place To Eat is a new fish restaurant in a central location in a busy city centre.

The owner has prepared the following forecasts for the first quarter of trading:

Sales	£32,000
Cost of sales are budgeted at 30% of sales	
Other expenses are fixed and per quarter are:	
Wages	£6,800
Salaries	£10,000
Rent and rates	£6,500
Depreciation	£3,500

a) Produce a simple budget from these values.

b) Prepare a flexible budget showing the effect of an increase/decrease in sales of 10%.

8. The Balance Sheet of Peter's Restaurants Ltd at 1st April 20x3 was as follows:

Non Current Assets	Cost	Depreciation	Net
Freehold Premises	900,000	900,000	
Kitchen Equipment	195,000	39,000	156,000
Furniture & Fittings	130,000	13,000	117,000
	1,225,000	52,000	1,173,000
Current Assets			
Stock		1,500	
Debtors		16,000	
Less Creditors - amounts falling due within one year			
Creditors	36,000		
Bank Overdraft	31,500	67,500	
Net Current Liabilities			(50,000)
			1,123,000
FINANCED BY:			
Share Capital		**Authorised**	**Issued**
		£	**£**
Ordinary shares of 10p each fully paid		1,200,000	1,000,000
Reserve			
Profit and Loss Account -			
Retained Profit			123,000
			1,123,000

You are required to:

The company has not previously used budget planning procedures, and you are required to prepare an Operating Budget and a Cash Budget for:

1. Accounting Period 1: 2 April to 29 April 20x3
2. Accounting Period 2: 30 April to 26 May 20x3
3. Accounting Period 3: 28 May to 24 June 20x3

4. Budgeted Balance Sheet at 24 June 20x3

You are also required to prepare a short commentary for management based on your figures that should include an analysis of the key ratios.

The following information has been forecast.

a) Sales-Accounting Period 1 - £80,000; Accounting Period 2 - £90,000; Accounting Period 3 - £100,000. Four-fifths of all sales are for cash, one-fifth is on one Accounting Period's credit. All debtors pay promptly, no cash discount is allowed.

b) The Gross Profit on Sales has been calculated at 55% for Accounting Period 1; 60% for Accounting Periods 2 and 3.

c) The level of stock remains at £1,500 throughout the period. All purchases are on one Accounting Period's credit. A cash discount of 2.5% is deducted when payment is made.

d) Direct wages, payable in the Accounting Period incurred: Accounting Period 1 - £20,000; Accounting Period 2 - £24,500; Accounting Period 3 - £26,000.

e) Direct Expenses, payable in the Accounting Period incurred: Accounting Period 1 - £4,000; Accounting Period 2 - £4,500; Accounting Period 3 - £5,000.

f) Depreciation is calculated on the Straight-Line Method at the following rates: Furniture and Fittings 10% on cost; Kitchen Equipment 20% on cost. The depreciation charge is allocated to Accounting Periods on the basis of 1/13th for each period. When new assets are purchased, depreciation is calculated on an Accounting Period basis.

g) The unissued Ordinary Shares are to be issued to shareholders for cash, at their par value, in Accounting Period 3.

h) The bank overdraft will be cleared.

i) A new issue of 500,000 10% Preference Shares of £1 each, at par, is to be made in Accounting Period 3. Authorised Preference Capital will be 1,000,000 shares of £1 each.

j) Additional Kitchen Equipment to cost £5,200 is to be purchased for cash in Accounting Period 3. Allow depreciation for this Accounting Period.

k) Selling and Promotion expenses are allocated as follows: Accounting Period 1 - £3,000; Accounting Period 2 - £4,000; Accounting Period 3 - £4,500. Accounting Periods 1 and 2 are payable in Accounting Period 3. Accounting Period 3 expense is not payable until Accounting Period 4.

l) Establishment Expenses are: Accounting Period 1 - £2,500; Accounting Period 2 - £3,000; Accounting Period 3 - £3,200, all payable in the Accounting Period incurred.

m) Administration Expenses are Accounting Period 1 - £6,000; Accounting Period 2 - £6,500; Accounting Period 3 - £7,000, all payable in the Accounting Period incurred.

9. Budget preparation

The Beach Restaurant and Function Rooms has the following Balance Sheet as at December 20x2. An operating budget and a cash budget need to be prepared for each of the months of January and February, and a budgeted balance sheet as at 28 February 20x3.

	Cost	Depreciation	Net
	£	£	£
Non-Current assets			
Freehold premises	4,355,000	80,000	4,275,000
Furniture and fittings	575,000	125,000	450,000
Kitchen equipment	720,000	150,000	570,000
		355,000	5,295,000
Current assets			
Stock		6,500	
Debtors		43,500	
		50,000	
Less: Creditors – amounts due for payment within 1 year			
Trade creditors	68,000		
Bank overdraft	10,000		
		78,000	
Net current (liabilities)			-28,000
			5,267,000
Financed by:			
Share capital		**Authorised £**	**Issued £**
Ordinary shares of £1 each fully paid		5,000,000	4,000,000
Reserve			
Retained profit			1,267,000
			5,267,000

The following information has been forecast:

a) Sales: January £160,000, February £170,000. Three-quarters of the sales are for cash, the other quarter is on 1 month's credit.

b) The gross profit on sales has been calculated at 70%.

c) Payroll and related costs are payable in the month incurred: January £40,000, February £42,000

d) The level of stock remains at £6,000 throughout the period. All purchases are on 1 month's credit.

e) Creditors are paid in the following month less a 5% cash discount

f) Direct operating expenses are payable the month incurred: January £12,000, February £14,000

g) Depreciation is calculated on the straight-line method at the following rates:
- Land and building – 5% per annum
- Furniture and fittings – 10% per annum
- Kitchen equipment – 20% per annum

Where new assets are purchased, depreciation is calculated on a monthly basis.

a) Sales and marketing expenses are allocated: January £12,000, February £14,000. However, these are not payable until March.

b) Property operation expenses are allocated: January £20,000, February £20,000. All are payable in the month incurred.

c) Additional kitchen equipment to cost £140,000 is planned to be purchased in February. Allow depreciation for the whole of the month.

d) Administration and general expenses are forecast to be January £16,000, February £15,000. All are payable in the month incurred.
- Prepare an Operating Budget and a Cash Budget on a month-by-month basis.
- Prepare a Balance Sheet as at 28th February 2023.
- Comment on the statements that you have produced including an issues arising.
- Explain how a business can benefit from effective Cash Budgeting.

References and further reading

Atrill, P. and Mclaney E. (2021) *Accounting and Finance for Non-Specialists*, 12th Edition, Pearson.

Harris, P. and Hazzard, P. (1992) *Managerial Accounting in the Hospitality Industry*, Nelson Thornes.

Hofsted, G. (1968) *The Game of Budget Control*. Routledge.

Otley, D. (1987) *Accounting Control and Organisational Behaviour*, Oxford: Heinemann/ CIMA

Ransley, J., Ingram, H. and Adams, D. (2022) *Developing Hospitality Properties and Facilities*. Routledge

Schmidgall, R. (2016) *Hospitality Industry Managerial Accounting*. Educational Institute of the American Hotel Motel Association.

Useful websites

www.finance4hospitality.co.uk An online community with bite sized content and resources developed by experts in hospitality accounting.

7 Management of working capital

About this chapter

In Chapter 3 the concept of cash flow was discussed in detail and guidelines were given for the preparation of the indirect style of cash flow in accordance with IFRS1 guidelines. The monitoring of cash flow is a vital task for all businesses regardless of size. This chapter introduces the concept of working capital, which focuses on the current assets and current liabilities from the balance sheet, highlighting the liquidity of the business. Each aspect of working capital will be reviewed with guidelines for managing the overall liquidity of the business.

Learning objectives

On completion of this chapter, you should be able to:

- ☐ Understand the importance of liquidity
- ☐ Understand the significance of cash flow management versus profit management
- ☐ Apply techniques for controlling inventory levels
- ☐ Understand the importance of managing debtor levels
- ☐ Apply techniques for monitoring creditors.

Introduction

A key feature consistent with many of the business failures in the UK has been the fact that businesses have been too late in realising the importance of short-term and long-term cash availability. Obviously creating profit is important but maintaining sufficient cash funds for financing the payment of suppliers (trade creditors) and payroll, as well as for financing capital expenditures, is vitally important for the long term success of the business. The business model will determine how and when cash is received. Tour operators often receive revenues in advance via deposits and final payment prior to the trip taking place, and this can greatly assist with cash flow management. For businesses such as those in the meeting and events sector, payment from customers may come after the event, increasing the risk to the business, which should be mitigated by taking deposits in advance where possible.

When there are insufficient funds in the form of cash, the business may at worst face liquidation if creditors are not being paid, but such a shortage also limits the ability of a business to pursue a strategy of expansion through revenue growth. This chapter considers the management of working capital in total, as well as a review of the key aspects of each of the components including the value of monitoring:

- ☐ Working capital cycles
- ☐ Working capital ratios
- ☐ Debtors (accounts receivable)
- ☐ Creditors (accounts payable)
- ☐ Stock or inventory levels
- ☐ Cash levels

Working capital

Working capital is normally defined as the cash value of current assets less the current liabilities. According to the ACCA (2023) working capital management is central to the effective management of a business because:

- ☐ Current assets comprise the majority of the total assets of some companies
- ☐ Shareholder wealth is more closely related to cash generation than accounting profits
- ☐ Failure to control working capital, and hence to manage liquidity, is a major cause of corporate collapse.

Poor management of the working capital can lead to:

- ☐ Inefficient use of resources if cash or inventory levels are too high and are not generating additional revenues. Too much beverage inventory held on site at a restaurant for example, represents cash tied up waiting to be released.
- ☐ Overtrading, which occurs when a business is growing, and trying to maintain a level of revenue to meet demand which is higher than the current levels of working capital can sustain. This can lead to a business struggling to keep up with purchasing sufficient inventory or investing on operational resources to meet demand.

When the current assets exceed the current liabilities at a particular point in time as illustrated by the balance sheet, this is known as positive working capital, where current assets are funded partly from the current liabilities such as trade creditors and bank overdrafts and also from long term sources of funds such as bank loans or equity. Negative working capital arises when current liabilities exceed current assets. In this case current liabilities are funding both current assets and a proportion of long-term assets.

In general, a business should seek to minimise the level of each type of current asset held such as stock, debtors and cash, and maximize the benefits from short term financing arising from the delayed payment of creditors. In practice this means only stocking the inventories required for immediate sale and reducing the credit offered to customers. However, other factors influence the working capital policy such as the possibility of lost sales through not offering credit to potential customers, lost sales through holding insufficient stocks when demand surges, and increases in operating costs due to poor supplier relationships. The management of working capital should be based on achieving a balance between these factors. The problem lies in the fact that the level of funds required is constantly changing, particularly where there are seasonal sales which will affect stock, debtor and creditor levels. As a result, forecasting working capital requirements becomes difficult in cases where the level of future sales and the timing of cash flows are not known with accuracy. However, it is essential that every attempt is made to accurately predict the business cash requirements and the increasing importance of monitoring the levels of cash generated in an operation is now widely recognised. It is recommended therefore to prepare forecasted cashflows on a regular basis, monthly, weekly and even daily for some businesses.

There are various approaches to monitoring cash levels and working capital requirements and these will now be considered.

Working capital cycle

In order to maintain liquidity in a business it is necessary to strike a balance to ensure that the level of available current assets is kept sufficiently high to cover payments to outstanding suppliers when they fall due. These cash balances mean that the business incurs an opportunity cost for interest lost or the earnings that could have been made if the cash had been invested elsewhere. The exact amount of idle cash held can be managed effectively by understanding and controlling the working capital or cash operating cycle. This calculation specifies the period taken in days between the cash payment to suppliers and the cash being received from customers for sales. In a business in the manufacturing sector where products are made in a factory environment, a large portion of the cash cycle will focus on days required to manufacture the finished product from the raw materials, and the incomplete finished goods are known as 'work in progress'. The cash operating cycle for a manufacturing business is illustrated below.

Number of days raw materials held in stock	*x* days
Number of days needed to produce goods	*x* days
Number of days finished goods held in stock	*x* days
Number of days debtors take to settle accounts	*x* days
LESS	
Number of days taken to pay trade suppliers	*x* days
EQUALS	
Cash operating cycle	*x* days

The aim is to reduce the cash cycle to zero so that a balance is achieved between the current assets and the current liabilities. A cash operating cycle above zero represents a less risky level of working capital but as the value increases more inefficiencies arise.

The typical restaurant operation for example, requires stock for almost instant usage and the emphasis is not on the management of the stock cycle but on ensuring that sufficient stocks are held for service without incurring the costs associated with overstocking. The following diagram shows in simplified form the chain of events in a restaurant operation which will affect the working capital cycle.

Number of days raw materials held in stock	x days
Number of days debtors take to settle accounts (probably zero)	x days
LESS	
Number of days taken to pay suppliers	x days
EQUALS	
Cash operating cycle	x days

Given the nature of the inventories with a large proportion of fresh goods the cash operating cycle may well be a negative value. Whenever a business is able to gain credit from suppliers this in effect finances part of the cash operating cycle. Consequently, large businesses such as hotel chains and contract caterers can operate with shorter or negative operating cycles if they are able to secure better credit terms from suppliers. Any delay in the time taken to receive cash from outstanding customers or additional time given in the credit terms offered will increase the length of the cycle.

The key factor for the successful control of the working capital cycle for the majority of businesses in the hospitality, tourism and leisure industries is in the management of debtors and creditors. However, in the case of large-scale production kitchens or other businesses that hold high levels of inventory for sale, there are obviously similarities with the manufacturing industries.

Measures for managing working capital

There are several performance evaluation techniques for monitoring the level of working capital. These include the calculation of a range of ratios based on the relationships that exist between the different types of current assets and current liabilities and also specific ratios for managing each type of asset. When calculated using internally reported values drawn from the monthly management accounts the results provide a useful tool for monitoring and evaluating performance. However, when values are taken from the published balance sheet it is important to remember that the financial statements are drawn up following a number of conventions and rules and that the asset values are simply those at that point in time, and that the relationships may have considerably changed since that date.

The current ratio

This provides a measure of the balance between the current assets and current liabilities. Usually, a business would seek to achieve a ratio in excess of 1:1 where the current assets equal the current liabilities, which communicates confidence to short term creditors by confirming the ability of the business to meet all its short term debts. Some advisors advocate a ratio of at least 2:1, that is current assets at twice the value of current liabilities, as being a safe measure. In practice the trading patterns of the business will dictate the level of a 'safe' ratio. In restaurants for example, current assets will consist of cash and fast-moving stocks with possibly little or no debtors. Therefore, all assets are in fairly liquid state, and it would not be unusual to see a consistent ratio of 1:1 or less with no working capital difficulties being experienced. Alternatively, a hotel operation may well have a considerable level of debtors and slow-moving stocks and the most efficient ratio will be higher than 1:1.

The acid test ratio

This is an adapted form of the current ratio where only the more liquid assets are included in the calculation. These are normally taken to be debtors and cash whereas stock may take longer to realise into cash and is therefore excluded from the current assets. However, it may also be relevant to exclude some of the debtors as well if the outstanding balances are difficult to realise. The target for the ratio is normally about 1:1 but again differences in industry operating practice means that these benchmarks should not be adhered to rigidly.

Managing debtors

Ideally if all sales could be for advance or immediate cash payment, liquidity problems would be less likely to occur. For many tourism and leisure businesses this is the case, but for some hotel businesses it is expected that credit will be available for customers and in many cases, this serves as a marketing tool to attract further business. The optimum level of debtors outstanding is established by achieving a balance between the cost of giving credit and the additional profits to be generated from credit sales. The cost of granting credit to a customer includes:

- **Loss of interest:** The supplier is in effect giving the customer an interest-free loan during the period in which the amount is outstanding.
- **Reduced purchasing power:** During the period that the debt is outstanding the supplier may suffer from insufficient funds to buy stock or pay staff.
- **Administrative costs:** Maintenance of a sales ledger will incur costs for record keeping and staffing.
- **Cost of bad debts:** these occur when an outstanding debt is not paid. The greater the length of debtor days the greater the risk of bad debts occurring.

However, costs are also incurred when credit is denied, the most significant being the loss of customer goodwill and sales.

In the hotel industry credit is extended at various levels, ranging from the house accounts where credit is extended during the guests stay until the point of check out when payment is made, to authorised credit extended to customers where the balance outstanding is shown on the sales or city ledger. Credit is also extended for a short period when a guest pays by credit card, where billing is made to the credit card company, usually incurring commission charges.

Credit policy

To avoid excessive bad debts occurring and to speed up the collection of outstanding invoices, an effective policy for giving credit should be established. This should be communicated to the team through training sessions and company manuals with standard procedures for collecting credit information. The company policy regarding credit should include guidelines for whom should be granted credit and references required, how much credit is to be granted and the length of the credit period to be extended. The credit application should be the most accurate document on customer details available and is, therefore, worth reviewing carefully.

In addition to the credit application form there are many sources available for gathering information about customer credit worthiness. These include:

- Credit ratings supplied by credit agencies
- Banks
- Trade associations
- Own company experience

To ensure that debtor management is efficient, it is important to monitor that invoices and statements are sent out promptly and accurately for those customers to whom credit has been extended. The sooner the invoice is sent out, the sooner the customer will respond to it and, ideally, make payment. An accurate clear invoice will also improve the speed with which the invoice is paid. Payment terms should be clearly worded, such as 'Please pay within 30 days of the invoice date' or 'Please ensure payment reaches us by the 25th of the month following the month of the invoice'.

A courteous but firm system of reminders and collection procedures should be operated, and the sending of statements, reminders and contact calls should all be logged. Most accounting systems will automatically generate reports to highlight outstanding invoice balances and the length of time outstanding.

Late payment of invoices by customers is clearly damaging to any type of business but it particularly affects the smaller business with less access to cash resources. Constant scrutiny is key to monitor outstanding debts. To avoid the problems associated with collecting debts, it may be relevant to consider debt factoring and offering discounts for prompt payment.

Debt factoring

Outsourcing some business processes can assist with achieving greater efficiencies, and there has been a growth in the usage of external debt collection agencies, with various services available depending on the needs of the individual business. The more common arrangement is that where the factoring organisation will pay invoices immediately up to an agreed percentage of the sales ledger, say, 80%, and receive in return a fee which maybe, say, 1.5% of the invoice total. Consequently, the business receives an immediate injection of cash but there are some disadvantages which should be considered. The most significant of these is that the outstanding customers will be contacted by the factoring company, and this may give the wrong impression to the customer, and with some contracts the debt reverts to the company after, say, 60 days. However, the advantages of factoring should not be dismissed because the process relieves the business of the administrative and financial burdens of granting credit but obviously at a cost. To assess the cost effectiveness of factoring it is necessary to evaluate the benefits, which might include reduced overdraft costs, reduced bad debts and reduced administration costs, and compare these with the cost of the factoring service.

Cash discounts

Discounts off the total amount outstanding may be offered to the customer for early payment, but care should be taken to ensure that the customer really is eligible. The offering of a cash discount for early payment is becoming less frequent and has never really been adopted by the hospitality, tourism and leisure industries, with many businesses preferring to offer special rates for immediate payment. In many cases the cost of discounting may mean that this is not a viable approach to reducing debtors. If a customer is offered terms of say '2/30, net 60' this means that payment is due within 30 days and will result in a 2% discount otherwise the full amount is due within 60 days. The customer has two options, he can either pay less 2% on day 30 or he can pay the full amount on day 60. The extra 30 days' credit costs the customer 2%.

This works out at approximately 360/30 = 12 times per year or an annual interest rate of 24%. The calculation can be worked out more precisely using the following formula:

$$I\,(\text{interest rate}) = (1 + \text{discount rate}) - 1$$

that is

$$I = (1 + 0.02) - 1 = 26.8\%$$

Unless the supplier's cost of borrowing is more than this figure it is uneconomic to offer this level of discount. The following example illustrates a cost benefit analysis calculated from the viewpoint of the creditor.

The following details relate to a debt of £1,000 owed by Sunshine Food Products to a food wholesaler. The terms are payment within 10 days to receive a discount of 5% or full payment within 30 days. The food company has an overdraft facility on which interest is payable at 15%. Should the food company take up the offer of the discount for early payment?

The benefit if the cash discount is accepted is a saving of £50 arising from £1000 x 5%.

The benefit if the discount is rejected is a saving in overdraft costs because the business would have 20 more days use of the money which represents:

$$£950 \times 20/365 \times 15\% = £7.81$$

Therefore, the benefit of a discount outweighs the cost of the overdraft incurred.

Interest charges

The reverse of offering a discount for early payment is to charge interest for late payment. The difficulty is in enforcing the payment of the interest. As mentioned it is often smaller businesses who suffer most from the late payment of invoices.

Bad debts

The cost of offering additional credit should be compared to the benefits of incurring additional sales. Offering credit will increase the likelihood of bad debts and increase administration costs. This needs to be reviewed in comparison to the benefit from additional sales. This example illustrates the cost benefit analysis.

Example

The current level of sales is £20,000 per month with an average credit period of 1 month. If the credit period is lengthened it is anticipated that sales will increase, and some bad debts will be incurred. There are considered to be three options the first of which is to continue with the existing policy.

Increase in credit period	Increase in sales above £20,000 per month	Percentage bad debt
NIL	NIL	NIL
1.5 months	£4,000	1
2 months	£10,000	10

The bad debt is only incurred on the new sales. The variable costs are known to be 60% of sales. Fixed costs are £50,000. There will be no increase in stocks required. Total investment in net assets, excluding debtors, will be fixed.

	Current situation	Increase by 1.5 months	Increase by 2 months
	£	£	£
Sales	20,000	24,000	30,000
Sales pa	240,000	288,000	360,000
Variable costs	144,000	172,800	216,000
Contribution	96,000	115,200	144,000
Bad debts	----------	480	11,000
New contribution	96,000	114,720	143,000
Fixed costs	50,000	50,000	50,000
Profit	46,000	64,720	93,000

Despite the bad debt increase extending credit to 2 months, this does provide an increase in profit.

The additional investment in debtors at cost is as follows assuming the cost of capital is 15%:

Debtor level	20,000	36,000	60,000
Value at cost	12,000	21,600	36,000
Opportunity cost	1,800	3,240	5,400

It is still worth offering additional credit to increase sales.

Debtor ratios

Ratios can also be used for debtor management and probably the most widely used is the debtor collection period. This calculated as follows:

$$\text{Debtor days} = \frac{\text{Average debtors x 365}}{\text{Annual credit sales}}$$

This value indicates the average time between the sale being recorded and payment being received. The ratio may be calculated annually or on a weekly or monthly basis substituting the relevant number of days. Most businesses calculate an average for the debtors in total and also values for individual accounts. The following time scales are averages of the periods normally used.

0 - 30 days	acceptable credit period
31 - 60 days	first chase communication
61 - 90 days	second chase communications and follow up
90+ days	restrictions imposed on further business

The average length of days for debtors in the UK is considered to be approximately 45 days, with the larger businesses often taking much longer. Beyond 90 days it may be possible to retrieve bad debts through a legal process, but this can be costly. It is better, therefore, to operate an effective credit policy to minimise the possibility of debtors being written off as bad debts in the first place.

Managing creditors

The process for paying suppliers is influenced by three important factors:

- Interest costs
- Administrative costs
- Supplier relationships

Creditors are an important source of short-term finance, and it is obviously beneficial to delay payment. Discounts may be offered by some suppliers as an attempt to improve payment settlement times. However, these should only be considered where the discount is greater than the opportunity cost of early payment as demonstrated by the previous example.

Large companies often take more than 30 days to settle an invoice, and this is due partly to administrative factors, particularly where invoices for individual units are settled centrally. Invoices for each supplier may be processed on a certain day each month and where the payment day is missed the supplier will need to wait until the following month. However, the delay in payment may be intentional, with companies taking advantage of suppliers who fail to follow up on outstanding invoices. Failure to pay on time may damage supplier relationships and could result in less cooperation from suppliers, increased prices, and delayed or erratic deliveries. A different approach to creditor management focuses on the relationship with suppliers, where communications are fostered to improve service and reduce the need for extensive stock holding. Companies who have taken this approach have reduced the number of suppliers used and have involved the supplier in strategic decision-making processes to reduce costs overall.

The management of creditors is achieved through the production of regular reports containing the credit payment period ratio which is calculated as follows:

$$\text{Creditor days} = \frac{\text{average or period end creditors x 365}}{\text{total purchases}}$$

The value calculated gives the number of days for which credit is taken. This ratio can be calculated annually or on a monthly basis using the relevant days in the month in the calculation.

Inventory control

Stock or inventory may be defined as any current asset held for conversion into cash. In manufacturing businesses such as factories, stock holdings may account for almost half of the total assets employed by the business and consequently stock management will require careful planning and control. In these types of business, the stock is classified into three types:

- **Raw materials:** stock held in the state in which it was purchased without any work having taken place
- **Work-in-progress:** stock which has been partially converted to the final state and the value is made up of material costs plus labour and expenses
- **Finished goods:** completed goods awaiting delivery to the customer.

In typical hospitality, tourism and leisure organisations, the stock holding levels are likely to be much lower and are often held solely in the raw material state with the transition to finished goods taking place at the point of consumption or simply held as finished goods ready to sell, such as retail products.

In hotels and restaurants, the most common stock will comprise of food and beverage, which will be fairly fast moving, and but also items such as disposables and stationery. The overall objective of inventory control is to minimize the costs associated with stockholding without losing potential sales through not having sufficient stock available. The cost of stock comprises of three elements: the purchase price, the holding costs and the cost to the business of being out of stock.

The cost of holding stock includes costs associated with the following:

- Lost interest on money tied up in stock
- Storage space
- Staffing, insurance
- Risk of obsolescence and pilferage
- Purchasing costs

The cost of being out of stock is difficult to calculate accurately. It is not easy to quantify the cost of the loss of customer goodwill and potential lost sales when insufficient stocks are available. In catering outlets for example, costs may be incurred as follows:

- Where production is halted in other areas, causing a delay in services,
- Through the loss of flexibility which exists when there is no buffer stock
- Administrative costs incurred from placing lots of small orders.

Stock management can be improved with the use of models to illustrate different scenarios and also the use of stock turnover ratios. The use of these methods will depend on the nature of the stock.

Models such as the Pareto principle and the A-B-C method are based on the condition that a small percentage of items comprise the greatest value of stock. The Pareto principle works on the assumption that 80% of the value of the stock may be held in only 20% of the items. This may well be close to reality in a hotel operation with several bars where liquor stocks often have the largest value per item. The A-B-C or 123 method of stock control is based on the principle that stock is classified into three groups depending on item value and degree of usage. The distribution of the value of these items may typically be illustrated as follows:

	% Stock volume	% Stock value
Category A	10	50
Category B	30	35
Category C	60	15
	100	100

Category A stocks will be essential items where the probability of a stock out is much higher and therefore levels must be monitored closely. Category B stocks will require less control and Category C stocks almost none. In practice all stock items can be effectively monitored using computerised inventory systems which can illustrate in real time how much stock is being held based on the opening stock and the sale of goods collected through the point-of-sale system.

Stock management models

The quantity of stock ordered from the supplier each time depends on the balance between the costs of holding stock over a period and the costs of a stock shortage, i.e. the loss arising when a sale cannot be made due to an item not being available. A common model is the Economic Order Quantity model (EOQ) which calculates the most efficient order quantity for each item given the costs. Many models operate on the assumption that the stock levels fall evenly over time until the stock runs out when it is replaced by a stock delivery, as illustrated in the diagram below. This assumption is not always necessarily true for hospitality operations.

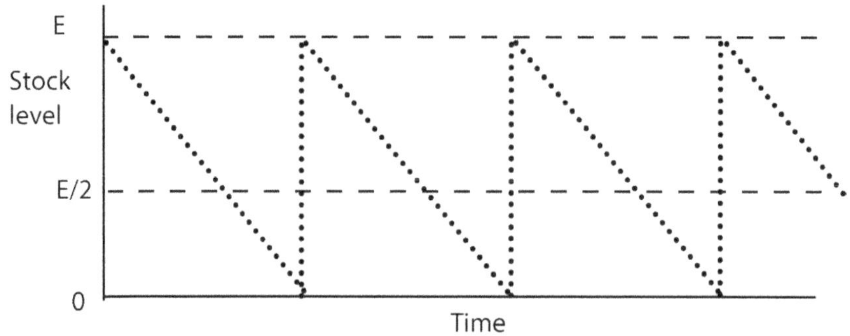

Figure 7.1: A graph of the stock level against time for an item of stock. An amount (E) of stock is delivered at time 0. This is steadily used until the stock level drops to 0, at which point a new consignment (amount E) arrives. The average level of stock is E/2)

This is the basis of the *Economic Order Quantity* model (EOQ), which calculates the most efficient order quantity for each item given the costs involved. The calculation is as follows:

$$EOQ = \sqrt{\frac{2\,Co \times D}{Ch}}$$

Where:

EOQ = Economic Order Quantity
Co = Cost of placing an order
D = Annual demand
Ch = Cost of holding stock

The assumptions underlying the model place limits on its use in the hospitality industry. They are that there is a known constant stockholding cost, a known constant ordering cost, the rates of demand are known and that there is a known constant price per unit. The seasonality of the hospitality industry may, in some cases, render the model less useful. However, the model may well have useful applications in the food production industries where production is constant. The concept is also useful in that it raises awareness of the costs involved.

The following example illustrates how the model is used.

Example

Ingredient X is required on a regular basis throughout the year. It is estimated that the annual demand is 4,095 kg and the cost of holding one kg in terms of refrigeration costs and other costs amounts to £4.00. It is estimated that it costs £4.85 to place and process a purchase order.

The Economic Order Quantity is calculated using the formula:

$$EOQ = \sqrt{\frac{2\,Co \times D}{Ch}}$$

Using the given values

$$EOQ = \sqrt{\frac{2 \times 4.85 \times 4095}{4.00}}$$

$$= 99.65\text{kg}$$

Assuming that demand is constant over the year purchase orders need to be made:

$$\frac{4{,}095}{99.65} = 41.36 \text{ times per year}$$

which is approximately equivalent to every 8 days.

Stock ratios

Stock control can be improved with the use of ratios. These are most effective when compared with budget, target or forecast figures. The most useful ratio is the stock turnover ratio which is calculated as follows:

$$\text{Stock turnover} = \frac{\text{Cost of sales}}{\text{Average value of stock}}$$

The greater the number of times the stock turns over the more efficient the stock control. The value can also be expressed in terms of the number of days the commodity has been sat on the shelf which is calculated as follows:

$$\text{Stock days} = \frac{\text{Value of stock}}{\text{Average daily cost of sales}} \times 365$$

The ratio may be calculated for stocks in total and also for individual items of stock to highlight slow moving items.

Cash and cash equivalents

Cash held by a business will be present in a variety of forms and may well include cash paid by customers, floats and cash held in bank accounts. It is essential therefore, that internal controls are maintained to minimise losses as follows:

- **Separation of duties.** This imposes checks on the individual where tasks are shared and individuals will need to collude to misappropriate funds.
- **Management authorisation** to raise payment for supplier's invoices, employee expense claims or cash advance requisitions.
- **Surprise checks** where cash is unexpectedly counted.
- **Regular bank reconciliations.**

No system of control can be perfect but internal checks can assist in preventing fraud and can reduce the likelihood of temptation.

Cash flow forecasts

A business needs to have cash in the bank available to meet day-to-day expenditure such as payment to suppliers and staff but it should also not be holding too much cash as this is an inefficient use of funds. Forecasted cash flow statements are essential for identifying peaks and troughs in cash requirements and may be produced with a simple receipts and payments approach or alternatively using the indirect style of cashflow approach as recommended by IFRS1, an example of which is included in Chapter 3.

Summary

The availability of working capital is essential for business survival. Too little in the form of stocks and cash will mean that the business will literally seize up. Too much will mean that extra costs will be incurred in holding too high a level of stock, cash and debtors. Creditors provide a valuable form of short-term finance, and a balance needs to be struck to ensure that creditors are maximised whilst ensuring that flexibility in supplier relationships remains.

Questions

1. The cash operating cycle

The Carmen Hotel has a bistro style restaurant which, due to growing demand, has been extended. A summary of its current year results are shown below:

	Food		Beverage	
	£	%	£	%
Sales revenue	150,000	100	100,000	100
Cost of sales	45,000	30	25,000	25
Gross profit	105,000	70	75,000	75

The following forecasts have been made for the coming year:

i) Sales of food and beverage will increase to £200,000 and £150,000 respectively.

ii) The amount of stock to be held will be:

Food - 10 days on average

Beverage - 25 days on average

iii) Of the total sales of food and beverage, 20% will be on credit and the debtors will be on average 45 days.

iv) Food suppliers will give 30 days' credit and beverage suppliers give 45 days.

v) Advance booking deposits from parties will amount to 5% of four weeks food sales.

a) Prepare a statement analysing the average working capital requirements necessary to fund the business during the coming year compared to the previous year.

b) Give illustrated examples of six key ratios which could be used to monitor the effectiveness of a restaurant operation.

2. The cash cycle

The West Hotels Group Ltd has been concerned with its liquidity position in recent months. The most recent Profit and Loss Account and Balance Sheet of the company are as follows:

Profit and Loss account for the Year ended 31st December 20x3

	£000
Sales	10,125
Cost of sales	2,997
Gross profit	7,128
Departmental expenses	1,767
Undistributed Operating Expenses	2,367
Profit before Fixed charges	2,994
Fixed charges	957
Net Profit	2,037

Balance sheet as at 31st December 20x3

	£000	£000	£000
Non Current Assets (net):			
Freehold property			17,600
Equipment & furniture			4,100
			21,700
Current Assets:			
Stocks of food & beverages			1,750
Debtors			2,250
Cash at bank			10
			4,010
Less creditors:			
(Amounts due within 1 year)			
Creditors		500	
Taxation		1,300	
Proposed dividend		1,100	
Bank overdraft		1,500	
		4,400	
Net Current Assets/ (Liabilities)			(390)
			21,310
Less creditors:			
(Amounts due in more than 1 year)			
10% Mortgage Debentures	20x0	8,400	
			12,910
Financed by:			
Ordinary Share Capital			6,910
Retained Profits			6,000
			12,910

You are required to:

a) Explain why West Hotels Group Ltd is concerned with its liquidity position.

b) Explain the term 'operating cash cycle' and discuss why this concept is important for a business.

c) Calculate the cash operating cycle for West Hotels Group Ltd based on the information in the statements above. Assume a 365 day year.

d) Discuss the strategies that can be followed to improve the cash operating cycle.

3. The Economic Order quantity

The Roasta Coffee Shop sells a particular brand of coffee and has the following characteristics:

Sales	10 cases per week
Ordering costs	£10 per order
Holding costs	30 per cent per year
Item cost	£80 per case

You are required to calculate:

a) How many cases should be ordered at a time?

b) How often should the coffee be ordered?

c) What is the annual cost of ordering and holding coffee?

d) What factors might cause the coffee shop to order a larger or smaller amount than the EOQ?

4. The role of the credit manager

a) Explain the role of a credit manager within a business.

b) Discuss the major factors a credit manager would consider when assessing the credit worthiness of a particular customer.

5. Business liquidity

These ratios are available for the Sands Hotel for three years of performance:

	2021	2022	2023
Current ratio	1.7	1.9	2.0
Acid-test ratio	1.3	1.4	1.5
Debtor days	35	38	40
Stock days	10	11	11

Use each of the above ratios to comment on the liquidity of the Sands Hotel from 2021 to 2023. What other information and ratios would be useful to give you full insight into the liquidity of the business and help you to interpret these values?

6. Managing inventory levels

A hotel is reviewing its stock ordering policy and has the following options available for the purchase of an item of cleaning materials used in housekeeping:

a) Purchase 100 cases of stock twice monthly

b) Purchase 200 cases per month

c) Purchase 600 cases every three months

d) Purchase 1,200 cases every six months

e) Purchase 2,400 cases once per year.

The purchase price for deliveries up to 400 cases is £10 per case. A discount of 5% is offered by the supplier for deliveries of 401 – 1000 cases. For orders in excess of 1,000 cases a total discount of 20% is available. Each order incurs administration costs of £25. Costs of holding the stock are estimated to be £2 per case.

Analyse the above information and give advice on the optimum order size. Consider what other factors should be taken into account when making this decision.

7. Economic Order quantity

The Alpha Food Service Company sells a particular brand of tea in all of its outlets. The tea is ordered centrally and then distributed to the outlets in order to gain the maximum discount from the supplier. The following data applies to the year 2021. Assume 52 weeks per year.

Sales	20 cases per week
Ordering costs	£20 per order
Holding costs (storage cost)	10%
Cost per case	£100

You are required to calculate:

a) How many cases should be ordered at a time?

b) How often should tea be ordered?

c) What is the annual cost of ordering and holding tea?

d) What factors might cause the company to order a larger or smaller amount than the EOQ?

e) How useful is the application of the EOQ model to be in the hospitality industry? Give examples of where its usage would be most and least appropriate.

8. Working capital

a) Explain what you understand by the term working capital

b) List the reasons why it is important to manage the level of working capital in a business.

c) What are factors which influence the level of cash which should be available to the business?

9. Controlling debtors

Seaside Hotels plc currently require payment from their customers month end after month of checkout. On average it takes them 60 days to pay. Credit sales amount to £1 million per year and bad debts are 4% of sales per year.

It is planned to offer customers a cash discount of 2% for payment within 30 days. It is estimated that 40% of customers will accept this facility but that the remaining customers, who tend to be slow payers, will not pay until 70 days after the stay. At present the company has a partly used overdraft facility costing 10% per annum. If the plan goes ahead bad debts will be reduced to 3% per annum and there will be savings in credit administration expenses of £3,000 per annum.

You are required to:

a) Advise Seaside Hotels plc on the viability of offering the new credit terms to the customers. You should support your answer with any calculations and explanations which you consider necessary. (Work to the nearest £)

b) Describe the costs incurred in offering credit to customers and recommend a code of practice to ensure effective debtor management.

10. Overtrading

a) Explain the term overtrading and describe what the possible consequences are arising from this condition.

b) What are the main causes of overtrading in the hospitality, tourism and leisure industry?

c) What financial ratios are useful for detecting signs of overtrading occurring?

11. Preparing a cash flow forecast

Note: Cash flow focuses on the timing of the business inflows and outflows.

Jane is planning to open a catering business to cater at local events.

The business will open in September with £2,000 in the bank account.

Jane estimates that she will attend two events per month and the average food revenue will be £1,500 per event, received in cash.

A potential client has offered her a contract to supply food at a regular event amounting to revenue of £250 per month for the next six months from October. The client requires one month credit and will pay in the following month.

The average cost of sales for materials will be 27% of revenue, paid in the month incurred.

An opening stock of food items, amounting to £100, will need to be purchased at the start of the business.

Jane will work from home for the first three months so there will be no office rental costs.

Jane plans to draw £1,000 per month as her salary.

Advertising costs are estimated at £500 for the first month and £200 per month thereafter, paid in the month incurred.

Accountancy costs will amount to £200 payable after six months of trading.

Equipment to be purchased in September for £4,000 has a life of three years.

Sundry costs including fuel amount to £200 per month.

Prepare a cash flow forecast for September, October and November.

References and further reading

ACCA Global (n.d.) *Working capital management.*www.accaglobal.com/gb/en/student/exam-support-resources/fundamentals-exams-study-resources/f9/technical-articles/wcm.html accessed 20/12/2023

Atrill, P. and Mclaney E. (2021) *Accounting and Finance for Non-Specialists*, 12th Edition, Pearson.

Ransley, J., Ingram, H. and Adams, D. (2022) *Developing Hospitality Properties and Facilities*. Routledge

Schmidgall, R. (2016) *Hospitality Industry Managerial Accounting*. Educational Institute of the American Hotel Motel Association.

Useful websites

www.finance4hospitality.co.uk An online community with bite sized content and resources developed by experts in hospitality accounting.

media.wiley.com/product_data/excerpt/57/07879538/0787953857.pdf excerpt from M. Dropkin & A. Hayden, *The Cash Flow Management Book for Nonprofits*

www.investopedia.com/articles/fundamental/03/061803.asp includes interesting case studies

8 Performance measurement

About this chapter

Tools and techniques for assessing business performance are essential requirements for understanding results, controlling revenues and costs and directing a business for the future. This chapter reviews the range of performance measures typically used and provides guidance on current practice in terms of both financial and nonfinancial performance measures widely used in the hospitality, tourism and leisure industries.

Learning objectives

On completion of this chapter, you should be able to:

- ☐ Understand and apply the range of operational measures used in the hospitality, tourism and leisure industries
- ☐ Understand and apply performance measures for assessing profitability, liquidity, asset usage and share performance
- ☐ Explain the factors to be considered when designing performance measurement systems

Introduction

The measurement of performance is central to control in both profit making and nonprofit making service organisations. It is essential to know **what** has happened, **why** it has happened and **what** can be done now to improve future performance. The details in the monthly management accounts should enable the management team to identify the strengths and weaknesses in the business and develop action plans for implementation to improve revenues, control costs and maximise profitability.

In the hospitality, tourism and leisure industries financial key performance indicators are used alongside non-financial measures to add a valuable additional dimension by providing information which attempts to quantify the competitive positioning of the business. As a result, many operations now try to use a mix of financial and nonfinancial measures, where intangibles such as quality and flexibility can be measured along with more traditional measures such as profitability and return on investment. The structure and size of the organisation clearly has implications for the scale and range of measures which are appropriate, with particular problems arising as organisations increase in size and change in structure.

Standards for performance measurement

There are generally five standards against which performance is normally measured.

- Performance of same unit or department in previous time periods
- Performance of similar units or departments both internal and external to the organisation
- Estimates of expected performance in the form of budgets and forecasts
- Estimates of what might have been achieved, set after the event
- Performance necessary to achieve desired goals.

The problem with setting standard targets for performance is that the process assumes that the environment remains the same throughout the period. In practice, changes in trading conditions may render the process of comparison useless. As a consequence, a system of this type is often perceived by managers as not being fair. Additionally, the process can fail to take into account what is achievable, with standards being set based on best performance rather than the average performance. This coupled, with the multiple natures of the objectives set, can lead to obsessive behaviours on the part of managesr as they attempt to meet all the targets, many of which are in conflict with each other.

To summarise, to develop effective processes for performance measurement it is important to consider the following major issues:

- Organisational objectives can be complex and not easily be summarized with a single measure of performance, such as the return on capital employed.
- Some aspects of performance, such as service levels, are difficult to measure in quantitative terms.
- Many organisational activities are interdependent and require cooperation between divisions, units or departments, and as a result performance measures should be tailored to the requirements of the organisation.
- The evaluation of performance must involve the exercise of judgment.

Financial measures of performance

Single ratio analysis, sometimes referred to as univariate analysis, is based on the calculation of individual ratios using data from the departmental operating accounts and the balance sheet. These ratios may then be used for comparison with previous trends, budget or with other similar operations. Ratios can be divided into those that can be used by any business in any sector and those which have been devised specifically for the hospitality, tourism and leisure sectors.

Ratios by type

Traditionally, financial ratios may be classified into five groups as follows.

- ☐ Profitability and operating ratios
- ☐ Asset utilisation
- ☐ Liquidity (control of cash and other working capital items)
- ☐ Capital gearing ratios
- ☐ Shareholders investment ratios.

The constituent ratios for each of these groupings are shown in more detail in Table 8.1.

Profitability and operating ratios
Return on net assets
Return on capital employed
Gross profit margin
Departmental operating income
Gross operating profit
Earnings before interest, tax, depreciation and amortisation
Net profit margin
Asset utilisation
Net asset turnover
Stockholding period
Debtor collection period
Creditor payment period
Capital gearing ratios
Debt to equity ratio
Number of times interest earned
Liquidity ratios
Current ratio
Quick assets ratio
Shareholders investment ratios
Return on shareholders funds
Earnings per share
Price/Earnings ratio
Dividend yield
Dividend cover

Table 8.1: Financial ratios for measuring performance by category

Many of these are standard ratios, used throughout many types of industry where benchmarks and guidelines for ratios are commonly cited, however, care should be taken as the magnitude of the ratios can vary considerably from one industry sector to another.

The following section aims to provide some guidance for the calculation and interpretation of these ratios when attempting to analyse company performance. It is worth remembering that ratio analysis is not an exact science and there are often a variety of methodologies quoted for the calculation of one particular ratio.

Profitability and operating ratios

There are a range of measures used across a range of business sectors to assess business performance. The return on capital employed (ROCE) ratio is widely used for comparing the return with the investment. Tthere are a number of methods for calculating this ratio, and individual organizations should select the methodology most suited to their needs. These represent the most typical approaches.

Return on net assets (return on capital employed) =

$$\frac{\text{Net profit before long term interest and tax}}{\text{Total assets less creditors due within one year (net assets)}} \times 100\%$$

This version of the ratio uses profit before interest and taxes due and the net assets. The usual level of profit to use with this ratio is operating profit or profit before interest and tax which then gives the profit available to both lenders and shareholders. By using the profit figure at this level in the profit and loss account the effects of taxation are avoided. This ratio is also often calculated using Earnings Before Interest, Tax, Depreciation and Amortisation (EBITDA).

Alternatively, the following version of the ratio is sometimes used:

Return on net assets (return on capital employed) =

$$\frac{\text{Net profit after long term interest and tax}}{\text{Total assets less creditors due within one year}} \times 100\%$$

The ratio should produce a value which is as high as possible without undermining the long-term success of the business. A short-term view will mean that earnings are increased through reducing expenditure in a number of areas such as training and maintenance and capital expenditure is reduced, but both of these policies will adversely affect the long-term viability of the business.

It is important to note that other alternative forms are sometimes used, such as return on total assets (fixed assets and current assets) and this will obviously produce a value which is quite different. Consequently, it is important to be clear as to the basis of the ratio being used.

The ROCE or return on investment (ROI) ratio is the most widely used financial measure of divisional performance and is closely related to the accounting rate of return (ARR) investment appraisal technique described in Chapter 10.

There are several important levels of profit in the Profit and Loss account which are monitored by comparing the profit to revenue as a percentage:

- Gross profit
- Departmental profit
- Gross operating profit
- Earnings before Interest and Tax

The gross profit margin ratio considers the proportion of sales revenue remaining after the expense of making the product is taken into account. Not all revenue generating departments sell a physical product – the rooms department in a hotel sell the use of the room space for example. The ratio is calculated and monitored extensively in food and beverage operations as follows:

Revenue – Cost of sales = gross profit

The gross profit margin is calculated as follows:

$$\frac{\text{Gross profit}}{\text{Sales}} \times 100\%$$

The scale of gross profit will depend on the pricing strategy of the firm. High volumes may be achieved with low prices or low volumes may be supported by higher average spends and consequently higher gross profit cash values. The other important factor associated with gross profit margin is sales mix. The combination of the products and services sold will impact on the average gross profit margin achieved.

Example

Use the following data to compute the cost of sales and the gross profit percentage for a café operation.

Opening stock 1 April	£22,184.00
April purchases:	
Meats	£11,501.00
Dairy	£6,300.00
Fruit and vegetables	£9,641.00
Other foods	£32,384.00
Closing stock at April 30	£23,942.00
Sales	£193,560.00

The consumption is calculated using the formula:

Opening stock + Purchases – Closing Stock = Cost of Sales

22,184.00 + 59,826 – 23,942 = 58,068

$$\text{Cost Of Sales \%} = \frac{58,068}{193,560} \times 100$$

$$= 30\%$$

$$\text{Gross profit \%} = 70\%$$

Departmental profits are calculated for revenue generating departments and these are usually clearly identified in the monthly profit and loss account. The departmental profit is calculated by deducting the departmental costs from the departmental revenue. Staff and labour costs are a significant expense in the hospitality, tourism and leisure industry and will often form a large proportion of departmental costs. Payroll is calculated on the basis of the various team members in the department and how much they earn. However, there are several additional payroll related costs that make up the final total:

- Employer National Insurance contributions
- Employer pension contributions
- Meals on duty
- Holiday pay
- Employee benefits

Employment costs have been rising for the service sector due to increases in the living wage and staff shortages. Techniques for managing the payroll cost include:

- ☐ Forecasting sales and volumes of customers accurately
- ☐ Multi-tasking / skilling employees to work in multiple areas
- ☐ Work scheduling to avoid idle time
- ☐ Monitoring ratios such as the payroll to revenue percentages

The importance of gross operating profit

The gross operating profit (GOP) is calculated by deducting the operational costs from revenue as follows:

Total revenue – Departmental costs – Undistributed operating expenses

The GOP is often used to assess the performance of a hotel business by reviewing the conversion of revenues to GOP in the form of a percentage:

$$\frac{\text{Gross operating profit}}{\text{Total revenue}} \times 100\%$$

Many hotels seek to achieve almost 50% conversion to gross operating profit. However, this is dependent on the control of the various costs.

Gross operating profit can be monitored using a range of measures, the cash value, the percentage to total revenue and as an asset usage ratio such as GOPPAR (Gross Operating Profit Per Available Room) and GOPPOR (Gross Operating Profit Per Occupied Room).

EBITDA (earnings before interest, taxes, depreciation, and amortization) is another significant measure of profitability and represents the profit after management fees have been paid but before interest on long-term loans, corporation tax, depreciation and amortisation. A common target for this is around 30%.

Once the remaining costs are included, the final net profit is distributed as dividends to the shareholders, with ideally some profit retained in the business to increase the equity in the balance sheet.

Asset utilisation ratios

These ratios are used to assess the effectiveness of the business in using its assets to generate revenue and profit. This includes both long- and short-term assets. The first of these is the net asset turnover ratio which focuses on net assets in total.

$$\text{Net asset turnover} = \frac{\text{Sales}}{\text{Total assets} - \text{current liabilities}} \times 100\%$$

The net asset turnover ratio enables judgment to be made on the extent to which the business has generated sales. The size of the ratio will be dependent on the nature of the business and a high ratio does not necessarily indicate profitability but generally speaking the higher the better.

The stock or inventory ratio focuses on the efficient usage of this short term asset and can be calculated in a number of ways which are dependent on the information available. When internal information is available it is possible to calculate a stock holding days value for every individual product line as follows:

$$\text{Stock holding period} = \frac{\text{Average stock held}}{\text{Stock consumption}} \times 365 \text{ days}$$

The ratio indicates the average number of days which stock remains in the firm before it is sold. The stock turnover ratio is the reciprocal of this, which is stock used divided by stock held. It is not possible to provide a standard figure as the days held will depend on the nature of the stock and the mix between fresh and dry goods. To maximise the use of working capital the figure should be as low as possible without a shortage arising. Another current asset requiring control is debtors, which are those customers who have yet to pay for goods and services received. Ideally the debtors' ratio should be calculated using credit sales but for analysis using published figures, normally only the total sales are disclosed.

$$\text{Debtor collection period} = \frac{\text{Trade debtors}}{\text{Credit sales}} \times 365 \text{ days}$$

This ratio tells us how long, on average, trade debtors take to pay. The figure should be low as possible and ideally it would be better to allow no credit sales. However, the provision of credit is essential for many business operations in the hospitality and tourism industry, but every effort should be made to ensure the bills are paid promptly and in full.

$$\text{Creditor payment period} = \frac{\text{Trade creditors}}{\text{Credit purchases}} \times 365 \text{ days}$$

This ratio tells us on average after a purchase on credit, the length of time the firm takes to pay its debts. A good credit policy will ensure that the business will take as much 'free credit' as possible without losing the goodwill of suppliers.

Liquidity ratios

These ratios are used to assess how well a business is using its working capital. The following ratio provides a measure of the business's ability to meet its short term liabilities by matching short term assets with short term liabilities.

$$\text{Current ratio} = \frac{\text{Current assets}}{\text{Creditors falling due within one year}}$$

A standard for the current ratio is often quoted as 1.5:1 which is ensuring that current liabilities are covered at least 1.5 times by current assets. However, companies in the hospitality sector have survived with ratios which are considerably less than 1, where current liabilities have exceeded current assets. The leisure sector in particular is typical, where sales are predominantly made for cash and stocks and cash holdings are kept at minimal levels and purchases are bought on credit. Consequently, a consistent ratio of 0.5 :1 can be expected. This ratio can be adapted to highlight liquid current assets.

$$\text{Quick assets or acid test ratio} = \frac{\text{Liquid assets}}{\text{Creditors falling due within one year}}$$

Liquid assets are normally taken to be cash and debtors excluding stock. However, in some cases the stock may be more liquid than the debtors. Again, the often quoted bench mark is 1:1 but the value very much depends on the nature of the business.

Capital gearing ratios

Capital gearing is concerned with the level of funding provided by shareholders and loan providers. Loan financing costs in practice tend to be cheaper than equity but loan funding exposes the shareholders to greater risk through the obligation to pay interest and the possibility of changing interest rates. The recommended value for this ratio changes from industry to industry and the assessment as to whether the value is high or low should be made in relation to industry values.

$$\text{Debt to equity} = \frac{\text{Borrowings (long and short term)}}{\text{Total equity (shares plus reserves)}} \times 100\%$$

A measure of what is considered to be high risk should be based within the context of the nature of the industry. Typically, hotel ventures, for example, require substantial investment at the start and a new operation with investment funding could initially be highly geared, possibly with debt exceeding equity in the early stages. As retained earnings increase the ratio is likely to change with equity becoming the dominant form of finance.

The gearing ratio is usually quoted with the following ratio which measures the ability to service the loan finance.

$$\text{Number of times interest earned} = \frac{\text{Net profit before long term interest and tax}}{\text{Interest payable}}$$

This ratio considers the profitability of the company from the viewpoint of the lender and assesses the ease with which interest is payable. A multiple factor of four times profit to interest is often suggested as a 'safe' value although there is little evidence to support this.

Shareholders investment ratios

These ratios consider the performance of the business from the viewpoint of the shareholder. Shareholders purchase shares to receive a regular income in the form of dividends and to hopefully also achieve capital growth when the share price increases.

Return on equity (Return on shareholders funds) =

$$\frac{\text{Net profit after long term interest and tax}}{\text{Share capital and reserves}} \times 100\%$$

This ratio considers return on capital specifically from the shareholders' point of view by considering the relationship between those profits which are attributable to the shareholder and their total funds invested. The following ratio, the earnings per share is an important measure of corporate performance.

$$\text{Earnings per share} = \frac{\text{Profit after interest and tax}}{\text{Number of ordinary shares in issue}}$$

This is the profit attributable to each share. The profit generated by the firm belongs to the shareholders whether it is paid out as dividends or not. The more equity increases, the greater the dilution of the earnings per share. This would indicate that funding from loan sources would serve to improve the resulting value. Although this is true, it should be remembered that loan finance carries its own risks associated with the commitment to pay interest and repay the capital sum. Earnings per share is normally linked with the following ratio, the price/earnings ratio.

$$\text{Price/Earnings} = \frac{\text{Current market price per share}}{\text{Earnings per share}}$$

This ratio can be seen as the number of years that it would take, at the current share price and rate of earnings, for the earnings from the share to cover the price of the share. The ratio indicates how much an investor is prepared to pay for the business earnings. The value of the ratio depends not only on the business itself but also on the industry in general. The following ratio is a measure of the return the investor is receiving on the current value of the investment.

$$\text{Dividend yield} = \frac{\text{Dividend per share (grossed up for tax)}}{\text{Current market price per share}} \times 100\%$$

This measure enables investments to be compared with each other and enables the investor to seek out those investments which outperform the market in general. The ability to pay the dividend is measured by the following rat io, dividend cover.

$$\text{Dividend cover} = \frac{\text{Earnings per share}}{\text{Dividend per share}}$$

This ratio indicates how comfortably the firm can meet the dividend out of current profits. A public limited company is under some pressure to provide a consistent dividend to maintain share price. However, failure to reinvest in the business can undermine the long-term viability of the operations.

To conclude, shareholder investment ratios are important for the manager of a business because of the power of the market in determining the fortunes of the business in the long term.

Operating statistics

Specific operating statistics, focusing on resource utilisation, are well used in the hospitality and tourism industry, and these may be usefully classified into two categories: those that focus on sales activity, and those that focus on cost reduction. Table 8.2 includes several key ratios highlighted in the Uniform System of Accounts for the Lodging Industry.

Food and beverage operations	
Sales related ratios	**Cost related ratios**
Restaurant occupancy by meal or by day	Salaries and wages in relation to sales
Average spend per customer	Material or product cost of sales
Sales revenue per employee	Stock turnover multiple
Percentage of beverage to food revenue	Stock held days
Percentage of food/beverage to rooms revenue	Expenses in relation to sales
Seat turnover (measure of seat usage in restaurants)	
Revenue per available seat hour	
Revenue per m2	

Rooms division	
Sales related ratios	**Cost related ratios**
Room occupancy percentage	Labour costs in relation to sales
Double room occupancy percentage	Laundry costs in relation to sales
Bed occupancy percentage	Cleaning cost per occupied room
Number of sleepers	Servicing cost per occupied room
Room revenue %	Costs per available room (CostPAR)
Average room rate per room occupied	Salaries and wages %
Average room rate per guest	Salaries and wages per occupied room
Total average spend of each guest	
Revenue per available room (REVPAR)	
Sales mix ratio	
Yield percentage	

Table 8.2: Ratios used in the Uniform System of Accounts for the Lodging Industry

Hotel revenue measures

Most of these measures are self explanatory but the following measures are worth noting as these are key for understanding hotel performance:

- ☐ Room Occupancy
- ☐ Average Room Rate
- ☐ REVPAR
- ☐ Yield statistic

The room occupancy measures the number of rooms occupied by paying guests as a percentage of the total rooms available. It is calculated as follows:

$$\text{Room occupancy \%} = \frac{\text{Rooms occupied by paying guests}}{\text{Number of rooms available}} \times 100\%$$

If a hotel has 100 rooms and 65 are occupied by guests and the room sales for the day are £6,500 then the Room Occupancy Percentage is calculated as follows:

$$\frac{65 \times 100}{100} = 65\%$$

Although room rates may vary seasonally, by market segment, or by room type within a property, most lodging properties calculate an overall average room rate, also called the average daily rate (ADR). The overall average room rate reveals the average rate charged per occupied room and is calculated by dividing total rooms revenue for a period by the number of rooms occupied during that period. Rooms occupied include rooms occupied on a paid basis, as well as rooms occupied without charge in connection with a promotion or contract. Complimentary rooms are not included in the denominator of the ADR calculation. The overall average room rate is calculated as follows:

$$\text{Average room rate} = \frac{\text{Total rooms revenue}}{\text{Rooms occupied}}$$

Using the previous data:

$$= \frac{£6{,}500}{65} = £100.00$$

RevPAR is calculated as follows:

$$\frac{\text{Revenue achieved}}{\text{Rooms available for sale}}$$

This measure assesses the overall earning power of the rooms available for sale and is a key measure for evaluating the usage of accommodation letting space. Using the previous data the REVPAR is:

$$= \frac{£6{,}500}{100} = £65.00$$

Note that the REVPAR can also be calculated by multiplying the average room rate by the occupancy percentage.

The yield statistic is the ratio of the actual revenue (generated by the number of rooms sold) to potential revenue (the amount that would be received from the sales of rooms in the hotel at a Rack Rate) and is expressed as the

$$\frac{\text{Actual revenue}}{\text{Potential revenue}}$$

This measure was discussed in more detail in Chapter 5 in relation to pricing strategies. A cost reduction approach may bring increases in profitability, but only increases in revenue can bring about an increase of cash flows into the business, and for high fixed cost industries increases in sales bring about substantial increases in profitability.

Another useful measure for monitoring revenues in the hotel sector is total revenue per available room (TRevPAR).

This measures the total revenue yield a property achieves relative to the rooms available in the property for a period. Total RevPAR can be used as one measure of total revenue change from prior period results or to compare actual to budgeted results. Since the total revenue is scaled by the number of rooms at the property, it can be used as one comparison of the revenue yield of a property to its competitors or comparable properties. For properties with significant revenue sources other than rooms' revenue, this may be a better indicator of revenue yield or growth as opposed to RevPAR.

Revenue measures for food and beverage operations

A useful measure for the food service industries focuses on the average spend for both food and beverage. This is calculated by taking the relevant revenue and dividing by the number of customers served (also known as the covers).

Per occupied room (POR) measures

Across the hotel P&L it is useful to analyse costs using the POR measure. This enables each cost to be evaluated in terms of the cost per room occupied and is particularly useful for variable costs. The result can then be compared to budget, prior year and industry data.

Measuring flow through

Flow through is defined by the USALI as the difference between the actual GOP achieved versus budget or last year divided by the difference in actual total revenue and the budget or last year values.

$$\frac{\text{Actual gross operating profit} - \text{Budgeted gross operating profit}}{\text{Actual revenue} - \text{Budget revenue}}$$

This provides an overall percentage measure of the conversion of the additional revenue to GOP which can be tracked when revenue both declines and increases. When both revenue and GOP has dropped, the USALI recommends that the Flex calculation be used.

$$1 - \frac{\text{Actual gross operating profit} - \text{Budgeted gross operating profit}}{\text{Actual revenue} - \text{Budget revenue}}$$

This is an excellent start to monitoring the GOP conversion. The next step is to understand how the source of revenue impacts on the conversion. The conversion rate of rooms revenue is quite different to F&B revenue, for example, because of the proportion of marginal or variable costs involved to deliver the sale. Within room sales, the additional revenue could arise through an increase in the Average Room Rate (ARR) or an increase in occupancy or a combination of both.

Using standard costing techniques, it is possible to split the revenue to determine the source of the change in revenues as well as calculating the additional cost likely to be incurred. We can start with the Sales Volume Variance, which is the difference between the actual and expected occupancy, i.e the number of rooms sold and then multiplied by the budgeted average room rate. The purpose of this variance is to separate out the change in GOP arising from the number of rooms sold. Then if we consider the Selling Price Variance, this is the difference between the actual and budgeted average room rate, multiplied by the actual number of rooms sold. The following steps illustrate how this can be achieved in practice.

	Actual	Budget
Rooms available	750	750
Rooms occupied	645	615
Occupancy %	86%	82%
ARR	£177.00	£163.00
Rooms revenue	£114,165	£100,245

Table 8.3: Rooms revenue calculations

From Table 8.3 above we can see that the additional total rooms revenue generated is £13,920. We can then split the increase in revenue into the two sources. The additional revenue due to the rooms occupied is:

30 × £163 = £4,890

And the additional revenue due to the average room rate is:

£14 × 645 = £9,030

We then need to consider the conversion rate of each of these sources of revenue to GOP. When additional rooms are sold there will be additional variable costs incurred, to clean the rooms for example. Whereas an increase in room sales due to the rate change will have a higher conversion to GOP.

As in all analysis there are various assumptions to be made throughout the calculations which some might argue renders the review less useful.

Competitor analysis

Effective competitor analysis lies in obtaining good, reliable and meaningful information about a relevant set of competitors. For the hotel sector, there are several excellent agencies available providing competitor set data where, for a fee, a hotel can receive a daily and monthly update on the hotel's performance in relation to a competitive set, normally comprised of four hotels chosen for comparison. To avoid issues with collusion, the data is always aggregated so that no one property is individually identifiable. To choose a competitive set it is useful to ask:

- ☐ If our guests were not staying with us, where would they stay?
- ☐ Does the competitive set represent all segments (or do you need multiple competitive sets)?
- ☐ Does your competitive set include 'aspirational' competitors?
- ☐ Do you have competition outside of your geographic area?

May 2016

	Occupancy (%)			ADR			RevPAR		
	My Prop	Comp Set	Index (MPI)	My Prop	Comp Set	Index (ARI)	My Prop	Comp Set	Index (RGI)
Current Month	74.3	76.5	97.1	189.85	181.26	104.7	140.97	138.63	101.7
Year To Date	72.2	74.1	97.4	183.77	179.74	102.2	132.66	133.24	99.6
Running 3 Month	75.1	77.6	96.8	182.70	180.80	101.1	137.18	140.23	97.8
Running 12 Month	68.8	70.4	97.6	180.77	175.82	102.8	124.30	123.85	100.4

May 2016 vs 2015 Percent Change (%)

	Occupancy			ADR			RevPAR		
	My Prop	Comp Set	Index (MPI)	My Prop	Comp Set	Index (ARI)	My Prop	Comp Set	Index (RGI)
Current Month	2.2	7.3	-4.8	3.1	1.7	1.4	5.4	9.1	-3.5
Year To Date	-2.8	1.0	-3.8	-0.6	0.5	-1.1	-3.4	1.5	-4.8
Running 3 Month	2.3	7.6	-4.9	-0.5	1.8	-2.2	1.8	9.4	-7.0
Running 12 Month	-1.4	-0.1	-1.3	1.1	1.4	-0.3	-0.3	1.3	-1.6

Table 8.4: A competitive set analysis report from STR Global. *Republication or other re-use of this data without the express written permission of STR is strictly prohibited.*

The relationship between the subject property and the competitor set is illustrated by indexing. If the subject hotels' results are lower than the competitor set, then the index will be lower than 100, whereas if the subject hotel has an index higher than 100 it is outperforming the competitor set. The measures most commonly used in competitor analysis are the occupancy percentage, the average room rate and REVPAR with REVPAR considered to be the leading measure.

Ratios for the airline industries
Operating costs per seat (£)
Group total profit/(loss) before tax per seat (£)
Airline total profit/(loss) before tax per seat (£)
Airline revenue per seat (£)
Airline cost per available seat kilometres (CASK)
Revenue per ASK (RASK)
Revenue per seat flown
CO2 emissions per passenger kilometre

Table 8.5: Operating ratios for the airline industries

Ratios for a tour operator
Average daily rate per bed
Referral Rate
Ticket yield per passenger
Spend per trip per person
Revenue per booking
Repeat customer rate
Booking by channels
Ratio of cancellations to bookings

Table 8.6: Operating ratios for the tour operator

Problems with using ratios

The use of ratios can be confusing where differing advice is offered as to how the ratios can be calculated. The choice of ratios used, the exact definition of the ratio and the conclusions drawn are very much based on personal judgment. Weaknesses in the use of ratios can also stem from the nature of the accounting information used in the analysis. There is a tendency for the profit and loss account to overstate the profit levels and a tendency for the balance sheet to misstate the value of capital tied up in the business.

The balance sheet figures represent the position at a single point in time and the figures may not be representative of the business in general. This creates problems for the interpretation of ratios, particularly where ratios are calculated using profit statement and balance sheet figures combined. Figures from the profit and loss account represent a series of transactions over a period of time, whereas balance sheet figures do not. Finally, the process of dividing one figure by another means that information is lost, therefore, the most useful way to analyse performance is to use the ratios with the original statements with an enquiring and critical approach.

Problems with specific ratios and performance measurement

The most common form of measuring business performance is to use some form of profit in the context of the investment needed to generate that profit, that is the return on capital employed or return on net assets. One problem with this ratio when it is used to compare managers' performance arises where managers attempt to 'manage' the ratio by reducing the level of investment rather than attempting to increase profit. Consequently, it may be useful to use a related concept called Residual Income (RI). The Residual Income is defined as 'controllable contribution', or profit less the cost of capital charge on the investment.

Economic value added (EVA TM)

The term 'residual income' has been redefined as 'economic value added', by the consultants Stern Stewart, and they advocate that it is the financial performance measure that comes closer than any other to capturing the true economic profit of a business. The EVA is calculated as follows:

EVA = Net operating profit after taxes (NOPAT) – (Capital x cost of capital)

NOPAT is defined as the Net Operating Profit After Tax.

The cost of capital is the cost of servicing the finance used in the business.

Research has suggested that a focus on EVA provides companies with a long term strategic approach to performance measurement although the measure is not widely applied in the hospitality and tourism industries.

Using key performance indicators

Given the plethora of performance measures available, it can be difficult to determine what the key measures in an organisation are. Many businesses, particularly those with public shareholders, are driven to focus on return on capital employed and shareholder measures. However, the results used in these are driven by a range of operational measures as the pyramid of measures in Figure 8.1 shows.

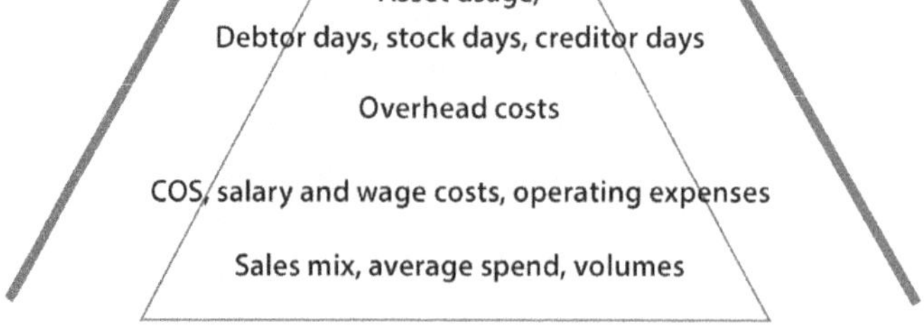

Figure 8.1: Pyramid of key performance indicators (KPIs).
ROCE: Return on capital employed; EPS: earnings per share; COS: cost of sales

Balanced Scorecard and performance measurement

The balanced scorecard concept was first launched by Robert Kaplan and David Norton in the article "The Balanced Scorecard - Measures that Drive Performance" in the *Harvard Business Review* in 1992. Kaplan and Norton's approach recommended broadening the scope of traditional financial measures such as return on capital employed and profit to sales ratios by including four key areas in the performance measurement process:

- ☐ Financial performance (how do we look to shareholders?),
- ☐ Customer knowledge (how do customers see us?),
- ☐ Internal business processes (what must we excel at?),
- ☐ Learning and growth (can we continue to improve and create value?).

This approach attempts to monitor not only how the business is performing now but also tries to assess the potential for the future. In recent years Kaplan and Norton's approach has been refocused beyond performance *measurement* but now includes the broader remit of performance *management*. Kaplan and Norton (1996) explain companies are using the balanced score card concept to achieve the following critical management processes:

- ☐ Clarify and translate vision and strategy into specific objectives and identify the critical drives of strategic objectives;
- ☐ Communicate and link strategic objectives and measures
- ☐ Plan and set targets in line with strategic initiatives
- ☐ Enhance strategic feedback and learning

A number of companies in the hospitality and tourism sector have adopted variations of the balanced scorecard approach as a means for evaluating and presenting business performance. The modern day equivalent is the dashboard of data available on a daily and monthly basis, which captures the essential key performance indicators for the business, including financial and non-financial measures.

Summary

This chapter has reviewed a variety of performance measures and where possible has attempted to use the measures to assess company performance. Single ratio analysis continues to be the most widely used technique for monitoring company performance but many companies in the service sector are supplementing these with operational measures based on nonfinancial criteria. In order to be effective ratio analysis requires standardization and consistency of the definitions used in the process to ensure success.

Questions

1. Shareholder ratios

You have received the following data with regard to a public limited company operating in the hospitality sector for the year 20x3:

a) The company has an issued share capital of 1,000,000 ordinary shares of £1 each nominal value. There are no preference shares.

b) The market price of the shares is currently £18.80

c) The net profit after taxation for the year was £800,000

d) The Directors are proposing a dividend of 80p per share for the financial year ended 31 December 20x3

You are required to calculate the following:

i) Dividend yield

ii) Dividend cover

iii) Earnings per share

iv) Price/earnings ratio

v) Comment on the results you have calculated.

2. The return on capital employed ratio is often the preferred measure for assessing the profitability of a business. Discuss the advantages and disadvantages of this particular measure and contrast this approach with that offered by the Balanced Scorecard approach.

3. "All businesses seek to 'profit maximise'". Comment on the validity of this statement with reference to key performance measures and other possible business objectives. Give examples of nonfinancial measures which are used in the hospitality industry to measure performance.

4. Below are the financial results of the Skyway Hotel for the years 2022 and 2023. The hotel has been operating since 1980 and its main activity is room letting.

Balance Sheets as at 31 December

	2022 £000	£000	2023 £000	£000
Non current assets (net)				
Land and buildings		640		780
Equipment and furniture		140		200
		780		980
Current assets				
Stock of food and beverages	40		150	
Debtors	24		100	
Cash	106	170	4	254

Current Liabilities				
Creditors	16		30	
Taxation	80		120	
Proposed dividend	50		60	
Overdraft	4	150	24	234
Net total assets		800		1000
Financed by				
Ordinary share capital		500		640
Retained profits		180		240
		680		880
10% Debenture (secured on property - 2025		120		120
		800		1000

Profit and Loss Accounts for year ending 31 December

	2022	2023
	£000	£000
Sales	1000	1400
Less Cost of Sales	200	280
Gross Profit	800	1120
Operating costs	640	880
Net Profit before tax	160	240
Less		
Corporation tax (50%)	80	120
Net Profit after tax	80	120
Less		
Proposed ordinary share dividend	50	60
Retained profits for the year	30	60

Note: 50% of total sales are on credit

You are required to:

i) Calculate 10 key accounting ratios for 2022 and 2023 to show liquidity, profitability and gearing.

ii) Comment on the strengths and weaknesses revealed by the ratios and any other information you consider relevant.

5. a) Review the statements below and prepare:

i) A comparative analysis of the two years of performance

ii) A range of ratio calculations to evaluate profitability, liquidity and asset utilisation.

b) Using the calculations, you have prepared, comment on the business performance and give recommendations for future courses of action.

Avon Hotels plc has been operating since 1960 and its main activity is room letting. The Actual Results for 2022 and 2023 are shown below:-

Profit & Loss Accounts for year ending 31 December

		2022		2023	
		£000's	£000's	£000's	£000's
Sales			3,000		3,800
Less:	Cost of sales		600		790
Gross Profit			2,400		3,010
Less:	Labour	750		1,050	
	Depreciation	70		100	
	Other Expenses	1,050		1,450	
			1,870		2,600
Net Profit Before Tax			530		410

Note: Other expenses includes interest

Analysis of Sales:

	2022	2023
Rooms	1,450	1,900
Food	800	1100
Beverage	600	600
Other	150	200
Total	3,000	3,800

Analysis of Cost of Sales:

	2022	2023
Food	240	340
Beverage	150	160
Other	210	290
Total	600	790

Balance Sheets as at 31 December:

	2022			2023		
	£000s	£000s	£000s	£000s	£000s	£000s
Non-Current Assets (net)						
Freehold Property			2,450			2,670
Equipment & furniture			280			400
			2,730			3,070
Current Assets						
Stocks of food & beverages		120			150	
Debtors		450			650	
Cash at Bank					45	
		570			845	
Less Creditors						
(Amounts due within 1 year)						
Creditors	75			90		
Taxation	80			85		
Proposed Dividend	100			120		
Bank Overdraft	85					
		340			295	
Net Assets			2,960			3,620

Less Creditors		
(Amounts due in more than 1 year)		
10% Mortgage Debentures 2024	340	340
	2,620	3,280
Financed By		
Share Capital		
Ordinary Shares of 10p each	2,260	2,690
Reserves		
Retained Profits	360	590
	2,620	3,280

Notes:

1) 50% of Sales are on credit, 50% for cash
2) The Debentures were issued in 2020
3) The current share price is £5.00

6. Explain the purpose and difficulties of using ratio analysis. Suggest a range of non-financial measures which could be used to monitor a hospitality business, using examples drawn from both your study and your experience.

7. Discuss the advantages which may be claimed for Kaplan and Norton's balanced scorecard as a basis for performance measurement over traditional management accounting views of performance measurement. Your answer should include specific examples of measures for each aspect of the balanced scorecard.

8. You have received the following data with regard to a public limited company operating in the hospitality sector for the year 2022:

a) The company has an issued share capital of 1,000,000 ordinary shares of £1 each nominal value. There are no preference shares.
b) The market price of the shares is currently £18.80
c) The net profit after taxation for the year was £800,000
d) The Directors are proposing a dividend of 80p per share for the financial year ended 31 December 2023

You are required to calculate the following:

1. Dividend yield
2. Dividend cover
3. Earnings per share
4. Price/earnings ratio
5. Comment on the results you have calculated

9. You are asked to write a succinct report to a potential investor who is taking a keen interest in the management and performance of two companies in the hospitality and tourism sector. Select two appropriate companies to consider. Research the results for each company for the last two years and the trends for the last five years, comparing these with the sector norms.

You should include an interpretation of the key financial statements with reference to aspects such as:

i) Long term cash flows

ii) Working capital controls

iii) Growth and Profitability

iv) Asset utilisation

v) Risk

using a range of methods for analysis.

Your report should advise the potential investor on the merits and weaknesses of each company and the prospects for return on investment.

References and further reading

American Hotel & Lodging Educational Institute, *Uniform System of Accounts for the Lodging Industry*, 11th Edition 2014. https://usali.hftp.org/

Atrill, P. & Mclaney E. (2021) *Accounting and Finance for Non-Specialists*, 12th Edition, Pearson.

Atkinson, H., Jones, T., Lorenz, A. and Harris, P. (2012), *Strategic Managerial Accounting: Hospitality, Tourism and Events Applications*, Goodfellow Publishers, Oxford.

Harris, P. (2013). *Profit Planning for Hospitality and Tourism*. Extended 3rd edition. Goodfellow Publishers, Oxford

Pizzam, A. (2015) *International Encyclopedia of Hospitality Management*, Elsevier

Ransley, J., Ingram, H. and Adams, D. (2022) *Developing Hospitality Properties and Facilities*. Routledge

Schmidgall, R. (2016) *Hospitality Industry Managerial Accounting*. Educational Institute of the American Hotel Motel Association.

Useful websites

www.balancedscorecard.org

www.evanomics.com/

www.skymark.com/resources/methods/balancedscorecard.asp

www.portfoliomgt.org/ForumItem.asp?itemID=1012

www.balancedscorecard.biz/articles.html

www.themanager.org/Knowledgebase/Management/BSC.htm

www.finance4hospitality.co.uk

www.portfoliomgt.org/ForumItem.asp?itemID=1012

www.valuebasedmanagement.net/methods_strategy_maps_strategic_communication.html

www.valuebasedmanagement.net/

Part 4: Strategic options

Developing the future strategy for an organisation is often the most important part of the strategic planning process, because it is at this stage that the long-term future directions for the business are determined. The strategic direction taken will depend on the existing position of the organisation and the current level of success at meeting the organisational key goals. Having established where the organisation is currently placed in terms of resources, efficiency and competitiveness, the process of formulating the future strategy can follow. The first step is normally to decide upon a fundamental strategy for the organisation and the nature of this can be summarised by the following five simple terms: conservative growth, high growth, status quo, survival and disinvest. Each of these terms is developed in more detail in Chapter 9.

A business can grow through either internal expansion by increasing sales, or by external acquisition by operating at more and more sites, which does not always require ownership of that site. The top 10 largest hotel group in the world, in terms of numbers of rooms, have used techniques such as management contracts, franchising and leasing of assets to fuel their expansion. One of the tasks of senior managers is to identify and evaluate potential investment opportunities and to proceed with those that should be successful. In this section the chapters are devoted to considering the sources of long-term funds, the financial tools available to help evaluate projects and a consideration of the merits, disadvantages and practicalities of each. The first step in evaluating a potential strategic decision is to perform a feasibility study.

Feasibility studies

A decision involving capital investment expenditure, i.e. investment for the long term, will require supporting information in the form of an in-depth analysis of the financial feasibility of the project. The nature of the investment may range from a decision to purchase new equipment through to a major new property development. A business operating in the hospitality, tourism or leisure sector may decide to expand by:

- Building new properties or sites with 100% or shared ownership – to include new hotels, extensions to existing hotels and facility additions
- Acquisition of existing competitor businesses or a group of businesses
- Partnering with an investor to operate the site as a management contract
- Partnering with an investor to receive franchise fees for the use of the concept
- Leasing a property or site on a long-term basis.

Typically, a feasibility study for a new operation should include an economic overview of the location, a site evaluation, an assessment of the competition and market research to estimate the demand for the facilities offered. Obviously, the financial content of the feasibility study is of paramount importance and should address the following issues:

- Calculation of capital expenditure required and the financing plan: this will include investment in non-current assets required, pre-opening expenses and working capital requirements.
- The expected useful economic life and an estimate of the residual value of the asset, i.e. value at the end of the project evaluation period. This requires attempting to place a valuation on the business at a point in time when the business can be realistically assessed to be stable. This typically involves considering a 5 or 10-year time horizon.
- Preparation of forecasted trading statements for the selected time period based on expected revenues and operating costs
- Preparation of cash flows to show income from trading, capital spend and repayments of debt. In the case of an hotel, this involves an assessment of room occupancy, room rates, food, beverage and other sales, wage costs and other cash expenses. From these cash flows are deducted costs such as management fees, property taxes and insurance.
- Sensitivity analysis to show a variety of different scenarios based on different possible trading conditions
- The impact of taxation
- The anticipated cost of capital associated with the financing of the project
- Evaluation of the project using capital budgeting methods such as NPV and IRR.

Several of the aspects described above are now given detailed consideration in the following chapters.

9 Funding growth

About this chapter

This chapter reviews the alternative forms of finance available from equity sources or from borrowing, for funding the development and expansion of businesses in the hospitality, tourism and leisure sectors. Each form of funding is considered in terms of the advantages and disadvantages of the use of that type. The industries in this sector are able to take advantage of a range of alternative approaches for funding investments, based on the separation of ownership from control, including approaches such franchising and management contracts, and the merits and the implications of these will be considered. Selecting which options to pursue and how to fund those options is an important aspect of the strategic process and this chapter and the following chapters focus on the issues relating to effective implementation of strategic developments.

Learning objectives

On completion of this chapter, you should be able to:

- List the main sources of financing a business
- Appreciate the factors to be taken into account when selecting long term funds
- List benefits and disadvantages of each type of financing
- List the alternative approaches for funding expansion available to the hospitality, tourism and leisure sectors.

Introduction

The strategic direction of a business can take a variety of formats as illustrated by Table 9.1.

A business selecting a strategy based on expansion will certainly need to consider additional sources of finance. The various sources of finance are illustrated in diagrammatic form in Table 9.2.

- **Conservative growth:** An approach to increase sales, profits etc, through the same or related businesses. This is achieved through the development of updated products and/or penetrating the markets for the existing business
- **High growth:** An approach to significantly increase sales by developing further existing or new products and services to be sold in existing or new markets. This approach can be typified by a strategy of acquisition of companies with similar or unrelated products or by buying 'supplying' or 'buying' companies known as 'vertical integration'
- **Maintenance:** An approach to maintain the status quo by maintaining sales and profit at historical levels of performance
- **Recovery:** The purpose of this strategy is to simply survive. This may involve reducing investment in and purchase of new assets, reducing operating costs and attempting to grow sales
- **Reduction:** This approach is to maximise the value of a declining business by salvaging remaining assets and liquidating the business. Alternative approaches might be to sell, negotiate management buyouts or franchise.

Table 9.1: Fundamental strategy goals and approach

Short term	Medium term	Long term
Trade credit	Bank loans	Debentures
Bank overdrafts	Credit loans	Other types of loans
Factoring	Hire purchase	Shares
Bills of exchange	Leasing	

Table 9.2: Sources of finance

There are a variety of sources and methodologies for gaining access to funding business expansion and the choice very much depends on a range of factors including the:

- Cost of raising the finance
- Cost of servicing the finance
- Obligation to pay a return on the capital
- Obligation to repay the finance
- Corporation tax implications
- Effect on the levels of ownership and control.

Risk and return

For many new businesses a variety of sources of investment are required in order to raise the necessary funds to purchase the required noncurrent assets and provide for working capital. The hotel sector within the hospitality and tourism industries is traditionally heavily long term asset based and often considerable sums of investment are required just to get started. Each of the possible sources of funds will have its own cost, that is the return required by the provider of the source of funds, and the size of cost is normally related to the size of the risk as perceived by the lender. In general, research in this area has indicated that investors expect and normally get higher returns in return for accepting increased risk.

For the small business just starting out, the proportions of borrowings to equity can be crucial to survival in the early years of trading. In the past it has been relatively easy to borrow 70% or even 80% of total funding secured against the assets of the business but this creates a burden in terms of the debt servicing costs in the form of interest payments. Experience has indicated that levels of 50% – 60% borrowing against assets can provide a workable level of debt without causing cash flow problems later. The other crucial factor to consider when raising finance is the maximum cost of the finance. In the case of long-term borrowings, such as loans, the cost of servicing the finance is determined by interest rates and the amount of interest to be paid. Changes in interest rates can have a significant impact on a business.

Case example: Impact of interest rates

During 2023 the UK government raised interest rates a total of 14 times to reach a rate of 5.25%, the highest rate for 15 years. This increase impacts all those businesses using debt to finance investments. The hospitality industry was the sector most impacted by the pandemic and many businesses took out loans to survive. The increase in interest rates adds additional costs to the business coupled with inflationary pressures on other costs such as food purchases and energy.

Increasing interest rates raises the cost of capital which means that some businesses are perceived as no longer being viable as the cost of capital exceeds the cash inflows from trading.

Source: Adapted from https://www.thecaterer.com/news/interest-rate-rise-bank-england-4-could-significantly-impact-viability-hospitality-businesses

Alternatively, equity funds are serviced by the payment of dividends which are often flexible in payment and size. However, despite this flexibility, experience indicates that equity investors, that are company shareholders, expect the highest returns in return for being subject to the highest risk. The relationship between risk and return is summarized in the Figure 9.1.

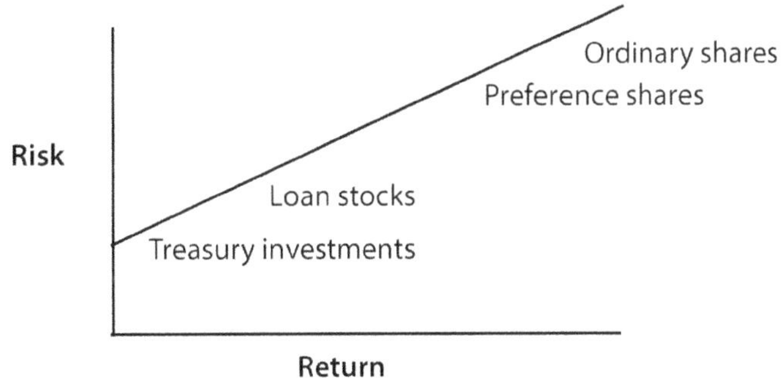

Figure 9.1: The relationship between risk and return

Equity capital

Equity capital comprises of three significant components:

- ☐ Ordinary shares
- ☐ Preference shares
- ☐ Reserves and retained earnings (profit)

Ordinary shares

When the business is first established, a decision is made to establish how much equity finance can be raised and the number of shares available to do this. The Articles of Association will specify the number of authorised shares available for issue. The most common form of equity is ordinary shares. When ordinary shares are first issued they are given a value known as the **par value** or the **nominal value** and this is typically around £1 in value. Once the company has become established its shares usually trade above the original par value price. This requires setting a price per share by which the total number of shares can be multiplied to calculate the total capital to be raised. A company wanting to issue new shares will do so at **market price** and the difference between market price and the nominal or par price is known as the **share premium**.

Preference shares

This category of shares form part of the shareholders' funds, or equity, although in practice they are known as 'hybrid' sources of finance with characteristics of both debt and equity finance. The issue costs are like those to be incurred when issuing new shares, whilst the servicing costs tend to be lower than for ordinary shares and are directly related to the nominal value of the share. Preference shares are often quoted with a specific percentage return, which is the limit of the return expected by the shareholders when dividends are available from profit to be paid. There is no obligation to pay preference dividends but where a dividend is to be paid the preference shareholders have priority over ordinary shareholders. Some preference shares are redeemable, and this fact needs to be built into the cash flow projections. Generally, preference shareholders have no voting rights so the balance of control within the business remains unaltered. Preference shareholders also have priority over ordinary shareholders for repayment of their investment in the event of the business closing, if sufficient funds are available. In practice the issue of ordinary shares remains by far the most common form of raising equity finance.

Reserves

It is a common mistake to assume that the reserves included in the balance sheet are the cash balances. The only cash available is that shown in the current assets of the balance sheet. The reserves can comprise of a range of items including the share premium account and retained earnings. The retained earnings represent the profits earned by the business in previous years and set the limit for the dividend which can be declared and be paid out. Retained profit is obviously an effective source of funds as there are no issue costs. However, it is not true to say that this is a free source of finance. Retained earnings are the property of the shareholders and consequently there is an opportunity cost incurred by reinvesting in the existing business. The business has, therefore, an obligation to ensure that the retained earnings produce a satisfactory return for the shareholders. Retained earnings represent the most effective method for funding expansion for most companies in terms of cost, and the distribution of control remains unaffected. However, projects which require an injection of finance over a period of years face uncertainty using this method of finance as the level of retained profits from year to year depends on the trading success of the business.

Other reserves in the balance sheet include the **revaluation reserve** which is created when the revaluation of the business assets, such as long-term assets, reveals a surplus over the stated book value.

Quoted companies

For quoted companies (that is companies with a Stock Exchange listing) there are the following principal markets in the UK:

- London Stock Exchange – the main market
- Alternative Investment Market (AIM)
- Sustainable bond market
- International Securities Market

AIM	Main Market
No requirement for a minimum number of shares to be held by the public	A minimum of 25% of shares to be held by the public
No requirement for historical trading reports to be available as this is for new companies	Normally a three year trading record is required
Prior shareholder approval required only for reverse takeovers and fundamental disposals	Prior shareholder approval required for significant transactions, including significant acquisitions, disposals and related party transactions
Admission documents not pre-vetted by the Exchange.	Prospectus pre-vetted and to be approved
Nominated adviser and broker required at all times	Sponsors needed for new applicants and significant transactions
No minimum market capitalisation value	Minimum market capitalisation of £700,000
Compliance required with a recognised corporate governance code	Compliance with the UK Corporate Governance Code

Table 9.3: Differences between the AIM and the Main Market

Source: Adapted from *A guide to floating on AIM - Listing in London* (pwc.co.uk)

The first two of these are markets for equities, with the latter being the markets for debt finance. Only shares in publicly traded companies are available to buy or sell on the stock exchange. In the UK, these companies have 'plc' or 'public limited company' at the end of their name. The market provides a listed company with access to a deep pool of international investor capital. The London Stock Exchange, according to the London Stock Exchange Group, is the world's most active international equity market, with companies from a range of sectors participating, including retailing, technology, finance and manufacturing. More than 1,000 companies, including more than 100 overseas companies, have securities which are quoted on this market (LSE, 2023).

The Alternative Investment Market, which opened in 1995, was specifically created to meet the needs of smaller and growing companies and is more lightly regulated than the main market. The benefits offered by this market are targeted at ease of access. There are no qualifying restrictions in terms of capital value, length of trading record or percentage of shares allocated to investors. Table 9.3 is adapted from an excellent publication from advisors, PwC.

Raising equity finance

Financing from equity is principally the most important source of finance in the UK, with the capital markets attracting both private and institutional investors, who become shareholders in a business. The ordinary shareholders are principally the owners of the business who through their voting rights have control over the business. As owners they carry the greatest risk of being the first to suffer if the business collapses. However, in the successful business, the shareholders are the principal beneficiaries as their return in the form of dividends and capital growth is directly related to business success. Access to funding depends on whether a company is quoted on the Stock Exchange, as a listing opens up far greater access to capital. The first step in creating a business is to form a limited company with one or more shareholders. Normally a limited company starts life as a private company. As the company becomes larger the need to raise additional finance increases beyond what is available from retained profits and loans, and a stock exchange listing is one option for raising additional funding. There are three main approaches to obtaining a quotation:

- ☐ **Offer for sale by prospectus.** Shares are sold to an issuing house and then offered at a fixed price to the general public including institutions
- ☐ **Via a placing.** Shares are placed with institutional investors by a merchant bank acting for the company
- ☐ **Offer by tender**

When a company chooses to sell shares via a prospectus the issue costs are much higher because of the volume of information which needs to be prepared. The issue price is crucial to ensure that the maximum number of shares is sold for the best possible price. When fixing the price of shares, it is usual to consider the key shareholder measures such as the Price/Earnings ratio, dividend yield and dividend cover. These ratios were considered in detail in Chapter 8. There are two ways in which the problem of price setting can be reduced. The first is to have the shares underwritten by a broker, but this process incurs additional costs. The second approach is to offer the shares for sale by tender. This is demonstrated by the following example.

A business wishes to issue 5 million shares by tender. After publishing an advertisement to attract potential buyers the following offers are received:

1m shares at £5.00 each

1m shares at £4.50 each

1m shares at £4.00 each

2m shares at £3.00 each

2m shares at £2.00 each

5m shares at £1.00 each

The share issue will be successful if priced at £3.00 per share as there are offers for £5 million shares at £3.00 and above. All the shares will be offered at this price.

The final consideration is the change in control which is likely to occur by inviting further parties to purchase shares.

Rights issues

A rights issue is one where existing shareholders are given the opportunity to purchase additional shares, often at favourable rates. The number of new shares available to each shareholder is usually dependent on their current level of ownership and does not, therefore, dilute their current level of control, whilst the price is often set at about 20 per cent below the market price for the period just prior to the issue. This ensures that the shareholder takes up the offer or sells the offer to avoid being disadvantaged in the future. The effect of the share issue will be to dilute the value of the share as more shares come into circulation. The price immediately after the share issue is called the 'ex-rights' price. This effect is demonstrated by the following example.

Balance Sheet extract (£000's)

Total net assets		5,000
Funded by:		
Share Capital	Authorised	Issued
Ordinary shares of £1 each	6,000	3,000
Reserves		
Retained profit		2,000
		5,000

When the market price of the share is £1.50 (premium of 50p over the par value) the company is said to have a market capitalisation value of:

3,000 shares at 150p = £4,500,(000)

If a rights issue is made on a 1 for 3 basis at a price of £1.20 when the market price is £1.50, a 20% discount on market price has been given. The effect is that 1,000,000 new shares are issued raising £1,200,000 in cash, if all the shares are taken up. This is shown in the balance sheet as £1,000,000 at nominal value and £200,000 as share premium.

The likely new share price after the share issue is theoretically:

$$\frac{£4,500,000 + £1,200,000}{4,000,000} = 142.5p$$

The value of the rights is calculated as being £1.50 less £1.425, that is 7.5p per share.

The effect on the balance sheet is as follows:

		£000
Total net assets		6,200
Funded by:		
Share Capital	Authorised	Issued
Ordinary shares of £1 each	6,000	4,000
Reserves		
Share Premium account		200
Retained profit		2,000
		2,200
		6,200

If a shareholder does not wish to take up the entitlement to purchase shares at a discount, the rights may then be sold to someone else, irrespective of whether they are an existing shareholder or not. However, for the majority of existing shareholders it is not financially viable to ignore the share offer, even if this means buying the rights to sell on immediately. This ensures that for many companies the rights issues are successful in terms of all the shares being sold and the required amount of capital subsequently raised.

Case study: Whitbread Hotels

In June 2020, Whitbread confirmed the successful completion of its rights issue, launched on 21 May 2020, raising £1bn with an acceptance rate of over 91%

Alison Brittain, CEO, commented:

"We are very pleased with the successful completion of Whitbread's £1bn equity raise, which achieved an acceptance rate of over 91%, demonstrating the high level of confidence in our strategy from both our institutional and retail shareholders.

Our strong balance sheet has for many years been a source of competitive advantage and has underpinned our long-term success. This equity raise enables us to maintain this competitive advantage and retains our financial flexibility. A strong balance sheet alongside our leading operating model and the power of our brands means that we will be in the best possible position to take advantage of enhanced structural opportunities that we expect to be available in both the UK and Germany. This will mean that we are in a position of strength to continue to invest, increase market share, support our colleagues and guests and create significant value for shareholders.

Source: https://www.whitbread.co.uk/rights-issue-successfully-completed/

Costs associated with equity capital

The costs associated with this form of finance include the issue costs and the servicing costs. The issue costs vary depending on the type of shares issued and can range from virtually zero up to about 15% of the value of the new finance raised. Such costs include legal and underwriting costs and for the introduction of new shareholders, advertising and prospectus costs.

Servicing costs occur in the form of capital appreciation of the value of the share and in the size of the dividend. The size of the dividend is at the discretion of the directors who have the right to withhold payment. However, this is often not the case as shareholders will soon display their displeasure by selling shares, causing the market price per share to drop, which in the majority cases is undesirable. A drop in share price down-values the company and creates opportunities for predator companies to engineer a takeover bid whilst the price is lower.

Equity finance offers the benefit of no obligation to repay the investment unless, of course, the firm is to be liquidated. However, a disadvantage lies in the fact that dividend payments are not deductible for Corporation Tax and this tends to make dividend payments more expensive than loan interest repayments which fall above taxation in the profit and loss account and are, therefore, tax deductible. A higher level of equity funding can increase the overall cost of capital for a business, and this will be discussed in more detail in Chapter 12.

Long term borrowings

There are three types of long-term borrowings:

- *Loan stocks*, or *bonds* or *debentures*, issued via the money markets for those companies with access to the capital markets or privately for those companies not listed
- *Term loans* via the banks or other institutions

The first of these are described as securities or bonds, and are issued through the capital markets with a fixed interest rate (the coupon rate) and a pre-stated repayment date to individual investors. When the securities are raised, the loan may be secured on the assets of the business (the loan is known as a *debenture*) or be simply based on a contract. The issue costs tend to be relatively low and the service costs in the form of interest are lower than those returns often expected by shareholders. Holders of loan stocks have the right to enforce payment of interest and the repayment of the loan itself and this can present a sizeable commitment to the business, particularly during periods of poor trading.

Convertible loan stocks bridge the gap between loan stocks and ordinary shares, being securities which are essentially loan stocks that at a pre-stated date may be converted by into ordinary shares. This can represent a cheap way to issue shares as the costs of issuing loan stock are lower than for shares. From the investors' point of view this represents a simple way of diversifying risk, in that loan stocks may be purchased during the early life of the company, minimizing risk, and these then converted to ordinary shares later with the potential for higher return when the company has become more established. The interest rate tends to be higher than for debenture stock because of the higher risk. A business which issues convertibles increases its gearing ratio, but this form of funding is particularly suited to a business with relatively high business risk but with strong potential for growth. This form of finance is available to both listed and private companies.

A *term loan* is a single loan negotiated from a bank or financial institution. These differ from loan stocks in that a single sum is received from one lender and is not passed from lender to lender, nor may it be traded in the capital markets. The usual source of this type of finance is a recognised financial institution and investment seekers should be beware of non legitimate sources of borrowings.

The remaining part of this chapter will consider what might be seen as less traditional sources of funds, but in practice represent some of the most effective and widely used routes to securing funds for expansion.

Franchising

Franchising represents an alternative approach to growth strategy by enabling a business to expand by forming strategic alliances. The British Franchising Assocation (BFA) describes franchising as a business relationship between two parties. This comprises of the franchisor, who owns the brand and business system, and the franchisee, who via a franchise agreement is able to trade under the brand.

Franchisees will pay an initial fee at the start of the relationship. In return they will receive a comprehensive package of training that will enable them to establish and run their business. There will also be monthly continuing fees throughout the term of the relationship. For this the franchisor will provide ongoing support, guidance and research and development to ensure the franchisee is successful. (BFA, 2023)

The origins of franchising can be traced back to the Middle Ages when King John of England granted franchises to tax collectors. However, the use of franchising as a business strategy gained prominence in the early 1900s when manufacturers attempted to establish links with retailers. Today franchising is used in many different business sectors as a means to achieving rapid expansion.

Franchising in the hospitality and tourism industries has long been associated with high street restaurant chains and hotel operators where it has mostly been highly successful.

Types of franchise strategy

Franchising is a form of strategic alliance and, compared to other forms of alliances, it is low in risk. In terms of cost, it has been found to be more expensive than licensing but cheaper than operating a joint venture. There are three types of franchise:

- ☐ Product trade name
- ☐ Business format
- ☐ Business conversion.

Product trade name franchising refers to alliances where the franchisee distributes a franchisor's products, and this model is popular in the retail sector. Business format franchising, also known as package franchising, provides the franchisee with a product or service, trade name, methods of operation and continuous guidance for aspects such as marketing, administration and staff training in return for a fee. This type of franchising is used most regularly in the hospitality industry.

In addition to the benefits arising from the support activities already described, the franchisor may well offer access to centralised reservation systems, yield management systems and property management systems.

Conversion franchising describes the development of a network of operations by attracting independent operators and persuading them to work together under a brand name, to attract customers and achieve cost savings through bulk purchasing power. This arrangement is best illustrated by consortia arrangements such as Best Western Hotels.

Advantages of franchising

For the corporate franchisor, the franchising arrangement offers considerable advantages primarily allowing a company to expand without using its own capital incurring relatively lower costs than with many other approaches to expansion. There are also less administrative problems as the individual franchisee takes over the workload. Many franchisors also own hotels themselves or operate properties under management contracts and franchising provides the opportunity to spread fixed operating costs over a range of properties. Finally, the franchisor can obtain greater purchase discounts from suppliers when individual outlets are tied to one supplier as part of the franchise agreement. There are, however, drawbacks for franchisors when loss of operational control over franchisees can sometimes harm the overall company image if standards start to drop. In general terms hospitality businesses with high quality facilities are less likely to franchise than those offering a more basic service. Franchise chains try to implement operational controls by regularly inspecting franchised units and specifying guidelines for operational standards.

Franchisors can also be limited by franchises with regard to future developments as restrictions maybe imposed limiting further expansion of similar units in the same region.

Xotels list the advantages for franchisees as:

- ☐ Strong brand portfolio
- ☐ Specific set of tools
- ☐ Strong approach to standards
- ☐ Good reputation
- ☐ Training programmes
- ☐ Consultation and advice service
- ☐ Marketing programmes

(www.xotels.com/en/glossary/hotel-franchise – retrieved 21/12/2023)

Benefits to the franchisees include the advantage of starting up with a proven name and a tried and tested concept. This reduces startup costs as the franchisor often provides management assistance in the areas of business location, facilities design, operating procedures, purchasing and promotion. This enables new units to gain a regular business clientele more quickly from target market segments. These factors obviously offer substantial benefits to the new operator as research has shown that the failure rate amongst new franchised businesses is much lower than amongst new small independent businesses. In return a fee is required and franchisees may also be tied to the company's nominated suppliers. It is critical for the potential franchisee to choose the correct type of franchise to suit local markets and trading conditions.

Where franchises fail, deteriorating relationships between franchisor and franchisee are usually cited as the key cause. Often the franchisee resents the royalty imposed by the franchisor and finds it difficult to assess the benefits being received in return. One way to overcome such a problem is to expand with partly franchised units and partly wholly owned units. This enables new products, equipment and management techniques to be evaluated and provides an example of 'best practice' for the franchisees.

Managing and controlling franchises

In the early days of franchises, the average length of period for a franchise was between 15 to 30 years. During this time the link between franchisor and franchisee can be highly intensive, with continual flows of information, funds, products and services, supplies, operations technology and administrative activity. Links between franchisees are also encouraged in some organisations such as McDonald's, Wendy's and Best Western Hotels, where franchisees face similar market conditions and can then cooperate on promotions and share costs. The coordination between franchisee and franchisor is based on legal documentation but also on trust. The franchisor can foster this by offering ,in addition to start up training, ongoing programmes to encourage the development of a culture of trust and shared values. This activity also ensures that standardization is maintained throughout.

Franchise fees

A franchise is a fee-based agreement between a business owner, the franchisee, and a brand owner, the franchisor. The scale of these fees vary from group to group depending on the nature of the contract. In the case of hotels, the basic fee is often around 4% to 10% of the room's net revenue. In addition to this there may also be a requirement for the franchisee to pay joining fees, royalties, reservation commissions and specific fees for other services provided by the franchisor.

Clearly franchisors need to be fairly large in order to generate significant profits, but with careful planning the process of franchising can provide the route for considerable expansion. Economies of scale ensure that for the larger franchisor the conversion of franchise revenue into profit may be as high as 95%.

Management contracts

This method of hotel operation separates ownership from management. The management contractor not only offers a license for the use of its brand name and reservation system but is also responsible for the day-to-day running of the operation and its performance. Many international hotel chains now include a number of managed hotels in their portfolio of total operations. The providers of equity for the investment range from individuals, governments, financial institutions and property developers.

The term of the management contract is the duration of the arrangement between the owner and the operator. The average length of contracts tend to be approximately 10 to 20 years.

The fees received by the operating company (the brand) include a base fee, which is a percentage of revenue, and an incentive fee based on the gross operating profit. The remainder of the profit remains with the owner of the property.

Independent white label operators

In recent years there have been a growing number of unbranded operators managing hotels for owners, offering the opportunity to switch between well-known brand names under a franchise arrangement with increasing flexibility. Traditional hotel management contracts tend to be rigid in structure and tie the owner in for long periods of time. Independent operators offer a more flexible arrangement and can often drive greater efficiencies and improved guest experience.

Lease contracts for land and buildings

This is another approach to expansion, based again on the separation of ownership and control. CIMA Management Accounting Official Terminology defines a lease as

> *'a contract between a lessor and a lessee for the hire of a specific asset. The lessor retains ownership of the asset but conveys the right to the use of the asset to the lessee for an agreed period in return for the payment of specified rentals.'*

The key difference between a management contract and a leasing arrangement is that whereas with a management contract a fee is made to the managing company, with a lease the managing company pays a rent to the owners and the remainder of the profits remain with the managing company. A lease is normally long term with the owner receiving rent on an annual basis. The most effective form of lease arrangement for the operator is one with a rental charge based on a proportion of turnover. This arrangement enables operators to build up the business without the commitment to fixed levels of rent. Fixed rental payments tend to be based on providing the owner with a target return on capital and could, in periods of recession, be more than the profit made for the period.

Sale and leaseback

This approach to funding is based on the sale of assets to a financial institution and these are then leased back. This form of funding is particularly popular during periods of high asset values and interest rates. At one time this could also be used as a form of off-balance sheet financing, whereby the asset itself was not required by accounting convention to be shown on the balance sheet. This served to improve return on capital calculations and reduce gearing ratios. Accounting conventions have now changed following the requirements of IFRS 16 where assets sold, and leased back are now required to be shown on the balance sheet as an asset and as a liability. This approach enables a business to raise funds, but the disadvantage is the loss of capital appreciation.

Alternatives to purchasing equipment

If the resources are available, buying a piece of equipment outright is often the most cost-effective approach and gives the freedom to make a purchase from a wide range of choices. However, if cash flow does not permit immediate purchase or uncertainty exists over the purchasing decision then other alternatives may be more suitable.

The principle of *free-on-loan* is widely used in the hot beverages markets, where dispensers are provided free of charge and will need to be filled with ingredients from the supplier of the machine. This may mean that a business is able to have access to equipment of a standard that it could not normally afford and be able to benefit from free upgrades as well. Renting the equipment presents an alternative option. These agreements are often fixed, being unchanged by changes in interest rates for example, and are fully deductible for tax purposes.

Leasing arrangements can be confusing when it comes to ownership and tax implications. With lease rental agreements, where the leasing company retains ownership at the end of the lease, all payments are fully tax deductible. However, with any financing agreement there is usually a premium to pay for saving money now and paying later.

Leasing equipment

Leases may be divided into two types:

- Operating leases
- Financial leases.

Operating leases equate to simply hiring the use of an asset and the ownership remains with the lessor, who carries out any necessary maintenance. Financial leases are effectively loans with the capital repayable in instalments. As described earlier, these used to be popular because although the effect is basically a loan, neither the asset nor the obligation needed to appear on the balance sheet. Changes in accounting practice now ensure that both the asset and the obligation appear on the balance sheet, ending the practice of off-balance sheet financing. Another important feature of leasing is the tax efficiency which may arise. Lease payments are shown as an expense in the Profit and Loss account and are therefore fully deductible for Corporation Tax.

Despite accounting changes in the treatment of leasing, this approach to funding remains popular as the implied interest rate in the leasing contract is often lower than that which the business would have to pay if it bought the asset itself.

The leasing decision

When the business is considering the purchase of an asset, the usual procedure is to assess the net benefit of owning the asset in terms of incoming cash flows, and to then discount those cash flows using an appropriate discount rate which reflects the level of risk in the project. When the resulting net present value is positive the project is worth pursuing. The decision to invest or not is a completely different decision from that regarding the source of finance. This is illustrated by the following example:

Example

A hotel has decided to purchase new equipment at a cost of £100,000. The decision to purchase has already been made on the basis of the expected savings to be gained. However, the subsequent decision is how to fund the purchase. The assets may either be purchased outright with a loan costing 12% per annum or the company could enter into a lease agreement. The terms of the lease are £20,000 to be paid starting at the date of the acquisition and for the next four years. After that date the lease may be extended by paying a nominal charge of £100 per year for a further 5 years. The differences in the financing should be assessed based on the fact that leasing incurs a timing difference in the cash outflows. This timing difference is assessed using discounted cash flow tables. (The principles of discounted cash flows are explained in more detail in Chapter 10) The future payments on the lease should be discounted using the cost of borrowing as a discount rate.

The net present value of the lease is calculated as follows:

Year	£000	Discount factor	Present value
0	20.0	1.00	20.00
1	20.0	0.89	17.80
2	20.0	0.80	16.00
3	20.0	0.71	14.20
4	20.0	0.64	12.80
5	0.1	0.57	0.057
6	0.1	0.51	0.051
7	0.1	0.45	0.045
8	0.1	0.40	0.040
9	0.1	0.36	0.036
Net present value (sum of the cashflows)			81.029

The lease option is worth pursuing as the net present value of the payments equates to £81,029 which is less than paying £100,000 now.

Taxation issues

Cash flows associated with taxation also need to be included in the project analysis and these will vary depending on the project and the nature of the taxation relief attracted. Capital allowances are forms of relief set against taxable profit based on the type of asset purchased, and are intended to stimulate certain types of investment. It is beyond the scope of this book to go into further detail apart from to note that there are generally two types of capital allowance available for the hospitality sector in the UK. These are Structure and Building Allowances (IBAs) and Plant and Machinery Allowances (PMAs) in the form of first year allowances and annual writing down allowances. There are also specific allowances which relate to hotel buildings provided they are used as 'qualifying hotels'. In order for a hotel to be classed as a 'qualifying hotel' there are a number of criteria to be met including:

- It is open for at least 4 months between April to October,
- It has 10 or more letting bedrooms used wholly or mainly for letting,
- The services provided normally include provision of breakfast and an evening meal.

Taxation affects cash flows from investments and further advice should be sought from specialized sources.

Real Estate Investment Trusts (REITs)

REITS were originally conceived in the US and today are available via the stock exchanges in various countries around the globe. A REIT comprises of a real estate mutual fund which permits small investors to participate in large professionally managed real estate projects. REITs are classified in the following categories:

- Equity REITs own and operate revenue generating assets
- Mortgage REITs lend money directly to asset owners and their operators, or indirectly through acquisition of loans or mortgage-backed securities
- Hybrid REITs are companies that both own properties and make loans to owners and operators.

According to REITComparison.co.uk to be a REIT the company has to comply with certain rules:

- 75% of the company's profit must be generated from rental income
- 75% of the company's assets must be properties available to rent
- 90% of the company's rental profit must be paid out to shareholders via dividends.

In the USA, REITs have been in existence since the 1960s but have been slow to be used as an investment vehicle in other regions of the world. In the UK the 2005 Budget confirmed the UK government's commitment to the introduction of the REIT concept, and these have now become forms of finance for real estate investments in the UK.

The majority of hotel REIT's are traded on the stock markets and investments can be bought and sold via a stock broker. The largest and most well-known hotel REITs include Host Hotels & Resorts Inc. (NASDAQ), Ryman Hospitality Properties Inc. (NYSE), Apple Hospitality REIT Inc. (NYSE) Park Hotels & Resorts Inc. (NYSE) and Pebblebrook Hotel Trust (NYSE).

Crowdfunding

Crowdfunding provides a route to funding a business via loans, donations or exchanging cash for rewards or shares in the business. This is usually carried out via a bespoke website. The advantages of this form of fund-raising centres around building a relationship with customers who often provide the funds for a project based on their loyalty and confidence in the business owners. However, the fundraising is not guaranteed and it maybe time consuming to achieve the desired outcome.

Summary

The purpose of this chapter has been to review the various forms of long-term finance available for expansion and to consider these in terms of the merits and disadvantages of each. Equity finance provides the vast majority of finance used by hospitality and tourism organisations which offers the benefits of low gearing although it should be remembered that the cost of servicing equity finance is often higher than that required for loan finance. Issue relating to cost of capital and gearing will be discussed in detail in Chapter 12.

Questions

1. List three sources of the following:
   a. short term finance
   b. medium term finance
   c. long-term finance.
2. Describe the alternative forms of financing available for funding a hotel asset and comment on the effects on the way the hotel is operated.
3. A large hotel and catering company is planning extensive expansion plans overseas. Describe the various forms of investment strategy available to a multinational business with access to the capital markets.
4. Rights issue

On 5th April 2023 the Riviera Hotels plc's shares were listed on the London Stock Exchange at £1.00 each. There were 25 million shares in issue. On 6th April Riviera Hotels announced to the press that it intended to purchase a smaller hotel group and the price of its shares rose to £1.20. On the 1st May the company announced that it was intending to raise £4 million to fund the purchase of the hotel group by means of a rights issue priced at 80p.

a. Calculate the market capitalisation of the business at 5th April 2023
b. How many shares will be issued to raise £4 million?
c. Why do listed companies normally make rights issues for new equity capital rather than public shares?
d. What factors can cause a movement in a company's share price?

5. Rights issues – theoretical ex rights price

In 2024 Sunshine Holiday Parks plc plans to acquire several new sites to expand the group. The new sites are expected to cost £52 million. The group's existing performance can be judged from:

Profit and Loss Account for the year ended 31 December 2023

		£ 000,000
Sales		96.8
Gross Profit		79.0
Less: Operating costs		
Staff costs	34.8	
External charges	25.4	
Depreciation	4.8	
		65.0
Trading Profit	14.0	
Less: Interest	4.0	
Profit before tax	10.0	
Less: Corporation Tax	3.0	
Profit after tax	7.0	
Less: Dividends	2.0	
Retained profit for the year		5.0

At present, 80 million shares have been issued and are currently valued at 160p each on the Stock Exchange.

The Directors aim to issue new shares to exactly finance the purchase of the new hotels (issue costs can be ignored). They propose to do this with a rights issue to be offered at 140p per share.

You are required to:

a) Calculate the theoretical ex-rights price per share.
b) Calculate the value of the rights per existing share.
c) Calculate the market value of each share after the rights issue, on the assumption that the new hotels produce an increase in profit after tax of £5.0 million and that the current Price/Earnings ratio is maintained.
d) Discuss the advantages and disadvantages of a rights issue over a public share issue.

6. A bond investment, with an annual coupon rate of 6%, face value of £1,000, and 8 years to maturity. What is the value of the bond when a 8% return is required?

7. Explain the advantages and disadvantages of using equity finance.

8. Explain the advantages and disadvantages of using debt finance.

References and further reading

Atrill, P. and Mclaney E. (2021) *Accounting and Finance for Non-Specialists*, 12th Edition, Pearson.

British Franchise Association (n.d.) *What is Franchising?* https://www.thebfa.org/what-is-franchising/ accessed December 2023

HMRC (n.d.) *IBA: Qualifying hotels: Period for which qualifying hotel conditions must be satisfied.* www.gov.uk/hmrc-internal-manuals/capital-allowances-manual/ca32403

Houchin, J. (2023) *The rising demand for independent white label operators*, https://boutiquehotelnews.com/features/rising-demand-independent-operators/

HVS. (2017). *An Overview of Hotel Management Contracts in Europe*. https://hvs.com/article/7993-hotel-management-contracts-in-europe

Lashley C. & Morrison A. (2000) *Franchising Hospitality Services* Routledge

LSE (2023) *The London Stock Exchange* www.londonstockexchange.com/discover/our-regions/united-kingdom

Miljković, N. and Critchley, J. (n.d.) *The Rise of Third-Party Operators of Hotels in Europe*, www.hospitalitynet.org/opinion/4114521.html

Ransley, J., Ingram, H. and Adams, D. (2022) *Developing Hospitality Properties and Facilities*. Routledge

Roper, A. (2017) *The Vertical Disintegration in the Corporate Hotel Industry*, Taylor and Francis

Schmidgall, R. (2016) *Hospitality Industry Managerial Accounting*. Educational Institute of the American Hotel Motel Association.

Useful websites

www.thebfa.org/

www.finance4hospitality.co.uk An online community with bite sized content and resources developed by experts in hospitality accounting.

www.xotels.com/en/glossary/hotel-franchise

www.hvs.com/article/9106-hvs-webinar-recap-hotel-franchising-why-is-a-hotel-franchise-worth-having

www.hvs.com/article/7993-hotel-management-contracts-in-europe

www.pwc.co.uk/risk/assets/pdf/guide-floating-aim-listing-london.pdf

10 Capital budgeting

About this chapter

Many of the options being considered in the strategic decision-making process will require an assessment of the viability of capital spending. AICPA & CIMA (2023) summarises the topic as follows:

> *'Investment appraisal involves a number of techniques used to identify the attractiveness of an investment. It helps you to assess whether or not to pursue a particular investment based on alignment with strategy, prioritisation of options, affordability and acceptable returns versus unacceptable risk.'*

This chapter reviews the number of techniques available for assessing the viability of a capital project.

Learning objectives

On completion of this chapter you should be able to:

- ☐ Explain the concept of discounted cash flows
- ☐ Apply the techniques of net present value (NPV), internal rate of return (IRR), payback, profitability index (PI) and accounting rate of return (ARR)
- ☐ Explain the advantages and limitations of each method.

Case study: London attracts hotel investment

According to research by Deloitte, gathered in the Deloitte European Hotel Industry Survey 2023, based on responses from 75 senior hospitality figures from across the world, including owners, lenders, developers, and investors, London is viewed as the most attractive European city for hotel investment in 2024. The majority of respondents expect to see London's Revenue Per Available Room (RevPAR) to grow in 2024. More than half (54%) expect the capital's RevPAR to grow between 4% to 7% (up from 41% last year), while 72% of respondents anticipate a RevPar of between 1% to 5% in the UK regions this year (up from 53% in 2022).

Hotel executives also showed improved optimism in their expectations for London's Gross Operating Profit per Available Room (GOPPAR) in 2024 compared to the last two years. The majority of respondents (58%) expect London's GOPPAR growth to be 1% to 5%, up from 38% last year. However, the pressures that high inflation, labour shortages and greater energy prices are putting on profits has led to more than one in four respondents (28%) expecting 0% or negative GOPPAR growth in London in 2024.

Source: Adapted from https://www2.deloitte.com/uk/en/pages/press-releases/articles/london-becomes-the-most-attractive-european-city-for-hotel-investment-in-2024.html

Introduction

Capital investment appraisal is concerned with long-term decisions based on major investments which will effect the future strategic direction of the organisation. The process includes planning the capital expenditure, evaluating and selecting projects, and finally controlling capital expenditures, which will generate future cash flows. Planning capital expenditure involves ensuring that the alternative projects selected by the organisation yield maximum returns whilst minimising or maintaining a certain level of risk. Generally, the basis for selecting the potential investment should be that only those projects which meet the objectives of the business should be considered and the expected rate of return should exceed the financing cost in order for the project to be worthwhile. Selecting which investment proposal to pursue and which to avoid is crucial to the business because of the large sums of finance often involved and the long-term nature of the commitment. Therefore, a long-term financial investment decision needs to fit with the strategic direction of the business and be financially justified by evaluating all the relevant costs and resulting cash inflows associated with the project. Several factors need to be taken into account including the:

- Size of the initial and any further investment
- Economic life of the project or the time period to be evaluated
- The final value of the investment
- Certainty of the returns and the expected economic environment
- Strategic importance to the company.

In the hospitality and tourism industries a capital investment could include expenditure on assets such as:

- New sites and new builds
- Replacement and new equipment, including technology
- Furniture and fixtures
- Building extensions
- Concept renovations

As a guideline, capital expenditure is spend which is likely to have benefit to more than one accounting year. If a business wishes to survive and to grow it will need to continually invest in capital projects in order to keep existing long-term assets in good condition and to expand the business.

There are several standard methodologies used in capital investment appraisal and these will now be considered in detail including the:

- ☐ Accounting rate of return (ARR)
- ☐ Payback period (which may also be discounted)
- ☐ Net present value (NPV)
- ☐ Internal rate of return (IRR).

Accounting rate of return

This method, also known as the Return on Investment (ROI), compares the average annual profits over the life of the project with the initial investment, expressing the outcome as a percentage.

$$ARR = \frac{\text{Average annual net profit before interest and taxation}}{\text{Initial capital employed on the project}} \times 100$$

This is the only method to be considered which uses profits rather than cash flows as the basis of the calculation, with the difference between the two being the annual depreciation charge. The profit forecasts, after straight line depreciation is deducted, is averaged for the estimated years of life of the project and the resulting percentage is then compared to some predetermined rate. Competing projects can then be compared with each other, and the project with the higher accounting rate of return being determined as being the more worthwhile as the following example demonstrates:

Example

Two projects are being considered both with a six year life and both with an original investment of £120,000. This value is to be depreciated in full over the life of the project using straight line depreciation (see Chapter 3 for more details on this). The anticipated profits for the projects are as follows:

		Project 1	Project 2
		£	£
Year	1	20,000	4,000
	2	16,000	6,000
	3	10,000	8,000
	4	6,000	10,000
	5	4,000	16,000
	6	2,000	18,000
Total		58,000	62,000

The average net profit over the life of each project is £9,667 for Project 1 and £10,333 for Project 2. The return on the original investment is

Project 1 $\frac{9{,}667}{120{,}000} \times 100\% = 8.06\%$

Project 2 $\frac{10{,}333}{120{,}000} \times 100\% = 8.61\%$

Using the Accounting Rate of Return, Project 2 is marginally better than Project 1.

The ARR can also be calculated using the average capital employed rather than the initial capital employed as follows:

$$\text{ARR} = \frac{\text{Average annual net profit before interest and taxation}}{\text{Average annual capital employed}} \times 100$$

The average annual capital employed is calculated using the formula:

$$\frac{\text{Initial capital employed + residual value}}{2}$$

Using the previous example

Project 1 $\frac{9{,}667}{60{,}000} \times 100\% = 16.11\%$

Project 2 $\frac{10{,}333}{60{,}000} \times 100\% = 17.22\%$

The benefits of the accounting rate of return approach can be summarised thus:

- The technique is easy to calculate and use
- The result is easy to understand without requiring financial expertise
- The principle is based on a widely used performance statistic, the return on capital employed.

The disadvantages are that the method is based on profit rather than cash flows, the latter now being recognized as a clearer indicator of company health. As a result, the method ignores the timing of the cash flows and hence the financing cost. The term 'profit' can be subject to different definitions, and it is not always clear whether the original value of the investment should be used or the average. The use of residual value in the average method means that the higher the residual value the lower the ARR. Returning to the above example where the timing of the profits are quite different for each project, Project 2 is favoured despite the fact that the majority of the profits are forecast to occur at the end of the six-year period and are subject to far greater uncertainty.

Where just one project is to be evaluated the decision is made on the basis of a comparison of the resulting ARR with the prevailing cost of borrowing, with targets often set 5–10% in excess of these rates. The ARR approach is acceptable as long as the meaning of the result is understood throughout.

Payback method

This technique is based on an assessment of how long it will take for the investment to pay for itself out of the cash inflows generated by the project. A project will only be selected if it pays for itself within a certain time period or alternatively competing projects will be selected on the basis of the project which pays for itself first. In order to use this method the following information is necessary:

- The total value of the investment
- The amount of the cash flows to be generated by the project
- The accounting periods in which the cash flows will fall.

This approach is very easy to use and interpret, although the basis of the decision is fairly simplistic. Setting suitable payback periods is a somewhat basic decision and too much emphasis on this aspect will ensure that only short term decisions are made. However, the acceptability of the payback approach can be improved by discounting the cash flows to take account of the changing value of the cash flows over time, although this still tends to emphasise cash flows prior to payback rather than those occurring in the long term. Cash flow is defined as the profit before interest and tax plus any noncash items (usually depreciation) which have been deducted to arrive at the profit figure. The method is illustrated using data from the previous example.

The anticipated profits for the projects are as follows:

	Project 1	Project 2
	£	£
Year 1	20,000	4,000
2	16,000	6,000
3	10,000	8,000
4	6,000	10,000
5	4,000	16,000
6	2,000	18,000
Total	58,000	62,000

The straight-line depreciation is based on the write off of £120,000 over 6 years with zero residual value will be £20,000 per year. Therefore, the anticipated cash flows are:

	Project 1	Project 2
	£	£
Year 1	40,000	24,000
2	36,000	26,000
3	30,000	28,000
4	26,000	30,000
5	24,000	36,000
6	22,000	38,000
Total	178,000	182,000

These cash flows can be used to identify the point when the original investment will be repaid. For Project 1 the payback period will fall between Year 3 and Year 4 and for Project 2 at some point between Year 4 and Year 5. On this basis Project 1 would be favoured despite the fact that Project 2 provides the greater cash inflow. Note that this result is opposite to that recommended by the Accounting Rate of Return method. The payback method is a relatively easy concept to understand and calculate but it does have a number of disadvantages as a technique for assessing viability of projects. In particular it is difficult to assess exactly when cash flows will be received and the overall total amount of the cash inflows is ignored. The focus on payback means that the overall profitability of a project is also ignored. Finally, the timing of the cash flows is not taken into account – for example a £1 received now is preferable to £1 received in three years time. However, this disadvantage can be overcome by discounting the cash flows. Despite the disadvantages of the method, it is widely used in the hospitality and tourism industry to assess both renovation and new investment decisions.

Discounted cash flows

Capital investment appraisal is based on an assessment of future returns forecasted to be generated by a project. The earlier the funds are made available, the sooner they can be used to make a further contribution to profit. The discounted cash flow attempts to analyse the timing and size of future cash flows. However, the difficulty lies in comparing a £1 of cash inflows received today with £1 received in the future as they can not be equal to each other. There are three reasons for this:

- ☐ Interest lost from other investments
- ☐ Inflation effects, that is, the changing value of £1
- ☐ Risk.

First, there is the interest foregone if the £1 were to be invested over the time period, and this represents an opportunity cost. So £1 invested for one year at 10% will be worth £1.10 at the end of this period. Second, inflation undermines the purchasing power of the £1 so that the same amount will not buy the equivalent value of goods and services in one year's time. Finally, risk needs to be considered because £1 received today has more certainty attached to it than the possibility of £1 being received in one year's time.

The process of discounting the cash flows aims to take into account the timing of the cash flows based on the interest foregone. Levels of inflation and anticipated risk are less easy to determine although a premium may be built into the discount rate used to compensate for these. Issues surrounding these aspects will be considered in Chapter 11. The procedure for discounting cash flows includes:

1. Calculate the future cash flows to be generated by the project
2. Estimate an appropriate discount rate based on the cost of capital
3. Multiply the net cash flows by a discount rate.

Discounted payback

This is a variation of the technique described earlier and is based on an assessment of how long it will take for the investment to pay for itself using discounted cash flows. The example below uses data from the earlier example.

Two projects are being considered, both with a six year life and both with an original investment of £120,000.

The anticipated cash flows are at discounted at 10% to give the Present Values (PV)

	Discount Rate	Project 1 £	PV £	Project 2 £	PV £
Year 1	0.909	40,000	36,360	24,000	21,816
2	0.826	36,000	29,736	26,000	21,476
3	0.751	30,000	22,530	28,000	21,028
4	0.683	26,000	17,758	30,000	20,490
5	0.621	24,000	14,904	36,000	22,356
6	0.564	22,000	12,408	38,000	21,432
Total		178,000	133,696	182,000	128,598

Project 1 pays back between Years 4 and 5 and Project 2 pays back between Years 5 and 6. Therefore, Project 1 would be preferred. Discounted payback has the advantage that it takes into account the changing value of money and will be based on more of the cash flows since the discounted payback period will always be longer than the simple payback method. However, the other disadvantages given for the simple payback method still apply.

Net Present Value

This technique for assessing capital projects is based on an assessment of future cash flows discounted to take account of the opportunity cost of the interest foregone. If we were to simply compare investing £10m held today at 10% for one year with an investment which is expected to be worth £12m to be received in one year's time, this would mean that the future cash inflow represents a better return than could be achieved with £10m invested at 10%. Alternatively, we could compare how much (*I*) would need to be invested now to achieve a return of £12m in one year's time at an interest rate of 10%.

$$\text{£12m} = I \times 1.10$$

I can be deduced to equal £10.9m and is called the present value. The present value of the future cash flows forms the basis of the capital appraisal technique known as net present value. Where the sum of the future discounted cash flows exceeds the initial investment, the project is deemed to be acceptable and is described as having a positive net present value. Where more than one project is to be assessed the one with the highest NPV is deemed to be the most acceptable. The discount factor is calculated from the interest rate where it is assumed that the cost of borrowing equals the cost of lending. After one year the discount factor at 10% will be

$$1/1.10 = 0.909.$$

To take account of several years the discount rate needs to be compounded, and although this can be done arithmetically, it is normal practice to make use of published tables giving discount factors for a range of interest rates over a number of years. These are published as an appendix in most accounting textbooks and can be found in Appendix 1 of this text. The following example demonstrates the net present value principle.

To calculate the NPV of a project the following steps are required:

1. Forecast the cash flows to be generated over the life of the project
2. Select an appropriate discount rate (how to do this will be discussed in Chapter 12)
3. Use tables to find the appropriate discount rates for multiplication with the annual cash flows
4. Sum the discounted cash flows
5. Compare the sum of the discounted cash inflows to the sum of the discounted cash outflows (cash flows in Year 0 are discounted by a factor of 1)
6. Consider whether the NPV is positive or negative.

This approach is demonstrated by the following example:

Example

A hotel owner decides to invest in renting an adjacent building to run as a restaurant. His initial feasibility study shows that it will cost £1,000,000 to prepare and equip the site for trading. The projected cash flows derived from net profit after tax with depreciation added back, for the next five years are as follows:

	£
Year 1	230,000
Year 2	235,000
Year 3	240,000
Year 4	250,000
Year 5	255,000
Total	1,210,000

The depreciated value of the furnishings at the end of this period is anticipated to be £120,000. Given these values the hotel owner appears to be gaining by investing in the new site. However, a more accurate picture emerges when the time value of money is taken into account. The future cash flows discounted at 12% are as follows:

Year 1: 230,000 x 0.893 = 205,390
Year 2: 235,000 x 0.797 = 187,295
Year 3: 240,000 x 0.712 = 170,880
Year 4: 250,000 x 0.636 = 159,000
Year 5: 255,000 x 0.567 = 144,585

Plus, residual value of the investment:

120,000 x 0.567 = 68,040
Total value of cash inflows =£935,190

Note that the residual value of the investment is also termed as a cash inflow and should be discounted at an appropriate rate. The cash inflows are less than the initial cash outflow and this creates a negative net present value to the value of £ 64,810. On this basis the project should be rejected because the investment is failing to achieve a 12% return.

With the use of discounted cash flows it is possible to identify for any project the present value for all future cash flows over the life of the project. The present value of the investment when taken away from the present value of the cash inflows produces the net present value, which indicates the financial benefit of going into the project in today's cash terms. The higher the present value the more attractive the project. The NPV approach is a logical method for assessing potential investments because the calculation takes into account the timing of the cash flows and the cost of financing the project as well as being practical and easy to use. Despite these benefits the method is not always widely used with many businesses preferring to use the other approaches.

The discount factor

The discount value applied to the calculations is obviously of critical importance. The higher the discount factors the lower the resulting net present value. If the factor chosen is too high there is the danger that profitable projects will be rejected whilst using a factor which is too low will result in loss making projects being pursued. Normally the factor is chosen by considering the cost of the funds being used for the project with additional premiums built in for risk as required. The calculation of the discount factor is considered in further detail in Chapter 12.

Cash flows

When discounting cash flows a number of assumptions are made. The first is based on when the cash flows actually occur. The discount tables assume that the cash flow is received in its entirety on the last day of the year. Obviously, this is not likely to be the case but in order to simplify the workings the last day principle is used, which means that the cash flows are always slightly understated in terms of value. Selecting which cash flows to put into a forecast can cause difficulty particularly when the project is based on existing assets. It is essential to determine the relevant cash flows, that is the future likely cash flows, and ignore past or sunk costs. Table 10.1 illustrates some examples of sunk costs.

1. Expenditure already incurred to make a site ready for development
2. Research and development costs already incurred
3. Feasibility study costs

Table 10.1: Examples of sunk costs in capital investment appraisal

Opportunity cost cash flows are cash flows which are not actually paid out but instead represent the benefit foregone by taking one course of action.

Internal rate of return (IRR)

An alternative to using discounted cash flows is the 'internal rate of return'. This approach assesses the rate of return required by the project to balance cash inflows and outflows. AIPCA & CIMA (2023) defines the internal rate of return (IRR) as the '*annual percentage return achieved by a project, at which the sum of the discounted cash flows over the life of the project is equal to the sum of the discounted cash outflows.*'

Solving the value of IRR manually is not easy and a process of trial and error is required. To assess a project only those with an IRR above a predetermined level are accepted or if competing projects are being assessed the one with the higher value is the one to be accepted. Using the data given for the NPV calculation the following workings demonstrate the IRR method:

The future cash flows were discounted at 12% as follows:

Year 1	230,000	x	0.893	=	205,390
Year 2	235,000	x	0.797	=	187,295
Year 3	240,000	x	0.712	=	170,880
Year 4	250,000	x	0.636	=	159,000
Year 5	255,000	x	0.567	=	144,585

Plus, residual value of the investment:

	120,000	x	0.567	=	68,040
Total value of cash inflows				=	£935,190

The cash inflows are less than the initial cash outflow and this creates a negative net present value to the value of £64,810. On this basis the project should be rejected because the investment is failing to achieve a 12% return. In order to find the IRR, it is necessary to discount the cash flows a second time to provide the basis for finding the discount rate which will give a net present value of zero.

The future cash flows are now discounted at 8% as follows:

Year 1	230,000	x	0.893	=	205,390
Year 1	230,000	x	0.926	=	212,980
Year 2	235,000	x	0.857	=	201,395
Year 3	240,000	x	0.794	=	190,560
Year 4	250,000	x	0.735	=	183,750
Year 5	255,000	x	0.681	=	173,655

Plus, residual value of the investment:

	120,000	x	0.681	=	81,720
Total value of cash inflows				=	1,044,060
Net present value				=	44,060

Therefore, the IRR must fall between 8% and 12%. The exact value can be pinpointed as follows. A factor of 12% gives a negative net present value whereas a discount factor of 8% gives a positive net present value. Therefore, a NPV of zero will fall between the two positions:

(64,810)-------------------0-------------------------- +44,060
12% ?% 8%

A change of 4% represents net present value of 108,870. The distance 64,810 to 0 is:

$$\frac{64{,}810}{108{,}870} \times 4\% = 2.38$$

Therefore, the IRR is 8% + 2.38% = 10.38%

The advantages of the IRR method are that the timing of the cash flows are taken into account and the method gives a clear percentage return on investment.

However, in practice it is not an easy concept to understand, and the method only gives an approximate rate of return. To identify the IRR it is necessary to apply alternative rates of discount to pinpoint the exact value and this can be time-consuming. However, the disadvantage can now be easily overcome with the use of electronic spreadsheets, such as Excel, which contain the function to automatically calculate IRR.

More importantly, there are a number of conceptual shortcomings associated with the IRR method which should be noted. First, it is possible for there to be more than one IRR associated with a project. This occurs when the cash flows are a combination of positive and negative values throughout the life of the project.

Under these circumstances it is not easy to identify the real internal rate of return and the method should be avoided. Second, although IRR is closely related to the NPV approach the two methods can sometimes give conflicting signals. This occurs when the two projects have different levels of investment because IRR is based solely on percentage returns rather than the cash value of the return. As a result, when considering a project one may have a return of say 10% another of say 13% but the 10% project may yield the higher NPV in cash terms and would therefore be preferable. Finally, IRR cannot cope with differing required rates of return. With NPV calculations it is possible to use different discount factors throughout the life of the project as the cost of capital changes, whereas IRR can only provide an average rate of return.

Despite these major shortcomings IRR continues to be popular approach to capital investment appraisal. The calculation of a percentage value is often preferred which can then be compared to a hurdle rate rather than the comparison of cash values for choosing between projects.

Comparing results from NPV to IRR

The NPV method tends to be the preferred method because the result is more easily understood – it indicates the amount by which the value of the company has increased. However, IRR has the benefit in that it provides a single percentage as the result, which is useful for comparison to a target or hurdle rate. However, it is always useful to use a range of capital investment appraisal techniques to ensure that all aspects of a project have been considered. The NPV and IRR methods should both normally give the same result – if the NPV using the discount factor of the cost of capital is positive then the IRR for the same project must be above the cost of capital. However, decisions become difficult to make when results provided by IRR and NPV are in conflict with each other.

Example

A leisure company has received two quotations for computer systems. The first will cost £12,000 and will save annual costs of £3,500 for five years. The alternative is a system which will cost £6,500, where the annual cost savings are £2,000 for five years. The cost of capital for both is 10% pa.

Option 1

	Cash flow	Discount rate 10%	Discounted cash flow	Discount rate 20%	Discounted cash flow
Year 0	(12,000)	1,000	(12,000)	1.000	(12,000)
Year 1	3,500	0.9091	3,182	0.8333	2,917
Year 2	3,500	0.8264	2,892	0.6944	2,430
Year 3	3,500	0.7513	2,630	0.5187	2,025
Year 4	3,500	0.6830	2,392	0.4823	1,68
Year 5	3,500	0.6209	2,173	0.4019	1,407
			1,268		(1,533)

To calculate the IRR:

10% ←——→ 20%
(1,268) (1,533)

$\frac{1268}{2801} \times 10\% = 4.53$

IRR = 10 + 4.53 = 14.53 %

Option 2

	Cash flow	Discount rate 10%	Discounted cash flow	Discount rate 20%	Discounted cash flow
Year 0	(6,500)	1.000	(6,500)	1.000	(6,500)
Year 1	2,000	0.9091	1,818	0.8333	1,666
Year 2	2,000	0.8264	1,653	0.6944	1,389
Year 3	2,000	0.7513	1,503	0.5187	1,157
Year 4	2,000	0.6830	1,366	0.4823	965
Year 5	2,000	0.6209	1,242	0.4019	804
TOTAL			1,082		(519)

To calculate the IRR:

10% 20%
1082 ←——→ (519)

$\frac{1082}{1601} \times 10 = 6.76$

IRR = 10 + 6.76 = 16.76%

According to the NPVs we should select the first alternative but the IRR results suggest we should select the second alternative. This conflict arises because of the differing sizes of the alternatives.

Using EXCEL to calculate NPV and IRR

The calculations can be performed very efficiently using the functionality of EXCEL as the following example demonstrates:

A hotel owner decides to invest in renting an adjacent building to run as a restaurant. His initial feasibility study shows that it will cost £200,000 to prepare and equip the site for trading. The projected cash flows derived from net profit after tax with depreciation added back for the next five years are as follows:

	£
Year 1	30,000
Year 2	35,000
Year 3	40,000
Year 4	50,000
Year 5	55,000
TOTAL	210,000

The depreciated value of the furnishings at the end of this period is anticipated to be £20,000.

Calculating NPV using discount tables

Given these values, the hotel owner appears to be gaining by investing in the new site. However, a more accurate picture emerges when the time value of money is taken into account. The future cash flows discounted at 12% are as follows:

Year	Discount Factor 12% Rate	Cash Flow £	PV £
1	0.8929	30,000	26,787
2	0.7972	35,000	27,902
3	0.7118	40,000	28,472
4	0.6355	50,000	31,775
5	0.5674	55,000	31,207
+ Residual Value of Investment	0.5674	20,000	11,348
TOTAL			157,491

The cash inflows are less than the initial cash outflow and this creates a negative net present value to the value of £42,509. On this basis, the project should be rejected because the investment is failing to achieve a 12% return.

Calculating NPV with EXCEL

The Net Present Value can also be determined using Excel (or another similar spreadsheet program). The formula used by Excel:

= NPV (*k*, CF*1* :CF*n*) + C   *k* = interest rate
CF = cash flows
C = cost of investment

Using the above example, the NPV is calculated using Excel:

	A	B	C	D	E	F	G
1							
2		K =	0.12				
3		Initial cost	-200,000				
4							
5		1	30000				
6		2	35000				
7		3	40000				
8		4	50000				
9		5	75000		Includes the residual value		
10							
11							
12		NPV	-£42,508.37		NPV(C2,C5:C9)+C3		

The formula for the NPV is shown next to the result. If the NPV is negative, the result will turn red. The initial cost must be entered as a negative figure in order for the formula to work.

Calculating IRR using trial and error

The future cash flows were discounted at 12% as follows:

Year	Discount Factor 12% Rate	Cash Flow £	PV £
1	0.8929	30,000	26,787
2	0.7972	35,000	27,902
3	0.7118	40,000	28,472
4	0.6355	50,000	31,775
5	0.5674	55,000	31,207
+ Residual Value of Investment	0.5674	20,000	11,348
TOTAL			**157,491**

The cash outflow was £200,000

The cash inflows are less than the initial cash outflow and this creates a negative net present value to the value of £42,509 (200,000 less 157,491). On this basis, the project should be rejected because the investment is failing to achieve a 12% return. In order to find the IRR it is necessary to discount the cash flows a second time to provide the basis for finding the discount rate, which will give a net present value of zero.

The future cash flows are now discounted at 4% as follows:

Year	Discount Factor 4% Rate	Cash Flow £	PV £
1	0.9615	30,000	28,845
2	0.9246	35,000	32,361
3	0.8890	40,000	35,560
4	0.8548	50,000	42,740
5	0.8219	55,000	45,205
+ Residual Value of Investment	0.8219	20,000	16,438
TOTAL			**201,149**

NPV 201,149 – 200,000 = 1,149

Therefore, the IRR must fall between 4% and 12% but fairly close to 4%. The exact value can be pinpointed as follows. A factor of 12% represents negative £42,509 present value whereas 4% represents positive £1,149. Therefore, a NPV of zero will fall between the two positions:

```
(42,509) ------------------------------------0----------------1,149
  12%                                       ?%                 4%
```

A change of 8% (ie 12% - 4%) represents net present value of 43,658 (ie 42,509 + 1,149). The distance from 1,149 to 0 is:

$$\frac{1{,}149}{43{,}658} \times 8\% = 0.210\%$$

Therefore, the IRR is:

$$4\% + 0.210\% = 4.21\%$$

Calculating IRR with Excel

The formula used by Excel:

= IRR (*C*, CF*1* :CF*n*) CF = cash flows
C = cost of investment

	A	B	C	D	E	F	G
1							
2		Initial cost	-200,000				
3		1	30000				
4		2	35000				
5		3	40000				
6		4	50000				
7		5	75000		Includes the residual value		
8							
9							
10		IRR	4.18%		IRR(C2:C7)		
11							

The formula for the IRR is shown next to the result. The initial cost must be entered as a negative figure in order for the formula to work.

EXCEL offers three options for IRR as follows:

- ☐ Standard IRR
- ☐ XIRR taking into account different size time periods
- ☐ Modified IRR, which considers the cost of borrowing the initial investment funds as well as compounded interest earned by reinvesting each cash flow

Profitability index

The final method to consider is the Profitability Index which relates the NPV to the size of the investment. It can be used to rank projects, with the highest ratios being given the highest priority, in capital rationing situations. To calculate the profitability index, divide the present value of cash inflows by the initial investment.

Case study: Capital investment appraisal techniques

The Advent Hotel Group plc are planning to build a 100-bedroom hotel operation in a city centre location in the UK. The feasibility study has included forecasts for:

- ☐ Room rate, room occupancy and yield
- ☐ Contribution to cash flows from food and beverage departments
- ☐ Contribution to cash flows for other income such as leisure sales
- ☐ Hurdle rate for the IRR at 20%
- ☐ Cost of capital at 10% – the project is to be financed using 60% equity and 40% loans.

The cash flows to be generated have been calculated using Gross Operating Profit less taxation, insurance, rentals, management fee and other costs before financing costs. A capital expenditure reserve has also been deducted representing 3%

of the investment value. The total cost of the investment includes a forecast for additional working capital (£1m) and capitalisation of the interest and pre-opening costs. The total investment amounts to £100,000 per room, i.e. £10,000,000 and the residual value at the end of five years is estimated to be 10 times the cash earnings for that year. The cash flows to be generated are:

Year	Cash flow £000
1	800
2	800
3	1000
4	1000
5	1000

The viability of the project is calculated as follows:

Year	Cash flow £000	Discount Factor 10%	Discounted value	Discount Factor 15%	Discounted value
1	800	0.9091	727.28	0.8333	666.64
2	800	0.8264	661.12	0.6944	555.52
3	1000	0.7513	751.30	0.5787	578.70
4	1000	0.6830	683.00	0.4823	482.30
5	1000	0.6209	620.90	0.4019	401.90
Residual value	11000	0.6209	6829.90	0.4019	4420.90
Total inflows			10273.50		7105.96
Original investment			10000.00		10000.00
NPV			**273.50**		**-2894.04**

The results indicate that, although the discounted cash flows exceed the cost of capital, the project does not make the target return of 20%. The difference between the two NPVs is 3,167.54 which represents 10%. The IRR is therefore, slightly less than 11%. We can prove this by discounting at 11% as follows:

Year	Cash flow £000	Discount factor 11%	Discounted cash flows
1	800	0.9009	720.72
2	800	0.8116	649.28
3	1000	0.7312	731.20
4	1000	0.6587	658.70
5	1000	0.5935	593.50
Residual value	11000	0.5935	6528.50
Total inflows			9881.9
Original investment			10000.00
NPV			-118.1

We can conclude from this that the project makes a return slightly in excess of the cost of capital but falls short of the target return of 20%.

Appraisal methods and hospitality organisations

All of the methods discussed here, along with hybrid versions, are successfully used in the hospitality industry. It is not unusual to see capital expenditure decisions in larger groups being split into two types. Those associated with refurbishment, which are assessed locally and are not subject to formal analysis; and those associated with development, where considerable larger sums of investment are required and a range of capital investment appraisal techniques may feature in the feasibility study. Table 10.2 is a summary of the relative benefits of the four investment techniques.

	ARR	PBP	NPV	IRR
Directly related to wealth maximisation	No	No	Yes	No
Accounts for timing of cashflows	No	No	Yes	Yes
Uses all relevant information	Yes	No	Yes	Yes
Easy to use and understand	Yes	Yes	Yes	Not
Comparison to WACC	Yes	No	Yes	Yes
Takes account of risk	Yes	Yes	Yes	Yes

Table 10.2: Summary of the relative benefits of the appraisal techniques

Capital investment control

The control and evaluation of capital investment projects is essentially concerned with ensuring that the achieved cash flows match the forecasted values and that the anticipated level of net present value will be achieved. Failure to achieve the forecasted NPV is primarily due to actual cash flows falling short of target and/or the discount rate used for discounting the cash flows being lower than that actually required.

A shortfall in cash flows may be due to the trading environment being less favorable than was originally forecast or the organisation's internal costs associated with the project being higher than originally anticipated.

An increase in the required discount rate can come about following an increase in either the prevailing interest rates or the company's own cost of capital percentage. Finally the initial spend on the investment may be considerable more than first anticipated and this will also reduce the forecasted net present value.

Consequently, the monitoring and control of capital projects is as important as the initial evaluation. The process of monitoring occasionally identifies that a project is no longer worth continuing with, and a decision needs to be taken as to whether the project should be abandoned or not. The final decision should be based on an NPV analysis of the relevant costs and the benefits of continuation relative to those associated with abandonment. Post-completion auditing is the process of reviewing the project once it has reached its conclusion in order to ensure that any errors in the investment decision process are not repeated. This process is less appropriate in the hospitality industry where investments tend to have a long life.

Case study

This case study examines the position of a fictitious company based in the South of England. The Ship Inn Company is a small business comprising of three sites which could be described as public houses with additional facilities. The company is jointly owned by two businessmen who have equal shares in the business.

The case is divided into the following sections and appendices as listed below.

1.0 Background to The Ship Inn Company

1.1 Human resources

1.2 Administration

2.0 The Case Problem

Appendix 1: Profit & Loss Account 2022/2023

Appendix 2: Balance Sheet at year end 2022/2023

1.0 Background to The Ship Inn Company

The Ship Inn Company was formed in 1982, when two businessmen invested their savings in their first public house, the Marie Rose I. One of the partners, Michael Donnelly, had previously worked in the licensed trade in the East End of London and was considered by those who had worked for him to be a tough but fair operator. The other partner, Peter Williams, had, in the past, been involved in a variety of business interests in a number of different areas. He saw himself as a shrewd business man with the ability to adapt to the needs of any business which appeared to be viable. He had already bought and sold several businesses, usually in the retail or computer industries, and always for a good profit. This business, The Ship Inn Company, was their first venture together in partnership and they formed an uneasy but successful liaison. Each had clear roles, Donnelly looking after the operational aspects, working long hours travelling from one unit to the other, whilst Williams dealt with the administrative details and also investigated other possible acquisitions to develop the partnership. A further two operations, Marie Rose II and Marie Rose III were purchased from a large brewery in 1984 but no further acquisitions have been made since.

1.1 Human resources

Each operation has its own bar manager, bar staff and cleaners. The workforce is generally made up of young part -time staff who have low levels of training and staff turnover in all outlets is high. The managers are normally college trained with a supervisory qualification and are individually responsible for cellar control and bar supervision. At Head Office there is one assistant, Betty Jones, who acts as secretary, administrator and book keeper.

1.2 Administration

Where possible, all administration is performed centrally enabling managers at each site to concentrate on the practical aspects of running the business.

The manager of each outlet may order their own stocks using the nominated suppliers and the invoices are received and paid for centrally. Prices from suppliers are negotiated by Donnelly who, as a result, decides which brands should be sold.

2.0 The Case Problem

Peter Williams has recently located a new potential site for an additional outlet and is particularly excited about its possibilities. The location appears to be perfect for an operation in the style of Marie Roses I and II, although,the purchase will involve buying an existing city centre unit, currently trading as a music store. This is not considered to be a problem as The Ship Inn Company will then commence the transformation to a bar and club resulting in a tailor made operation. Williams feels that it is reasonable to forecast that the new outlet will open for trading within six months from purchase. Williams has also produced some financial projections and these are illustrated below. Given these forecasts, Williams feels confident that the venture will return a satisfactory level of profit. However, Donnelly has some reservations about the new acquisition as he feels that the partnership may be over-stretched both financially and operationally by the introduction of a fourth unit. He has consequently asked Williams to prepare some detailed financial projections for them both to discuss and consider. The details relating to the project are given below.

Forecasted projections

Williams has conducted a market survey costing £150,000 which has yet to be paid.

The initial capital expenditure is subject to straight line depreciation and requires additional working capital to support the project.

The project is to be evaluated over 6 years and requires capital expenditure of £6,000,000.

At the end of year 6 the residual value of the capital expenditure is forecast to be £1,000,000. The working capital requirements are forecasted to be:

Stocks	£250,000
Cash	£50,000
Creditors	£50,000

The best forecasts for sales over the life of the project are:-

Year	£
1	6,000,000
2	6,000,000
3	8,000,000
4	8,000,000
5	8,000,000
6	10,000,000

The variable costs are estimated to be 60% of sales.

Fixed costs are estimated to be £2,500,000 which includes an apportionment of the total business overheads of £500,000. The actual additional overheads to be incurred by this project are £300,000. The estimate for fixed costs also includes a charge for depreciation.

The directors are uncertain as to how to fund the project. One approach would be to fund the project partly from reserves and partly with a loan of £6,000,000 repayable in full at the end of the six years. Donnelly favours this option because he argues that using loans is cheaper than raising additional equity. Williams argues equity funds are less risky and would therefore, be preferable. The business weighted average cost of capital is estimated to be 12% pa and it has a marginal borrowing rate of 8% pa. It uses 20% pa as an initial target return.

Williams has approached a variety of lenders requesting a loan for £6,000,000.

Appendix 1: Profit and Loss Account

	2022	**2023**
	£m	£m
Sales	200	280
Less: Cost of Sales	40	56
Gross Profit	160	224
Less: Wages and Staff Costs	56	80
Operating Profit	104	144
Less: Expenses	65	86
Less: Depreciation	7	10
Trading Profit	32	48
Less: Corporation Tax	11.2	16.8
Profit after Tax	20.8	31.2
Less: Dividend	10.0	12.0
Retained Profit	10.8	19.2

Appendix 2: Balance Sheet - 31 December

	2022	**2023**
NON CURRENT ASSETS (net)	£m	£m
Freehold Property, at cost	128.0	156.0
Equipment and Furniture, at cost	28.0	30.0
	156.0	186.0
CURRENT ASSETS		
Stock	8.0	10.0
Debtors	20.8	20.0
Bank Balance	6.4	2.8
	35.2	32.8
Less: CREDITORS - Amounts due in less than one year		
Creditors	5.2	6.0
Dividend (proposed)	10.0	12.0
Taxation	11.2	16.8
	26.4	34.8
NET CURRENT ASSETS	8.8	(2.0)
TOTAL NET ASSETS	**164.8**	**184.0**

CAPITAL AND RESERVES

	£m	£m
SHARE CAPITAL		
Ordinary Shares	100.0	100.0
RESERVE		
Profit and Loss Account - Retained Profit	64.8	84.0
CAPITAL EMPLOYED	**164.8**	**184.0**

Summary

This chapter describes the various theoretical approaches to assessing investment opportunities. In practice it is the accountants in the business who will select the methodologies to be used for evaluating project but mangers needs to understand the methodologies if they are to put forward projects for successful appraisal. Academically the net present value approach is considered to be the most accurate as it takes account of a range of factors including the changing value of money, future cash flow expectations and risk. Despite this a range of methods are used in practice and it is not uncommon in the hospitality and tourism industries for emphasis to be placed on the accounting rate of return and the payback period. In order to use investment appraisal techniques successfully it is essential that other practical considerations are addressed such as taxation, inflation, risk and sensitivity analysis and these will be discussed in the following chapter.

Questions

1. Describe the payback method of capital investment appraisal. List the advantages and disadvantages.
2. What is discounting in the context of capital investment appraisal?
3. There are many different capital investment appraisal techniques available. Evaluate the advantages and disadvantages of the following techniques:
   a) Payback period
   b) Accounting Rate of Return
   c) Net Present Value
   d) Internal Rate of Return

4. Calculating net present value and the internal rate of return

The Exclusive Club is considering adding fresh home baked breads to its menu. However, an oven that costs £30,000 will have to be purchased. It has an estimated seven-year life and the owners have calculated that the club will sell £20,000 of breads annually with a food cost of 30% and a labour cost of 35%. The residual value of the machine at the end of seven years is forecast to be £5,000.

The target return is 15% per annum.

You are required to:

a. Calculate the net present value for this investment.

b. Calculate the internal rate of return.

c. Comment on your findings. Do you think the machine should be purchased?

d. Describe the different capital investment appraisal techniques available and give the strengths and weaknesses of each. Which method do you feel is the most effective and why?

5. Using capital investment appraisal methods

Fairview Productions is considering the purchase of new food production equipment. The introduction of the automated equipment will save labour costs. The business is considering two types of pieces of equipment and the following data is forecast:

	Equipment A (£000's)	Equipment B (£000's)
Initial Cost	400	260
Estimated Life	6 years	5 years
Residual Value	150	120
Working Capital	none required	none required

Annual labour cost savings arising from purchase (equivalent to cash flows generated):

		Equipment A (£000's)	Equipment B (£000's)
Year	1	120	90
	2	120	90
	3	120	60
	4	50	60
	5	50	60
	6	50	n/a

The weighted average cost of capital is 10%. The target rate of return for investment is 20%.

You are required to:-

a) Calculate the viability of each piece of equipment assuming a purchase is made. The following capital investment methods should be used.

  i) Average accounting rate of return.

  ii) Net present value.

  iii) Internal rate of return.

b) Write a report to the Director reviewing your findings. You should also include in your report comments to address the following issues:

  i) A review of the advantages and disadvantages of the capital investment methods which could be used.

ii) Comment on how the risk associated with the project could be quantified and monitored.

iii) Your conclusion as to what action the business should take.

6. The owner of "Fish 'n' Chips 4All", a chain of five fish and chips restaurants in London, is considering renewing all the frying machines of his restaurants. The cost would be £100,000 for all the machines and installation, and a saving of £2,500 per year in oil and wastage for each restaurant is expected. The estimated useful life of the machines is considered to be 10 years with zero residual value. The weighted average cost of capital is 8%

a) Calculate the net present value at a cost of capital of 8%

b) Calculate the internal rate of return

c) Calculate the payback period

d) Calculate the accounting rate of return

e) Discuss your results and the implications for the business

7. Explain the differences between DCF methods of investment appraisal and ARR. What do you consider to be the main weaknesses of the ARR method?

References and further reading

AICPA & CIMA (2023) Welcome to investment appraisal, www.aicpacima.com/resources/article/welcome-to-investment-appraisal

AICPA & CIMA (n.d.) 3 ways to calculate internal rate of return in Excel, www.aicpa-cima.com/news/article/microsoft-excel-3-ways-to-calculate-internal-rate-of-return-in-excel

Arnold, G. C. and Hatzopoulos, P. D. (2000) The Theory-Practice Gap in Capital Budgeting: Evidence from the United Kingdom. *Journal of Business Finance & Accounting* 27 (5/6): 603

Atrill, P. & Mclaney E. (2021) *Accounting and Finance for Non-Specialists*, 12th Edition, Pearson.

Mclaney, E. (2009) *Business Finance: Theory and Practice,* Prentice Hall.

Ransley, J., Ingram, H. and Adams, D. (2022) *Developing Hospitality Properties and Facilities*. Routledge

Schmidgall, R. (2016) *Hospitality Industry Managerial Accounting*. Educational Institute of the American Hotel Motel Association.

Useful websites

www.finance4hospitality.co.uk

www.inlandrevenue.gov.uk/capital_allowances/investmentschemes.htm

www.investopedia.com/terms/i/irr.asp

11 Practical aspects of investment appraisal

About this chapter

The purpose of this chapter is to consider how capital investment appraisal techniques can actually be put in to practice as part of the process for evaluating strategic options. A range of important issues are to be considered including the practicalities for:

- Forecasting accurate cash flows
- Assessing the life span of project
- Calculating the residual value
- Allowing for working capital requirements
- Taxation and inflation effects
- Measuring risk.

Learning objectives

On completion of this chapter, you should be able to:

- Understand how to forecast accurate cash flows
- Appreciate the factors to consider when assessing the life span of project
- Understand the significance of working capital in investment appraisal
- Appreciate the impact of taxation and inflation effects
- Apply techniques for measuring risk.

Introduction

Several writers have commented on the misuse of capital investment appraisal techniques for assessing the viability of projects, with the effect that companies are under-investing because they misapply or misinterpret discounted cash flow techniques. Surveys have indicated that companies are regularly underestimating cash flow forecasts and using excessive discount rates to evaluate projects, resulting in projects that would be viable being rejected.

Appraising capital investment

A number of factors need to be taken into account to when appraising capital investment, particularly for those investments focusing on the construction of long term assets such as hotels and resorts. Increasingly sustainability is becoming more important and can deliver commercial value to capital projects.

- ☐ Material costs savings can be achieved.
- ☐ Capital projects can be made more resilient, or future-proofed, against emerging sustainability risks.
- ☐ The costs of inaction are potentially material.
- ☐ Taking into account sustainability drives innovation in your supply chain.
- ☐ Demonstrating your sustainability commitment can build trust and reinforce or enhance your licence to operate.
- ☐ Adopting sustainability practices can help to reduce financing costs and increase access to capital.

Source: Adapted from The A4S Essential Guide to Capex.pdf.downloadasset.pdf (accountingforsustainability.org)

Which capital investment methods are preferred?

Several studies on the use of capital investment appraisal methods in organisations from the manufacturing sector conclude that the most frequently used method is payback although this is often used alongside other methods. In the hospitality, tourism and leisure sectors, capital projects are often evaluated using the IRR method to give a percentage value for comparison to cost of capital for example. The rate of return is also often used despite the problems associated with this method. Many organisations attempt to formally analyse risk through the sensitivity analysis and incorporate estimates for inflation into the calculation.

In view of the arguments against the use of IRR described in the previous chapter, it is perhaps surprising that the use of the method is so widespread. This may be due to the fact that the workings provide a percentage result which is easier to interpret than the NPV result, and IRR provides a ranking of projects of different size and timescales without the need for a predetermined discount rate, as is required by NPV. IRR is also very easily calculated using spreadsheets.

The value of accurate forecasting

For capital investment appraisal to be successfully carried out, it is essential that the forecast data be as accurate possible. In practice this means reliance on management experience and standard relationships unique to the hospitality industry.

The information required to prepare a forecast includes:

- ☐ The scale of the initial investment
- ☐ Sales growth rate and operating profit margins
- ☐ The timings associated with the projected earnings

- ☐ The working capital requirements
- ☐ The residual capital value
- ☐ The magnitude of recurring levels of maintenance, capital expenditure and any additional investment required
- ☐ The cost of capital.

Many feasibilities are built using recognised industry metrics, such as the investment per bedroom for hotels and the estimated yield using the 'Rule of Thumb method' discussed in Chapter 1. Margins and costs are often based on industry averages, however, care should be taken to test all the of the assumptions made.

It should be noted that capital investment techniques assume that cash flows will occur at the year end for discounting purposes. Discount tables can be produced on a month-by-month basis but the use of these would considerably increase the nature of the workings. As a result the year end assumption means that cash flows are marginally over-discounted and are, therefore, included in the calculation at a slightly lower value than would be the case in reality. The effect of this is to marginally increase the payback period and to understate the net present value and internal rate of return.

Feasibility studies

To arrive at a set of accurate cash flows, a feasibility study is required. This may be carried out by the investing organisation or an independent consultant. The aim is to ensure that all possible aspects of the suggested project have been considered and that the forecasts for sales, volumes and costs are as accurate as can be possible. The typical steps in a feasibility study are illustrated in Figure 11.1

Figure 11.1: Typical stages in a feasibility study

The first steps require a detailed knowledge of the business environment and current trends, in order to forecast the likely sales volumes, average spends and sales mix. Knowledge of the cost structure in terms of fixed and variable costs is critical for ensuring that the profit and cash flow forecasts are practical. These aspects were considered in Part 2 of this text. The initial financial evaluation is then subject to a sensitivity analysis. CIMA (2023) defines sensitivity analysis as *'a modelling and risk assessment procedure in which changes are made to significant variable in order to determine the effect of these changes on the planned outcome.'* With the financial forecasts agreed the financing for the project can be confirmed and the detailed operational aspects of the project specified.

Life span of the project

The determination of life span for a project can prove awkward to forecast in the hospitality and tourism industries, where investments are considered to have an indeterminate life. A piece of equipment is normally considered to have a certain working life and is then depreciated on the basis of this. This type of investment is, therefore, simple to analyse in terms of initial spend, cash savings and residual value. Projects involving long term investments obviously cannot be evaluated over an indefinite period as the value of the forecasted cash flows becomes virtually meaningless. As a result, hospitality and tourism projects are normally evaluated over a five to ten year period and the accuracy of the residual value at this point is of prime importance. The residual value may well be in excess of the initial spend and the determination of this figure will require an understanding of valuation techniques.

Residual value or exit value

This is the value of the project at the end of the evaluation period. A simple approach to arriving at a valuation figure would be to revise the purchase or construction cost in line with the Retail Price Index. Other methods may be appropriate, such as the current market price or the depreciated replacement cost.

The *'Income Capitalisation'* approach is achieved by using either discounted cash flows or by the use of a method called the *'Earnings Multiple'*. The discounted cash flow approach is based on the capitalisation of the anticipated net cash flows for an operation by discounting at the appropriate discount rate. The Earnings Multiple approach requires the application of a multiplier to the maintainable earnings, which are defined as the adjusted cash flows, expressed in present values, which can be sustained over the foreseeable future.

Working capital

In addition to the capital investment most projects will require an injection of working capital. This will normally be required throughout the life of the project to fund and maintain stock levels and to allow for credit sales, whilst enabling the suppliers to be paid. It is fair to suppose that this part of the investment will be substantially released at the end of the project, and should therefore be shown as a cash inflow in the final year. However, at the end of the project, its value will be considerably reduced due to the changing value of money over time. Consequently it is normal practice to discount the working capital released, with the discount factor rate prevailing at the conclusion of the project.

Taxation

The complexities surrounding taxation and capital appraisal are beyond the scope of this text. However, the basic principles will be discussed briefly and more detailed sources of information are supplied in the further reading suggested at the conclusion of the chapter. Capital expenditure may attract tax relief for a business in the form of capital allowances, and this should be reflected in the forecasted cash flows. The capital allowance amounts to a reduction in the taxable profit in order to relieve expenditure on fixed assets, and acts as an incentive to industry to encourage investment. There are several categories of fixed asset, each with its own rules and level of capital allowance. However, the two most widely used categories are Plant and Machinery and Industrial Buildings.

The first of these, Plant and Machinery, includes a wide range of assets, and a business may deduct 25% of the cost of the asset from the profit for the period during which the asset was acquired. In each subsequent year of ownership, 25% of the balance may be deducted.

The second group is that of Industrial Buildings, which includes buildings used directly or indirectly in manufacturing, the transport industry and other restricted purposes excluding shops and offices. Relief is given by allowing a business to deduct 4% of the cost from the taxable profit for each year the asset is in use. Other types of asset attract capital allowances and these include, in particular, hotels. The important aspects of taxation for the hospitality industry include:

- ☐ Ensuring that all allowances are claimed for, particularly for Plant and Machinery, as this represents an important resource;
- ☐ Assessing the effect of taxation on the investment decision;
- ☐ Assessing the benefits to be derived from alternative methods of funding, for example, outright purchase versus rental.

Plant and Machinery allowances

These allowances can be important to the hospitality and tourism industry where there is substantial investment in this form of assets, and yet this is often an under-utilised resource. The difficulty in gaining the maximum benefit from these allowances lies in the complexities of separating out those items which are allowable from those which are not. This is particularly difficult to achieve where contractors are involved to complete work, the value of which includes equipment costs as well as installation costs. The contractor may be unwilling to reveal the Plant and Machinery figures within the total cost and a separate valuation may be required. The definitions for plant and machinery eligible for capital allowances are often quite complex and specialist advice will ensure that the maximum benefit is achieved. This example illustrates the calculation of capital allowances.

A restaurant purchases a delivery van for £15,000. The capital allowances would be calculated as follows:

Year	Balance	Capital allowance	
2020	£16,000	4,000	25% of £16,000
2021	£12,000	3,000	25% of £12,000
2022	£ 9,000	2,250	25% of £9,000
2023	£ 6,750	1,688	25% of £6,750

This pattern is continued until the asset is scrapped or sold.

Taxation effects on the investment decision

A serious implication for capital investment appraisal occurs when taxation distorts the investment decision by converting a viable investment into a non-viable investment. This can occur when profits are different to cash flows generated by the project,which may be the case when equipment is purchased and capital allowances are set against the profit and loss account.

The level of distortion depends on the level of sophistication of the tax system. It is important to realise that tax rules change, and specialist advice should be sought to ensure that the current rates and benefits are being fully utilised.

The impact of inflation

The term inflation means the erosion of the purchasing power of currency due to the increase in price of goods and services, and is a condition which affects most economies of the world at some time. Even relatively low levels of inflation can affect purchasing power over long periods and therefore the implications need to be assessed in the capital investment appraisal workings. The use of discounted cash flows is not sufficient to take account of the full effect of inflation. The general principle is that cash flows stated in real terms, that is without adjusting for inflation, should be discounted with a rate which also includes inflation in order for like to be compared to be compared with like. Where sales and costs and have been adjusted for inflation then a rate incorporating an adjustment for inflation should be used.

The difficulty in forecasting for inflation lies in the fact that, in reality, the individual cash flow elements such as sales, material costs, labour costs and others may not all be subject to the same degree of inflation.

Measuring risk in investment appraisal

Any project which is to be assessed over the long term must be subject to some risk or uncertainty. *Risk* describes the situation where it is possible to identify all the likely outcomes and their likelihood of occurring, without being absolutely sure what will actually occur. *Uncertainty* describes the situation where it is not possible to be sure of all the likely outcomes. All business decisions are subject to some uncertainty and risk but it is really only the latter which can be identified and subsequently assessed.

There are many possible sources of risk which may cause actual revenues and costs to be different from those initially forecast and these may be classified as

- Business risk
- Operating risk
- Financial risk.

The first of these, business risk, occurs as the result of changes in the economic and business environment and all businesses will be subject to this. It can arise from a variety of sources, such as changes in the nature of the competition, technological innovation, and from fluctuations in the national or world economy.

Operating risk arises from the cost structure of the operation and occurs when variable costs are substituted by fixed costs. Substantial fixed costs mean that a certain level of revenue is required to simply cover those costs. In times of good business conditions this can be an advantage, but losses will soon be incurred during periods of recession.

Financial risk arises from the method of financing used by the business and is reliant on the cost of servicing the debt. Sources of funds derived from borrowings incur an interest charge which must be paid regardless of the level of profit. The relationship between equity funds and interest bearing funds is called *gearing* and is described in greater detail in Chapter 12. During periods of good trading conditions, high gearing, that is where the majority of funds are provided from borrowings, can be beneficial. The interest charge is fixed and once this has been paid the remainder of the profits can be used for dividend payments or reinvestment. However, during periods of recession, the fixed interest charge must be met regardless of the level of trading, which means possibly incurring an even greater loss as result of paying interest.

It is vitally important to take account of risk, whatever the form, and this should be done on a formal basis for each investment project. The methods to be discussed in the remainder of this chapter are:

- Sensitivity analysis
- Probability and expected value.

Sensitivity analysis

Sensitivity analysis is used to evaluate the effect of a change on each of the factors contained in the forecast. In the capital investment appraisal calculation a variety factors will need to be forecast. These include the:

- Value of the initial investment
- Length of the project
- Sales projections based on volume
- Selling price and sales mix
- Cost projections:
- Predicted discount rate.

All of the values are subject to change either individually or as a result of dependence on another variable. Simple calculations can easily be performed where just one variable changes, and it is possible to determine the likely effect on the project. More complex relationships may require the use of computer simulations, and even a basic spreadsheet can be of assistance for modelling '*what if*' situations. The following example illustrates a basic approach to sensitivity analysis, where each variable changes independently of the others.

Example

The Riverside Hotel PLC has the opportunity to invest in a new cafe to support its existing activities. The demand is estimated to be 10,000 covers per year for a minimum of five years. The following data relates to the decision:

- The restaurant is estimated to have no residual value and will cost £140,000 payable immediately
- The average spend per cover is estimated to be £10
- The variable costs are estimated to be £6 per cover (£3 for labour and £3 for materials)
- Overheads are not expected to be affected by the decision
- The firms cost of finance for such a project is estimated to be 10%
- The project is not expected to require any additional working capital
- The effects of taxation are to be ignored.
- All cash flows occur at the year end.

The annual cash flows will be:

10,000 x £(10 - (3 + 3)) = £40,000 each year.

Thus the project's cash flows are forecasted to be:

		£
Year	0	(140,000)
	1	40,000
	2	40,000
	3	40,000
	4	40,000
	5	40,000

The discount factor is 10% and this can now be used to calculate the Net Present Value of the project.

Year	Cash flows £	Discount Factor	Present Value £
0	(140,000)	0	(140,000)
1	40,000	0.909	36,360
2	40,000	0.826	33,040
3	40,000	0.751	30,040
4	40,000	0.683	27,320
5	40,000	0.621	24,840
		3.791	11,600

The annuity factor for five years at 10%is 3.791. The NPV is therefore:

$$-140{,}000 + (40{,}000 \times 3.791) = 11{,}600$$

The project has a positive NPV and is therefore, favourable. The aim of sensitivity analysis is to assess the effect of a change in the input factor on the overall acceptability of the project.

The factors used in the above example to calculate NPV are:

Original investment	I
Annual sales volume	V
Selling price per unit	S
Labour cost per unit	L
Material cost per unit	M
Annuity factor	A
Cost of capital	C
Life of the project n	

The workings above can be represented by a single equation:

$$-I + (V \times (S - (L + M)) \times A = \text{NPV}$$

To carry out the sensitivity analysis each factor will be considered in terms of what change is required to reduce the NPV to zero which is the point when the project would no longer be acceptable.

1. Original investment

$$-I + (10{,}000 \times £(10 - (3 + 3))) \times 3.791 = 0$$
$$I = 151{,}640$$

2. Annual sales volume

$$-140{,}000 + (V \times £(10 - (3 + 3))) \times 3.791 = 0$$
$$V = 9232$$

3. Selling price per unit

$$-140{,}000 + (10{,}000 \times £(S - (3 + 3))) \times 3.791 = 0$$
$$S = £9.69$$

4. Labour cost per unit

$$-140{,}000 + (10{,}000 \times £(10 - (L + 3))) \times 3.791 = 0$$
$$L = £3.30$$

5. Material cost per unit

$$-140{,}000 + (10{,}000 \times £(10 - (3 + M))) \times 3.791 = 0$$
$$M = £3.30$$

6. Cost of capital

$$-140{,}000 + (10{,}000 \times £(10 - (3 + 3))) \times A = 0$$
$$A = 3.5$$

Looking at tables the annuity factor is closest to 13% for a project 5 years in length

7. Life of the project

-140,000 + (10,000 x £(10 - (3 + 3))) × A = 0

A = 3.5

Looking at tables the annuity factor is closest to 4 1/2 years for a project with a 10% return.

The results are summarised as follows:

Factor	Original estimate	Value for zero NPV	% difference
Original investment	£140,000	£151,640	8.3
Annual sales volume	10,000 units	9,232 units	7.7
Selling price per unit	£10	£9.69	3.1
Labour cost per unit	£3	£3.30	10.0
Material cost per unit	£3	£3.30	10.0
Cost of capital	10%	13%	30.0
Life of the project	5 years	4 1/2 years	10.0

This highlights those factors which are the most sensitive and are most likely to undermine the profitability of the project, which in this case are selling price and sales volume.

The above example illustrates a simplistic view of sensitivity analysis but even this level of analysis enables the decision maker to gain a grasp of the critical factors in the project.

Use of probabilities

The use of probabilities enables a whole range of possible outcomes for each factor to be considered, providing that it is possible to assess the probability of each outcome occurring. It is then possible to calculate a range of NPV's for the project. In practice this can be difficult to achieve, but as with sensitivity analysis the exercise offers the opportunity for the decision maker to become familiar with the key factors in the project.

Using the above example it will be assumed all factors are known with certainty, except sales volume and the material costs. In practice all factors should be assigned probabilities as none can be determined with certainty. However, this would produce a large volume of calculations which, in practice would need to be calculated with the aid of a computer. Extensive market research indicates that annual demand will either be:

a) 11,000 covers (0.3 probable)

or b) 10,000 covers (0.5 probable)

or c) 9,000 covers (0.2 probable)

The possible outcomes are:

NPV at 11,000 units = -140,000 + 11,000 (10 - 6)3.791

= 26,804

NPV at 10,000 units	= -140,000 + 10,000 (10 - 6)3.791
	= 11,640
NPV at 9,000 units	= -140,000 + 9,000 (10 - 6)3.791
	= (3,524)

This could then be combined with possible outcomes for a second factor.

Independent of sales volume the cost of materials will either be:

a) £3 per cover (0.6 probable)

b) £4 per cover (0.3probable)

c) £2 per cover (0.1 probable)

The situation now becomes more complicated because there are a total of nine possible outcomes based on three alternatives for sales volume and three alternatives for material costs.

The possible outcomes are:

a) Material costs of £3 per cover

A	NPV at 11,000 units	= -140,000 + 11,000 (10 - 6)3.791	= 26,804
B	NPV at 10,000 units	= -140,000 + 10,000 (10 - 6)3.791	= 11,640
C	NPV at 9,000 units	= -140,000 + 9,000 (10 - 6)3.791	= (3,524)

b) Material costs at £4 per cover

D	NPV at 11,000 units	= -140,000 + 11,000 (10 - 7)3.791	= (14,897)
E	NPV at 10,000 units	= -140,000 + 10,000 (10 - 7)3.791	= (26,270)
F	NPV at 9,000 units	= -140,000 + 9,000 (10 - 7)3.791	= (37,643)

c) Material costs at £2 per cover

G	NPV at 11,000 units	= -140,000 + 11,000 (10 - 5)3.791	= 68,505
H	NPV at 10,000 units	= 0,000 + 10,000 (10 - 5)3.791	= 49,550
I	NPV at 9,000 units	= -140,000 + 9,000 (10 - 5)3.791	= 30,595

In order to asses the probabilities of two events occurring, the probabilities need to be combined and this is achieved by multiplying the two values together. The following list indicates the possible outcomes and probabilities.

Possible outcome	NPV	Probability
A	26,804	0.18
B	11,640	0.30
C	(3,524)	0.12
D	(14,897)	0.09
E	(26,270)	0.15
F	(37,643)	0.06
G	68,505	0.03
H	49,550	0.05
I	30,595	0.02
		1.00

Using the above data, only one of the above options can occur. Only projects with a positive NPV should be accepted and from the above data it is possible to conclude that there is 58% chance of a positive NPV occurring (A+B+G+H+I).

Questions

1. Briefly discuss the techniques used to analyse risk in capital budgeting.
2. Explain the distinction between business risk, financial risk and operational risk.
3. Select a business from the hospitality and tourism sectors and describe the types of risk associated with investment decisions. Suggest how the scales of these risks can be assessed in practice.
4. Your hotel company is an international player looking to expand its presence in Asia and is considering the suitability of an investment in the Islamic Republic of Iran. You have been asked to prepare a presentation outlining the full range of risks the investing company is likely to be exposed to with this investment. Use an appropriate range of risk management models to structure your analysis.

Summary

This chapter investigates the important practical issues that have to be considered when evaluating capital investment projects. The general manager needs to be aware of the implications of inflation, taxation and risk on the capital investment decision and how to assess the effect of these factors in practice. Specific issues such as taxation will need the input of specialist advice to determine the current implications for a particular organisation. However, a major requirement of general management is to be able to assess and manage risk to ensure that exposure is minimised, and there are a range of financial techniques available to assist in this. These include an analysis of key ratios and cash flows. The techniques described in this chapter can be effectively used and developed further with the use of computer software such spreadsheets or more complex simulation packages.

Further reading

Atrill, P. and Mclaney E. (2021) *Accounting and Finance for Non-Specialists*, 12th Edition, Pearson.

Mclaney, E. (2009) *Business Finance: Theory and Practice*, Prentice Hall.

Ransley, .J, Ingram, H. and Adams, D. (2022) *Developing Hospitality Properties and Facilities*. Routledge

Schmidgall, R. (2016) *Hospitality Industry Managerial Accounting*. Educational Institute of the American Hotel Motel Association.

Website links

www.finance4hospitality.co.uk An online community with bite sized content and resources developed by experts in hospitality accounting.

www.inlandrevenue.gov.uk/capital_allowances/investmentschemes.htm

http://www.insurancejournal.com/magazines/midwest/2004/08/23/coverstory/45573.htm Hotels make room for risk management

www.hotel-online.com/Trends/Aon/index.html

12 The cost of funds

About this chapter

The purpose of this chapter is to illustrate the relationship between the cost of capital and the sources of finance, and to demonstrate how the cost of capital can be calculated for each source of funds. From this overall cost, value can be determined, reflecting the capital structure of the business. Establishing the cost of capital accurately is essential for evaluating projects, as was illustrated in Chapter 10, but in practice can be difficult to achieve. The aim of this chapter is to provide a simple overview of the key issues surrounding the cost of capital calculation, in order to enable the reader to understand the principles involved.

Learning objectives

On completion of this chapter, you should be able to:

- Understand the concept of gearing and financial leverage
- Explain the meaning of the weighted average cost of capital (WACC)
- Understand the relationship between wacc and the gearing ratio
- Appreciate the factors which impact on the selection of capital for the financing of a business or capital expenditure.

Introduction

The potential sources of funds available to an organisation have already been described in Chapter 9. These can be divided into two main groupings: equity sources and those termed as borrowings or debt capital. Equity sources include:

- Ordinary shares
- Preference shares
- Reserves and retained profits.

Debt financing can include:

- Bank loans
- Debentures
- Convertibles
- Bonds
- Mezzanine finance
- Creditors.

It has already been noted that equity sources can expect a varying level of return whereas borrowed funds normally require a fixed return in the form of interest. In general, the providers of the finance expect a level of return which is directly linked to the perceived level of risk. The higher the risk, the greater the expected return. The advantages of debt financing include the cost of the funding which is usually lower than equity financing. This is because:

- The pretax rate of interest is lower than that expected by shareholders, as share capital is perceived to be riskier, as the return – i.e. the dividend – is not guaranteed
- Debt interest falls above taxation in the structure of the profit and loss account, reducing the overall cost of the interest
- The administrative costs of debt capital, such as the issuing costs, are normally lower than those required for issuing share capital.

Cost of capital

CIMA (2023) defines the cost of capital as:

> *"The minimum acceptable return on an investment, generally computed as a hurdle rate for use in investment appraisal exercises. The computation of the optimal cost of capital can be complex and many ways of determining this opportunity cost have been suggested."*

If a company is to survive in the long term it must achieve a return in excess of the cost of the funds invested in it. The total cost is dependent on the cost of funds from equity sources and on those from borrowings. The return on equity is made up of the dividends paid to shareholders and the funds that belong to shareholders which have been retained within the company for reinvestment. The simplest approach to finding the cost of capital requires estimating the cost for each source of funds and combining these to provide a single value using a weighted average.

The cost of equity

Equity consists of the share capital and the retained profits invested in a business. Retained profits are often, mistakenly, considered to be a free source of finance. However, this is not the case, because there is an opportunity cost associated with using these funds. The calculations for the cost of equity should therefore reflect this fact. The cost of equity can be calculated in two ways. The first of these, the dividend growth model, provides the simplest approach to determining the cost of equity. The second approach, the capital asset pricing model, is more complex and will only be considered briefly here. However, some of the issues surrounding the second approach are of importance and these merit further discussion.

The dividend growth model

This approach calculates the cost of equity from the annual dividend payment and the current market price of the share as quoted on the capital markets, this being the dividend yield ratio.

$$\text{Dividend yield per cent} = \frac{\text{Dividend}}{\text{Market Price}}$$

This simple ratio only represents the cost of capital when the dividend remains the same for each following year and of course this is not always the case. Additionally, the method faces difficulty with a dividend payout of zero.

The dividend growth model is an attempt to overcome the issue regarding fluctuating dividends by building into the equation an estimate for future increases in dividend levels where:

$$\text{Cost of Equity} = \frac{d1}{M} + g \times 100$$

where d = the expected dividend to be paid out
g = expected dividend growth rate in percentage terms where investors expect the dividend to grow at a constant rate into the future
M = the market price of the share

This formula is demonstrated with the following example.

Where a company will pay an expected dividend of 14p per share and the current market price of the share is 200p, if the anticipated growth rate is 5% the cost of equity (Ke) will be:

$$Ke = \frac{0.14}{2.00} + 0.05$$

$$= 12.0\%$$

This model provides a simple approach to finding the cost of capital but the relationship should be used with care. In practice it is difficult to establish a value for g, the growth rate, with any certainty. The model also assumes that g will be less than the cost of capital. This is proven by rearranging the formula to show the market price of the share, M.

$$M = \frac{D(1+g)}{Ke - g}$$

If the long run the growth rate is equal to the cost of capital, the formula solves to show the value of the company as infinite which is clearly not practical.

The capital asset pricing model

This approach to estimating the cost of equity is based on the returns expected by the investor for buying the share. It assumes the greater the risk the greater the expected return. The level of risk is measured via a factor known as *beta*. This is combined with two other factors to determine the cost of equity. These are the risk free rate of return and the market risk premium.

- ☐ **The risk free rate of return** represents the most secure rate return which could be achieved and this is normally quoted as being the rate available from government gilts in the region where the investment is taking place.
- ☐ **The market risk premium** represents the excess return above the risk free rate which investors expect in order to compensate them for holding riskier investments. This calculated by using the average return from the capital market less the risk free rate of return.

Beta is the measure of systematic risk, which is the riskiness implied by a specific business activity and the way in which it is financed.

Risk measured by beta is that part of the total risk a business faces which cannot be diversified away. The beta can be measured in a number of ways, but the most usual approach is to estimate it using standard regression techniques based upon historical share prices. This is the approach adopted by the London Business School's Risk Measurement Service which publishes beta values for industry use.

The graph in Figure 12.1 illustrates the relationship between market return, the risk free rate of return and beta.

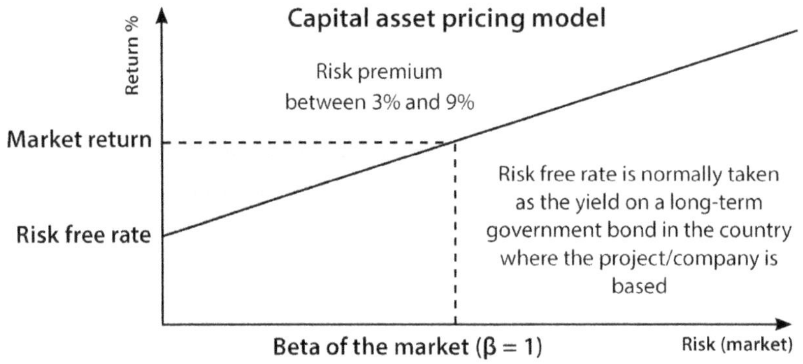

Figure 12.1: The relationship between market return, the risk free rate of return and beta. Source: https://corporatefinanceinstitute.com/resources/valuation/what-is-capm-formula

If the beta for a company is equal to 1, it means that the volatility of the expected returns from the company is equal to the average market return, i.e. the company performance will follow the market.

If a company's beta is equal to 1.2 then the average returns have a 120% with the volatility of the market average. When the stock market increases in value the company value will increase by a multiple of 1.2 and similarly when the stock market value drops.

A beta of -1 means that a company has a perfect negative correlation with the market.

Table 12.1 illustrates some beta values for a variety of different companies.

Table 12.1: Beta values from a selection of sectors. *Source*: Yahoo Finance

	At Feb 23	At Dec 23
Glaxo Smith Kline	0.14	0.27
Starbucks	0.92	0.96
IHG	0.97	0.89
Whitbread	1.11	1.01
Marriott	1.59	1.55
Zoom	-0.23	-0.1

The cost of equity is thus calculated with the following formula.

Cost of equity = risk free rate of return + (beta × market risk premium)

To apply this formula in practice requires knowing the beta factor for a particular business. These are published for companies, whilst estimates for the other two factors are freely available in the UK.

Example

A business financed 100% from equity has a beta of 0.8. The risk free rate of interest is 4% and the expected rate of return on the market portfolio is 10%.

Cost of equity = risk free rate of return + (beta x market risk premium)
= 4% + 0.8 (10 – 4)
= 8.8%

This approach to calculating the cost of equity is also useful for unquoted companies where there is no available market price for the shares. In this case a beta factor for a similar company might be used to enable the cost of equity value to be calculated. The CAPM approach has generally become an acceptable approach to calculating the cost of capital. However, there are still some problems associated with this method.

Evidence suggests that it is not always possible to summarise the market-related risk with a single indicator such as beta. The approach also assumes that the past is an accurate indicator of the future. This is not necessarily true in a changing economic environment. Despite these disadvantages CAPM remains a superior approach to the Dividend Growth Model.

Cost of loan capital

A second element in the cost of capital calculation is the cost of the long term borrowings. There are different types of loans, ranging from a bank loan through to debt raised through the capital markets in the form of bonds or debentures. Loans can be classified into types:

- ☐ **Irredeemable** where only interest is required to be paid
- ☐ **Reedeemable** where both interest and capital repayments are required

The majority of loan capital is redeemable – that is with capital repayments of the principle borrowed during or at the end of the lifetime of the loan.

The cost of the loan is based on the interest paid and the value of the debt:

$$\text{Cost of debt} = \frac{\text{Interest}}{\text{Market value of the loan}}$$

A simple bank loan will not change in value, but debt raised on the capital markets will change in value in response to changing interest rates in the external environment. When the debt is redeemable or repayable in full, the cost of capital is found by discounting the future cash flows arising over the life of the loan. The discount rate, which equates the present value of the future cash flows to the current market value of the debt, is the cost of capital for those borrowings. The following example illustrates this.

Example

Loan stock was originally issued at a par value of £100. The current market value is £93. The repayment of the original amount is due in five years' time and interest of 10% is due annually on the original amount. The cost of the loan stock is calculated by considering the cash flows over the next five years.

	Cash flow	Discount factor	Present value
	£		£
Year 0	(93)	1.000	(93)
1	10	0.909	9.09
2	10	0.826	8.26
3	10	0.751	7.51
4	10	0.683	6.83
5	110	0.621	68.31

At 10% discount factor a positive present value of £7 is achieved. If a discount factor of 12% is used, the resulting net present value is almost zero and this, therefore, equates to the cost of debt. The drop in the value of the loan stock has occurred because the return of £10 or 10% must be below the market rate of interest. As a result the perceived value of the stock fall belows the original value of £100.

Normally businesses might have more than one source of debt finance. The overall cost of the debt can be calculated by taking a weighted average of the individual components.

Loan capital and tax relief

The interest payable on borrowings attracts Corporation Tax relief so the true cost of loan capital should reflect the benefit derived from this. This due to the positioning of interest in the profit and loss account where interest is deducted from profits prior to the corporation tax calculation. The true cost of the interest payment is calculated as follows:

$$\text{Cost} = i(1 - T)$$

where:

T is the Corporation Tax rate

i is the interest rate

For example, if the interest rate is 10% and the corporation tax rate is 20%, this means the true cost of debt finance falls from 10% to 8%.

The weighted average cost of capital (WACC)

Having calculated a cost of capital for each element of the capital structure the resulting cost of capital is calculated by combining these values as a weighted average as shown in the following example.

Example

At present a company is funded by a combination of equity and debt capital. The equity shares were originally issued at £0.60 and have a current market price of £2.70. The current dividend is £0.10 per share and this has been growing at a rate of 10% per annum in recent years. The loan capital issued by the company is irredeemable and has a current market value of £95 against an original cost of £100. Interest is paid out at a rate of 12%. The corporation tax rate is 20% The company has 70% of its operations funded by equity with the remainder funded by borrowings.

The weighted average cost of capital is calculated from the cost of the two sources of funds. The cost of equity is found using the dividend growth model.

$$\text{Cost of equity} = \frac{10p\,(1 + 0.10)}{270p} + 10\%$$

$$= 14.1\%$$

The cost of the borrowings is found as follows:

$$\text{Cost of debt} = \frac{12}{95}$$

$$= 12.6\%$$

After tax is taken into account this becomes 12.6% x 0.8 = 10.08%

The weighted average cost is found from

(70% x 14.1%) + (30% x 10.08%) = 9.9 + 3.0 = 12.9%

The effect of gearing on the cost of capital

A very large proportion of businesses have some level of debt finance and the relation with the equity is called *gearing* or financial leverage. It is important, therefore, to consider the relationship between gearing and cost of capital. The more common approach is known as the traditional view and that is based on the assumption that as gearing increases, the perceived risk increases and equity investors and lenders will require a higher return. It is suggested that at lower levels of gearing, neither investor group requires greatly increased returns and as loan sources tend to be cheaper than equity sources the weighted average cost of capital will decrease.

At higher levels of gearing, risk becomes more important to investors and the WACC starts to increase significantly. As a result there is a point where the WACC is at a minimum and this is described as the optimum level of gearing. This effect is shown in Figure 12.2.

This approach was questioned in the fifties by Miller and Modigliani (1958), who published what is now considered to be an extremely significant article questioning the basis of the traditionalists' view. They argued that it is not possible for a business to borrow additional funds and by so doing reduce its weighted average cost of capital. Their view is that when additional cheap loan finance is introduced, the weighted average cost of capital is not affected because there is a corresponding increase in the cost of equity. The effect is illustrated in Figure 12.3.

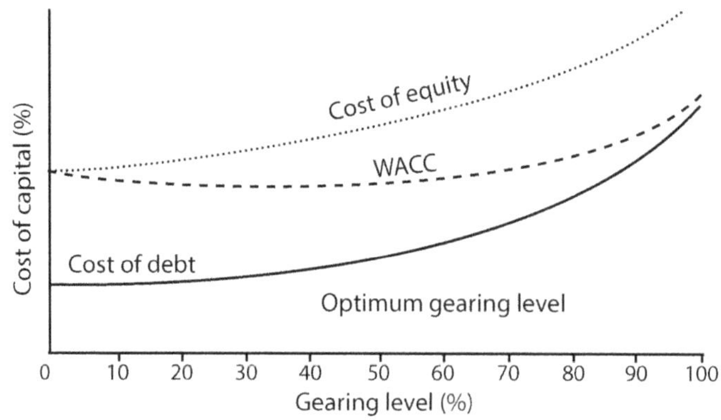

Figure 12.2: Weighted average cost of capital (WACC): traditional view

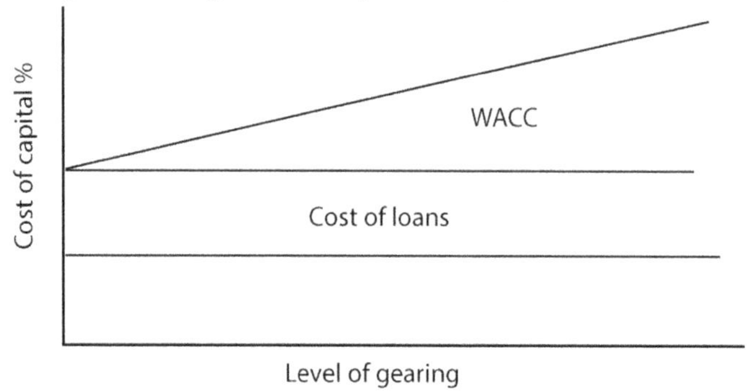

Figure 12.3: Cost of capital for varying levels of gearing – the MM (pretax) view

As a result, Miller and Modigliani conclude that there is no optimum level of gearing. Since they proposed their theories there has been much debate by academics on the issue of cost of capital and gearing. It has since been shown that some of the assumptions underlying their approach are incorrect, although there is some logic in the theory. As a result, a compromise position is recommended, whereby WACC is likely to fall as gearing increases, but that this trend will change when equity holders and lenders become increasingly conscious of risk.

Summary

The cost of capital is an important concept for all types of organisation using a range of sources of finance. All sources of funds have a cost of servicing associated with them, either in the form of variable or fixed charges. Accurate determination of the cost of capital is vital as this figure represents the discount rate used in capital investment decisions. If a figure is calculated which is higher than the actual level, this may result in profitable projects being rejected. Conversely an estimate which is too low means that unprofitable projects will be accepted. There are different approaches to the calculation of the cost of capital value and each of these has its inherent difficulties. The level of gearing in a company is thought to affect the cost of capital of the component sources of finance, based on the perception of risk. It is generally believed that increased gearing up to a certain level reduces WACC, however Modgliani and Miller have proposed that gearing makes no difference to the cost of capital. The theories remain unproved and consequently the general consensus is that gearing does have some bearing on the resultant cost of capital.

Questions

1. What is the cost of equity in the following case:

Share price is £2.70

Past dividend growth is 5%

EPS is £0.24

Dividend cover is 4 times

2. The Directors of Venus Hotels plc are considering opening a new resort facility. The finance director has provided the following information:

Initial capital investment £2,750,000

The following is an extract from the balance sheet of Venus Hotels plc for the year ended December 31 2023:

Creditors due in more than one year	
10% Debenture	£500,000
Long term loan – variable rate	£900,000
Capital and reserves	
3,000,000 shares at 25p each	£750,000

The authorised share capital is 5 million shares; the current market price per share at December 31 2023 is 145p ex-dividend. The dividend growth factor (g) is estimated to be 8%. The current market price of debentures is £75 (ex-interest) and interest is payable each year on 31 December.

The interest rate on the long-term loan is 18%.

The debentures are non-redeemable. Ignore taxation.

You are required to:

a) Calculate the average weighted cost of capital for Venus Hotels plc as at 31 December 2023.

b) Comment on why it is important to calculate the cost of capital with care.

c) Explain the distinction between business and financial risk.

3. Forest Caterers plc is a major hospitality company wishing to expand. Currently the company has £500 million of long-term capital and proposes to raise a further £100 million to finance the expansion.

At present 60% of the Forest Caterers plc finance comes from equity and the rest from loan stock. However, one of the Directors feels that more loan stocks could be introduced as these are a cheaper form of finance than equity and suggests introducing additional loan finance so that only 50% of funds are classified as equity after the additional finance has been raised.

A second Director argues that the best way to finance the project would be to use retained profit as this represents a 'free' source of finance to the business.

Currently the shares, which have a nominal value of £0.50, are being traded at a market price of £1.25. The dividend at present is £0.05 per share and recently has been increasing at a compound rate of 10% per annum.

The average cost of the loan stock after taxation is 10%.

a) Calculate the WACC for Forest Caterers plc for each of the scenarios described and comment on the remarks made by each of the Directors.

b) Calculate the amount of finance the Directors wish to raise and comment on the business plan to increase the gearing of the business.

c) Explain the term 'Cost of Capital' and discuss why a company should calculate its cost of capital with care.

4. Malvent Hotels plc is a major hotel company wishing to expand. Currently the company has £400 million of long-term capital and proposes to raise a further £90 million to finance the expansion.

At present 80% of the Malvent Hotels plc finance comes from equity and the rest from loan stock. However, the Directors feel that more loan stocks could be introduced and plan to introduce additional loan finance so that only 60% of funds are classified as equity after the additional finance has been raised.

Currently the shares, which have a nominal value of £0.50, are being traded at a market price of £3.25. The dividend at present is £0.10 per share and recently has been increasing at a compound rate of 8% per annum. The company always issues irredeemable loan stock and its loan stock, issued in 1989 at par, has a current market value of £120 per £100 nominal. This loan stock pays 14% interest at the end of the year.

The tax rate is 25%.

5. Autumn Café has common stock currently trading at £40 per share. The stock is expected to pay a dividend of £3.00 at the end of the year and the dividend is expected to grow at a constant rate of 6%. What is the cost of the common stock?

6. The Marchwood Restaurant Group has the following capital structure which it considers to be optimal:

Debt	30%
Preferred Stock	10%
Common Stock	60%

The following data is also applicable:

a) Corporation tax rate is 20%
b) The expected dividend growth rate is 9%
c) Dividend last year was £3.60
d) Market price of common stock is £54.00
e) Preferred stock pays a dividend of £10.00 with a market value of £90.00
f) The debt interest rate is 12%

i. What is the cost of capital for each element of capital?
ii. What is the WACC?

7. XZZ Plc has a beta of 0.7. The yield expected on Government stocks is 6%. The market risk-free premium is 5% and the average return on equity in the past year was 15%. What is the cost of equity using the CAPM formula?

8. Hadyn Restaurants has the following capital structure:

   Debt – 20%
   Preferred stock – 10%
   Common stock – 60%

   The tax rate is 40% and dividends grow at 6%. The last dividend paid was £3.80 and the market price of a share is £70. Treasury bonds yield 6% and the market risk premium is 5% with a beta of 1.3. The preferred stock has a value of £90 per share and a dividend of £10 per share. The cost of debt is 8%.

   What is the WACC?

9. In theory the WACC will decrease as the gearing of the business increases. Explain what happens to the WACC in practice and illustrate your answer with a relevant graph.

10. In the CAPM formula, *beta* is used to measure the riskiness of the company. Explain how a *beta* of more than 1 or less than 1 reflects the riskiness of a company.

References and further reading

Atkinson, H., Jones, T., Lorenz, A. and Harris, P. (2012), *Strategic Managerial Accounting; Hospitality, Tourism and Events Applications*, Goodfellow Publishers

Atrill, P. & Mclaney E. (2021) *Accounting and Finance for Non-Specialists*, 12th Edition, Pearson.

Miller, M. & Modigliani, F. (1958) The cost of capital, corporation finance and the theory of investment. *American Economic Review* 48(3), 261-97.

Ransley, J., Ingram, H. and Adams, D. (2022) *Developing Hospitality Properties and Facilities*. Routledge

Schmidgall, R. (2016) *Hospitality Industry Managerial Accounting*. Educational Institute of the American Hotel Motel Association.

Watson, D. & Head, A. (2013) *Corporate Finance: Principles and Practice*, Pearson Education.

Website links

www.cimaglobal.com/

www.finance4hospitality.co.uk

www.valuebasedmanagement.net/

www.sternstewart.com/

www.youtube.com/watch?v=etlv7qTQUSY&t=8s What is beta?

1

Part 5 Strategic implementation and evaluation

Recent worldwide events such as the disruption caused by the global pandemic have impacted the hospitality, tourism and leisure industry in a variety ways and have proven that it is essential for businesses to continually monitor market trends and adapt internally to meet each new challenge.

Structural changes in the industry have led to the emergence of a range of international players with a geographically dispersed portfolio, often as a consequence of extensive merger and acquisition activity. The traditional patterns of ownership have been replaced with a complex arrangement of franchising, management contracts, joint ventures and strategic alliances, aimed at reducing the cost and risks associated with development whilst providing the opportunity to expand more rapidly.

Technological developments in systems, processing capability and connectivity have revolutionised marketing, revenue management and customer expectations. At the time of writing, the UK is experiencing continued optimism in the strength of the staycation and business travel markets, which is driving record levels of hotel development, but the PwC UK Hotels Forecast 2023-2024 shows an increase in rooms supply comes as the post-Covid 'revenge travel' bounce fades, inflationary pressures reduce, and the UK economy remains flat.

The rapid developments in the use of information technology and artificial intelligence are providing the capability and opportunity for business managers and operators at all levels to operate with increased levels of data about their business and the competition. The provision of monthly reporting of business performance, for example, is now available in some hospitality businesses just three days after the month end, whereas this activity would have taken at least two weeks or more just a decade ago. As a consequence, managers in the hospitality, tourism and leisure industries are now required to take an active role in budgeting and forecasting performance and to use business data for decision making and evaluation of business performance.

In this final section of the book, we consider the impact of strategic decisions on the overall value of the business. Chapter 13 reviews the problems associated with valuing a business and focuses in particular on issues associated with the hospitality and tourism industries. The final chapter reviews some of the forecasts and predictions currently being proposed for the future of management accounting in the hospitality, tourism and leisure industries.

13 Measuring the value of a business

About this chapter

The principle aim of business activity is often stated as being to maximise shareholder value. In todays' world, businesses are more conscious of their impact, and many focus on the 3 Ps: People, Planet and Profit. Increasing regulation means that sustainability and impact on the environment will rapidly become a requirement for reporting in the annual accounts, and the accounting profession is preparing for the challenges this will bring. Several factors drive the value of a business and in this chapter these factors will be considered, with an evaluation of the alternative approaches for attempting to arrive at an estimate of business value. For businesses with a market listing on the Stock Exchange, the valuation is derived by calculating the market capitalisation value, which is the current share price, multiplied by the number of shares in issue. However, as was discussed earlier in the text, a large proportion of the sector is made up of private organisations. For these organisations alternative approaches for determining business value are relevant. This chapter will consider the application of a variety of widely used approaches to business valuations with a specific focus on hotels, including:

- Market capitalisation methods
- Dividend yield and price/earnings ratio
- Net assets
- Comparable sales
- Earnings multiple
- Rebuild value
- Net present value using forecasted discounted cash flows
- Intangible values
- Impact of sustainability strategies.

Learning objectives

On completion of this chapter, you should be able to:

- Understand the factors which drive the value of commercial real estate
- Use a range of methods to determine an estimate of the value of a business
- Appreciate the difficulties experienced by the hospitality, tourism and leisure industries when attempting to estimate the value of a business.

Introduction

The principle purpose for measuring the value of a business is to provide a monetary measure which accurately reflects the true worth of that business. In general terms, research has indicated that a number of factors determine business value when seeking to purchase an existing commercial asset, and these include:

- ☐ Potential for revenue growth
- ☐ Construction costs for a new build, in terms of long-term assets and working capital, less the wearing out of the asset
- ☐ Value of the intangibles, such as brand or intellectual capital
- ☐ Cost control and profit margins – past and forecasted
- ☐ Predicted residual value, i.e., the predicted value after, say, 10 years of operation

The issue of business valuations and the choice of appropriate methodology is somewhat controversial in accounting circles and the UK hospitality industry has been particularly troubled in this area.

There are many valuation techniques available and often the most appropriate method will depend on the subsequent use of the valuation. These potential uses include providing a balance sheet figure for accounts preparation purposes as well as setting a value for acquisition purposes, for insurance assessment, for investment monitoring purposes, such as return on capital employed measures, and possibly to provide a figure to banks as the basis of collateral valuations when raising a loan. The most appropriate method depends not only on the end purpose of the value but also on the size and type of business. Hotel valuation experts, HVS, estimate that the last significant economic event, the global financial crisis in 2008/09, depressed European hotel values by an average of 23% resulting in a recovery period of some six years. According to HVS, the factors influencing buyers and sellers and the determination of hotel price can be summarised as illustrated in Table 13.1.

Table 13.1: Factors influencing willing buyers and willing sellers. *Source*: www.hvs.com/article/8876-the-impact-of-covid-19-on-the-european-hotel-sector

Downwards Factors	Upwards Factors
Unprecedented revenue and EBITDA decline	Improved business operating model
Economic recession	Return of positive operating leverage
Longer recovery of MICE business	Yield-hungry funds creating competition
Uncertainty regarding normal travel patterns	Low cost of capital likely to continue
Potential for prolonged recovery, re-infection	Some lenders will wait for values to rise before losses are recognised
Cash drain may force owners to sell	

HVS report that in 2020, the year of the COVID-19 outbreak, hotel values in Europe saw average declines of between 5% and 15% compared with the previous year. In general, hotels in gateway cities with a stable infrastructure have seen less decline, whilst hotels with weak offers have been the most severely impacted.

Despite the impact of the pandemic, numerous investors have remained active throughout this period and transactions relating to 'trophy assets' have remained strong according to real estate experts, Savills (2021).

Market capitalisation

The larger sized business, which has shares trading on an apparently efficient stock market, can be evaluated by simply multiplying the shares in issue by the current share price. This provides an estimate for the value of the entire company and the figure is known as the market capitalisation value. However, many companies in the sector are operating as private companies, i.e. they are not listed on a Stock Exchange, and hence no current market price per share is available. In other cases, it is not the total value of the company which is sought but instead a value required for a particular asset or group of similar assets. In these cases, other approaches are required.

Dividend yield basis

This approach to valuation is based on the principle of estimating the value of the total equity within a business and uses the dividend yield ratio introduced in Chapter 8 as its basis. The methodology assumes that the ordinary shares of two different businesses should have a similar dividend yield ratio provided that they are similar in size, activity, capital gearing and proportion of profit paid in dividend. If the shares of one of these businesses is quoted then this will enable the price to be set for the unquoted business. The value of the business in question can then be found by applying the following ratio.

$$\text{Gross dividend yield} = \frac{\text{Dividend paid}}{\text{Current market price per share}}$$

where

$$\text{Current market price} = \frac{\text{Dividend paid}}{\text{Gross dividend yield}}$$

The following example demonstrates the method in practice.

Z Ltd is a small business which at the end of the last financial year paid out a dividend of £120,000 gross. The dividend yield value for a similar listed business is 8% gross. Using this a market price for the business can be estimated.

$$\text{Estimated market price} = \frac{120{,}000}{8\%}$$

$$= £1{,}500{,}000$$

There are a number of inherent difficulties in using this approach in practice. It may well be difficult, if not impossible, to find a similar business for comparison purposes, and even if this were possible the approach assumes that the dividend paid always reflects the level of the market price for the share, which may not be valid.

Price/earnings basis

This approach is based on the ratio between current market share price and the earnings of the business. The ratio is as follows.

$$P/E = \frac{\text{Current market price per share}}{\text{Post tax earnings per share}}$$

where

$$\text{Current market price} = P/E \times \text{earnings per share}$$

The method assumes that the P/E ratio will be the same for similar firms and therefore can be applied to calculate a share price which can be used to estimate a value for market capitalisation. The following example demonstrates the method in practice.

A Plc and B Ltd are two businesses of similar size, activity and capital structure. A is quoted on the Stock Exchange whereas B is not. The P/E ratio for A is 10 and the annual earnings after tax for B have been a static £0.50 per share. B has 1 million shares in issue. Using the formula then,

$$10 = \frac{\text{Current market price per share}}{£0.50}$$

The market capitalisation of the business is estimated to be £5 million.

The choice of P/E ratio to be used is often dependent on one or more of the following factors:

- Prevailing economic conditions
- Type of industry
- Size of operation
- Market confidence
- Potential forecasted profits
- Levels of equity and debt.

As a result, it can be quite difficult to establish an appropriate value to use and it is not uncommon for a specific sector to have a wide range of values.

Net assets basis

This approach is based on the book value of the assets as stated in the balance sheet and the valuation is based on the net assets less outstanding long-term loans.

The practice of valuing assets

The approaches described so far are fairly theoretical and do not provide the solution to finding the value for specific assets. This section will consider this particular problem.

The Companies Act allows UK companies to adopt accounting policies other than purely historical cost accounting when preparing their financial statements. As a result, tangible long-term assets, such as property, may be stated at either market value on the date they were last valued or at current cost. Where market values are used the valuations should be kept up to date, but the difficulty occurs in establishing what this market value should actually be.

Establishing a true value for the assets of a business is required for a variety of purposes. In general, the shareholders and investors expect to see the assets stated at current value so that profit performance can be assessed in relation to the capital investment via the return on capital employed ratio. The shareholder will also want to make comparisons with the performance of other companies in the sector and with companies in other industries, and it is therefore, essential that the bases used for valuation are realistic and adequately disclosed.

The responsibility for ensuring that the valuation of assets has been correctly stated is that of the directors of the company and this is monitored by the auditors whose job it is to ensure that the prepared financial statements give a true and fair view. On a practical level, within the accounting system the various fixed asset accounts identified should be backed up by detail of the physical holdings of assets. For all assets, there should be maintained separately a fixed asset register to show:

- The organisation's internal reference number
- The manufacturer's serial number; description of the asset
- Location of the asset
- Department which 'owns' the asset
- Purchase date
- Cost
- Depreciation method and estimated useful life
- Net book value.

Consequently, the fixed asset register needs to be reconciled to the nominal ledger to make sure that all additions, disposals and depreciation provisions and charges, have been posted. It is essential that the company inspects all the items in the fixed asset register and keeps the fixed asset register up to date.

Comparable transactions

This approach is based on the market value for the business if it is sold for its existing use. An existing hotel operation, for example, might typically include the land and buildings, items such as fixtures, furniture, equipment, computers, goodwill and stock. All of these assets are classified as being tangible, excluding goodwill and brand value which are intangible assets and can be identified as being derived from the location, the operational strengths of the site, the personal flair of the existing management team and the value of the brand name. An estimate for all of these should be included in the valuation, although in practice this can be quite difficult to achieve. The total value of the site can be set by simply considering similar and comparable transactions, where competitive operations have already been sold for what is considered to be a fair value, using a measure such as the price per room achieved. It may be necessary to increase or decrease the measure used, depending on how the strengths of the operation compare to the competitive operation.

This approach is often more practical for the smaller operation where there may be many similar businesses on which to make a comparison. However, for the larger, possibly more individual, operation in a unique position it may simply not be possible to determine the value by considering similar transactions. In this case it may be necessary to use an alternative approach.

Earnings multiple

This approach is based on simply applying a multiple to maintainable earnings, which are defined as the adjusted net cash flows, in present value terms, which can be sustained over an extended time period. The resultant estimate of stabilised earnings will be capitalised at the appropriate multiplier, reflecting all appropriate considerations. Whilst the maintainable earnings can be estimated fairly easily, the determination of the multiplier must reflect the perceived risk or security associated with the investment.

Example

A hotel has a sustainable annual EBITDA of £1,500,000 which is based on assuming that REVPAR, Occupancy % and ARR have all now stabilised with a consistent revenue mix between room sales and other operating revenues such as Food and Beverage. The Departmental Expenses and Undistributed Operating Costs are all considered to be stabilised. A capitalisation rate of 10% has been deemed as the most appropriate for the region. (These rates often come from consultancies with access to transaction data operating in the region). The capitalisation is based on a multiple calculated by assuming that the EBITDA is to be 10% of the final value. The multiple to use is calculated from 1 / 0.10 which is 10 times. Therefore, the valuation for the property is 10 times £1,500,00 equalling £15,000,000.

Net present value

The value of an asset or a business in total can be estimated by predicting the future cash flows and then discounting these with an appropriate cost of capital. The particular elements which need to be considered in the valuation process are:

- Revenue growth rate and gross operating profit margins
- Timings associated with the projected cashflows
- Working capital levels
- The asset value at the end of the analysis
- The magnitude of recurring levels of maintenance, capital expenditure and any additional investment required
- The cost of capital.

Theoretically, this approach is the soundest in that it takes into account the timing and value of future earnings. However, it is dependent on an accurate forecast for the future cash flows and the correct estimation of the appropriate discount rate. The following is an example to demonstrate the methods in practice:

Example

A colleague of yours is considering purchasing a chain of 21 public houses, the summarised accounts of which appear below.

Balance Sheet at 31st December

	2022		2023	
	£m	£m	£m	£m
Non current assets (net of depreciation)	8.0		8.5	
Current assets				
Stocks	3.3		5.6	
Debtors	0.5		0.8	
Bank balances	0.3		0.1	
		4.1		6.5
		12.1		15.0
Current liabilities: (amounts falling due within one year)				
Creditors	3.8		3.3	
Bank overdraft	0.3		1.5	
Dividends	0.7		0.9	
Taxation	0.7		1.0	
		5.5		6.7
Total assets less current liabilities		6.6		8.3
Long term liabilities (amounts falling due after more than one year)				
Long term loan @ 10%pa		1.4		1.4
		5.2		6.9
Financed by:				
Called up share capital				
4 million ordinary shares @ £1		4.0		4.0
Share premium		0.2		0.2
Reserves		1.0		2.7
		5.2		6.9

The financial record for the business for the last two years is summarised below:

Profit & Loss Account Year ended 31st December

	2022	2023
	£m	£m
Revenue	15.40	17.50
Profit before interest	2.34	3.74
Profit before taxation	2.20	3.60
Taxation on profit	0.70	1.00
Profit after taxation	1.50	2.60
Dividends	0.70	0.90
Retained profit	0.80	1.70

Industry analysts advise that quoted companies in similar industries have an average P/E ratio of 5, a dividend yield of 15% and a cost of capital of 12%.

You estimate the net cash flows to be achieved following the purchase to be:

Year 1 - 5 £800,000 per year
Year 6 £1,200,000 per year.

A value for the business can be calculated using a range of approaches.

The dividend yield valuation can be worked out as follows:

$$\text{Market price} = \frac{0.9}{15\%} = £6 \text{ million}$$

The price earning valuation is as follows:

2.6 x 5 = £13 million

The net assets as quoted at book value amount to

£8.3million - £1.4million = £6.9 million

allowing for repayment of the long term loan.

The calculation for net present value is as follows:

Year	Cashflows (000s)	Discount factor	Net present value (000s)
1	800	0.893	714.4
2	800	0.797	637.6
3	800	0.712	569.6
4	800	0.636	508.8
5	800	0.567	453.6
6	1,200	0.507	608.4
			3,492.4

The purchase price is approximately £3.5 million.

Intangible value

It is now widely recognized that for many successful enterprises there is not always a correlation between the value of the net assets figure shown in the balance sheet and the market capitalisation of the business. In the business world today there are a growing number of operations whose market value is dependent on a range of intangible assets including:

- Intellectual capital – the value of the knowledge held by the operating team within the business
- Brand value
- Potential – arising from the location of the business, forward bookings and reputation.

The value of these intangibles can be defined as the difference between net book value of assets and the market capitalisation of the business.

ESG and business value

ESG stands for Environmental, Social, Governance. Together these three concepts form a framework for understanding and measuring how sustainably a business is operating. ESG takes a holistic approach to sustainability rather than limiting it to environmental issues alone. The regulation landscape is changing with an increased requirement for businesses to report both financial and non-financial data relating to ESG activities.

The Greenhouse Gas Protocol is an internationally accepted, step-by-step guide for companies & organisations to quantify & report their GHG emissions. The hospitality and tourism industries are some of the most significant contributors to the level of GHGs and business value can be directly impacted by both how the site is constructed, materials used etc. and also how the business is operated.

Summary

Considerable difficulties face the hospitality industry in setting asset values. This is particularly true in an economic environment where asset values are more likely to go down than to go up. Case histories indicate that the current methods are far from satisfactory, and the best approach is based on discounted cash flows. Academically this approach is superior because it is based on forecasted cash flows and a discount rate which should be calculated using the cost of capital, anticipated risk, and predicted inflation.

Questions

1. You are considering the purchase of a chain of restaurants, the summarised accounts of which appear below:

Balance Sheet as at 31 December 2023

Long term Assets	**£000**
Cost	16,000
Accumulated depreciation	3,000
Net book value	13,000
Current Assets	
Stock	4,000
Debtors	5,500
Cash	500
	10,000
Less Creditors: Amounts falling due within one year	
Trade creditors and taxation	4,500
Bank overdrafts	7,800
Dividends payable	900
	13,200
Total Assets, less Current Liabilities	**9,800**

Less: Long term loans	5,000
	4,800
Capital and Reserves	
6 million ordinary shares of 50p	3,000
Reserves	1,800
	4,800

Profit & Loss Account as at 31 December 2023

	£000
Turnover	38,000
Profit before interest and taxation	3,400
Interest payable	2,300
Profit before taxation	1,100
Taxation	275
Profit after taxation	825
Dividends (net)	400
Retained Profit	425

Additional Information

- ☐ Similar companies have a price earnings ratio of 15
- ☐ Forecasted cash flows for the first 5 years of trading are estimated to be £900,000 per year. An appropriate discount rate will be 12%

a) Estimate the value of the business using:

i) Assets valuation

ii) Price earnings ratio

iii) Forecasted cash flows

b) Comment on the merits of each valuation technique.

2. Research the latest annual report and accounts for a company operating in the hospitality, tourism and leisure industries. (Most large companies post their accounts to their website where you can freely download the information). Using the published profit and loss account and balance sheet:

a) Review the proportion of fixed assets to current assets

b) Review the proportion of tangible fixed assets to intangible fixed assets. Use the notes to the accounts to determine what the intangible assets represent

c) What are the components of the current assets

d) Can you find any notes on the company asset revaluation policy?

Research the financial press to find the share price and the market capitalisation of your chosen business. Do you think the share price is overvalued or undervalued?

References and further reading

Atrill, P. and Mclaney E. (2021) *Accounting and Finance for Non-Specialists*, 12th Edition, Pearson.

Cornell SC Johnson (n.d.) *ESG Innovations in Hospitality,* https://business.cornell.edu/hub/2021/05/06/esg-innovations-in-hospitality/ accessed December 2023

Harper, D. (2008) *Valuation of Hotels for Investors*, Taylor & Francis

PSC (2023) *Hotels Forecast 2023 - 2024*, www.pwc.co.uk/industries/hospitality-leisure/insights/uk-hotels-forecast.html

Knight, D. (1999) Performance Measures for increasing intellectual capital, *Strategy and Leadership* 27(2)

Koller, T., Goedhart, M. and Wessels D., (2010) *Valuation: Measuring and Managing the Value of Companies*, McKinsey & Company Inc.

Ransley, J., Ingram, H. and Adams, D. (2022) *Developing Hospitality Properties and Facilities*, Routledge

Schmidgall, R. (2016) *Hospitality Industry Managerial Accounting*, Educational Institute of the American Hotel Motel Association.

Useful websites

www.finance4hospitality.co.uk An online community with bite sized content and resources developed by experts in hospitality accounting.

corporatefinanceinstitute.com/resources/knowledge/other/esg-environmental-social-governance/

www.hospitalitynet.org/news/4111726.html

www.pwc.co.uk/issues/esg.html

www.hvs.com/article/8876-the-impact-of-covid-19-on-the-european-hotel-sector HVS, *The Impact of COVID-19 on the European Hotel Sector 2021*

14 The way forward

About this chapter

The role of the financial controller or unit accountant in the hospitality, tourism and leisure industries has changed considerably in recent years. Advances in integrated technology have enabled the management accountant's role to be more wide ranging, with less time spent entering and processing data and more time dedicated to supporting the management teams in decision making. Extensive restructuring of the finance function has resulted in flatter organisational structures, with many organisations no longer reliant on a full accounting team located at every business unit. In the larger hotel groups for example, it is not unusual for the finance function to be structured on a cluster basis with a team supporting a number of outlets. Independent hotels may choose to outsource part or all of the finance function as an alternative to employing a full team on site.

It is widely recognised that data management and information sharing is the key to organisational success and competitive advantage. Clearly the finance role has a significant part to play in ensuring that trends and analysis is extracted from the raw data available and then shared across the organisation. In this final chapter we will explore some of the current models used in the hospitality, tourism and leisure industry for ensuring effective control and usage of business assets in the sector.

Learning objectives

On completion of this chapter, you should be able to:

- ☐ Appreciate the changing role of the finance function in the hospitality, tourism and leisure industries
- ☐ Appreciate the current factors impacting on the provision and use of information for business control and planning
- ☐ Understand the factors which have driven the nature of change in the hospitality, tourism and leisure sectors.

Introduction

During the last 30 years the international hospitality industry has witnessed a period of tremendous change, which in turn must surely have implications for all of the functional activities within the business and the finance function is no exception. The growth in size of the multinational operations, with both diversified investors and interests, highlights the growing need for accurate and timely information for performance measurement and control. Competitor analysis is key for ensuring that each investment is maximising its potential and providing value for investors. Research into the future of the finance function from the accountancy membership bodies for management accountants such as CIMA and AICPA, indicates that the finance team has a mandate to go beyond its core accounting role. This changing mandate doesn't discard core accounting; it's still an essential foundation of the finance function. However, enabled by new technologies, the function is now capable of assessing a broader range of information and becoming a more influential player within an organisation. The research highlights the fact that the modern controller in the hospitality, tourism and leisure industry is increasingly faced with the challenge of harnessing the tremendous potential to be derived from the continuing application of information technology to the systems for measurement and control, to ensure that optimum benefit is being provided. Increasingly hierarchical structures are perceived as no longer relevant and instead a flatter team-based structure approach is more appropriate.

The role of the manager in the hospitality industry is also changing, with more emphasis being placed on commercial skills and entrepreneurship in many of the larger organisations. A general manager at a managed or franchised hotel can expect to have monthly meetings with the investors to discuss not only the profitability of the property but also the cash flow, asset management and the competitor analysis. This can mean that unit manager and departmental heads are increasingly required to take a more active role in strategic planning, forecasting, and budgeting and monetary control. The provision and management of 'business intelligence' is crucial.

The purpose of this book has been to highlight weaknesses in the traditional approaches to management accounting in the hospitality and tourism industries, although it is widely recognised that management accounting in many industry sectors has failed to keep up with advances in other aspects of business practice and strategy. It has been noted in Chapter 1 that there are a number of specific issues currently impacting on the hospitality and tourism industry which will have a far-reaching effect on the future nature of hospitality finance systems.

Changing roles

Traditionally the role of the accounting function has been heavily biased towards the comparison of costs with revenues whilst focusing on the internal operations of the business. Accounts by definition are historical and inward looking, and accounting practice is governed by the underlying principle of prudence. In many hospitality and tourism operations, the accountant is still traditionally viewed as the 'bean counter' focusing on historical results. Obviously, there is still some relevance in this role; however, in most modern organisations it has become essential to produce accounting information with a strategic perspective. In practice this means not just reviewing internal operations but also the external environment and the role of the competition.

A typical job description for a hotel financial controller includes managing or overseeing:

- The business regulatory accounting and financial management requirements
- The provision of monthly management accounts by department
- Preparation of regular forecast updates
- Regular preparation of the cash flow forecast
- Supporting the general manager and the department heads in the annual budget preparation
- Advice and tactics for revenue generation and cost control
- Monitoring product and service profitability
- The different elements of working capital, inventory management, accounts receivable and accounts payable
- Provision of data for monitoring the competition.

According to generic research by the Fitzgerald et al. (2023), focusing on the finance operating model of the future, financial managers will see their role shift from leading a silo of resources to coordinating various teams to focus on coordinated enterprise performance. Consequently, increasingly the accountant's role in the hospitality and tourism sector is to be viewed as a member of the management team bringing specific expertise to the decision-making process.

The role of the operational manager in the hospitality and tourism industry has also dramatically changed in response to the increasingly competitive environment where decisions need to be made locally and quickly. Failure to make the right business decision can lead to loss of profitability or even business demise. As a result, to make quick, frequent, and correct decisions the available supporting information needs to be timely and of the necessary quality. Research by Hodari and Sturman (2014) found that hotel general managers in both independent and hotel chains are required to make decisions and take actions that will have an impact on the hotel's performance and results. This is particularly important for hotel operating companies where the company has been recruited by the owners to improve the operating performance over and above that of the competition.

Consequently, the finance function's role is to deliver high quality decision support services to the users of the financial information. The finance function needs to consider the following questions carefully:

- Who are the users of our information?
- Do we need to clarify the information produced to assist managers to make decisions based on this information?
- What services do other functions in the business need from us?

- ☐ What is our strategy for the production and delivery of information?
- ☐ How do we monitor whether we have met our user's needs?

Critical success factors for the industry

Management accounting in the hospitality, tourism and leisure industry is governed by the operational features of an industry which is characterised by fixed supply of certain resources, such as rooms, space, staffing and investment, perishability and seasonality of the product, and high fixed costs, in particular, labour and maintenance.

Effective cost control throughout the business requires applying well known techniques, such as process engineering, consistently and thoroughly in every aspect of the operation. Payroll is the largest single controllable cost in most hospitality and tourism operations and savings in this area will have a dramatic effect on profitability. Several businesses, particularly those in the contract catering sector, are now employing sophisticated labour scheduling tools to ensure that payroll costs are strategically managed. For catering operations, the cost of materials is a significant cost, and the larger companies are developing partnership arrangements with suppliers to reduce unit costs. The impact of this has been a marked reduction in standard cost of sales ratios over the past decade. In recent times, due to economic pressures, there has been a focus on utility costs and the investment required to switch to cheaper and more sustainable solutions.

In hotels and resorts, fixed costs are clearly the most significant cost, with each sale providing a contribution towards covering these costs. Ongoing site maintenance, for example, can be as much as 20% of revenues, in order to maintain the quality of five-star operations, and many businesses in the hospitality and tourism industries have outsourced some of these activities to specialist organisations in a bid to strategically reduce costs but maintain or indeed improve these areas.

Historically, medium- and long-term planning is often an activity which the hospitality industry has failed to address adequately, and as a result a traditional incremental approach is often adopted. However, evidence suggests that increasingly operational mangers at unit levels are being actively encouraged to improve their financial awareness skills and deploy these, producing regular forecast updates for planning future performance and the effective use of resources.

The role of artificial intelligence

It is already becoming clear that intelligent systems, known as artificial intelligence (AI), will take over more and more administrative tasks from human workers. According to research from the ICAEW (2018) in order to build a positive vision of the future, it is necessary to develop a deep understanding of both how AI can solve accounting and business problems and the practical challenges, and the skills accountants need to work alongside intelligent systems. Advances in artificial intelligence have the power to transform the finance function but the full benefits are yet to be harnessed. Machine learning will enable computers to move far further into decision making processes. Table 14.1 is adapted from research at the ICAEW on the key features of artificial intelligence systems and capabilities which will have an impact on the accounting processes of the future.

Table 14.1: Key features of Artificial Intelligence and accounting processes

Features of AI systems	How accountants deploy technology
They can process large volumes of both structured and unstructured data.	Using better and cheaper data to support decision making
They can pick up weaker and more complex patterns than are detectable by human intelligence	Generating new insights from the analysis of data
They are more consistent decision makers with less bias that humans	Freeing up time from data collection to spend more time on decision making

Source: Adapted from ICAEW Thought Leadership (2018) '*Artificial Intelligence and the future of accountancy*' https://www.icaew.com/-/media/corporate/files/technical/technology/thought-leadership/artificial-intelligence-report.ashx

Knowledge sharing

In recent years the concept of knowledge management and sharing has been the subject of considerable interest in management literature. All organisations can be considered as 'constellations of interacted practice' or 'communities of practice' (Wenger, 1998) but typically we tend to classify organisations on the basis of formal structures with communication and reporting based on lines of command. In a seminal article published in 1991, Seely Brown and Duguid suggested that organisations are typically structured on the basis of responsibility, enhancing internal competition and creating boundaries for secrecy and privacy. They suggest that to create synergistic collaboration between workers, learners and innovators, a conceptual reorganisation is required. The notion of competitive advantage through effective use of information and communications technology is widely recognised (Senge, 1990; Castells, 1996). Castells suggests that the overall aim must be to create competitive advantage by leveraging economies of scale from all the business assets, including intellectual capacity and knowledge about suppliers and markets. Senge uses the term 'learning organisation' with the objective of developing collective intelligence. Much has been written about the success that the social capital resident in communities of practice (CoPs) has had on improving business performance. In their research, Lesser and Storck (2001) highlight four areas of organisational performance that have been impacted on by the ongoing activities of CoPs. These include:

- Decreasing the learning curve of new employees
- More rapid response to customer needs and inquiries
- Reducing rework and preventing 'reinvention of the wheel'
- Spawning new ideas for products and services

Clearly fostering knowledge sharing practices and opening up communication channels in the hospitality, tourism and leisure industries is not only the responsibility of the accounting function but requires a strategic approach across all functional areas in the business.

Assessing profitability by market segment

Traditionally the business has structured its management accounts on a departmental basis, focusing on the products and services provided, rather than the markets served. In the hospitality industry, the management accounts are based on the recommendations of the Uniform Accounting System, which was first developed by the Hotel and Catering Economic Development Council in 1969 followed by the US system, the Uniform System for Accounts for the Lodging Industry, which was first published by the Hotel Association of New York City in 1926. The Uniform System may be defined as a manual of instructions for preparing standard financial statements and schedules for the various operating and productive units which make up an operation. The purpose of this manual is to provide a simple formula for the classification of accounts which could then be adopted by any hotel regardless of size or type. In practice most of the major hospitality companies do use the system or an abridged version. The Uniform System is based on departmental accounting, using product and service type as the basis for monitoring revenues and profitability. However, there is increasing interest in customer and market profitability. This includes gaining a better understanding of what drives customers to use the business services, what value the customer receives and what value each customer grouping adds to the business. This is known as the process of market segmentation, and is critical for understanding the profile of the different types of customers engaging with the business.

Risk management

Increasingly organisations are required to develop a coordinated strategy with regard to managing risks. A recent report from the Institute of Internal Auditing (2023) entitled *2023: Risk in Focus* suggests that a state of crisis is the new normality. Climate-related natural disasters, looming recession, an accelerating cost of living catastrophe in Europe, food shortages, employee welfare and skills deficits, and a rapidly industrialising cyberattack landscape are overlaid by intensifying geopolitical tensions and the very real threat of financial liquidity and solvency risks for businesses.

> *The Board has ultimate responsibility for risk management throughout the Group and determines the nature and extent of the risks we are willing to take. Certain responsibilities, such as overseeing the systems of risk management and internal control, have been delegated by the Board to the Audit Committee, which completes an annual review of the effectiveness of these processes. Risk is managed proactively by the Executive Committee. Our individual business units complete an annual review of the risks relevant to the achievement of their strategic goals, while also taking into account key operational risks, which are updated regularly.*

Whitbread Hotel Group Annual Report 2020/21 retrieved from https://cdn.whitbread.co.uk/media/2021/05/21175600/23076_Whitbread_AR2020_web-1.pdf

The following diagram adapted from the IIA, illustrates the typical interlocking risks.

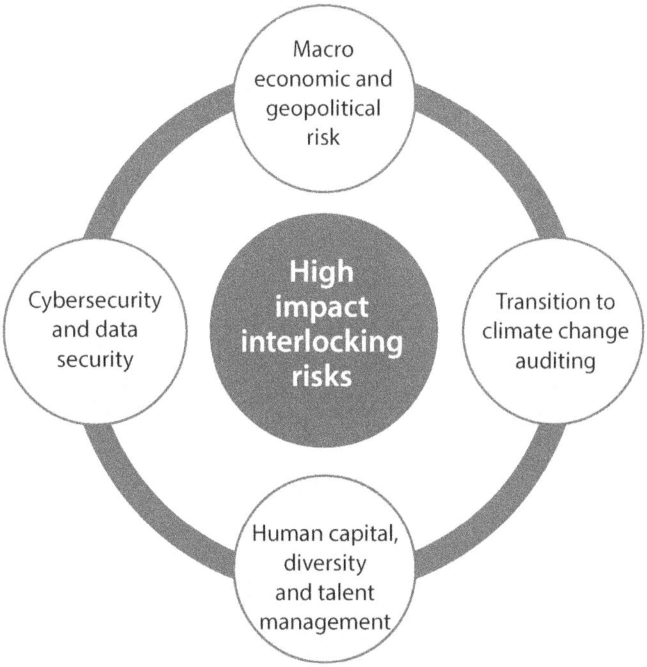

Figure 14.1: Interlocking organisational risk

Source: Adapted from Institute of Internal Auditing (2023) 2023: Risk in Focus, https://www.iia.org.uk/media/1692515/risk-in-focus-2023.pdf

Sustainability accounting

Many hotels and resorts have become much more focused on social responsibility, including managing and monitoring their impact on the environment. The United Nations World Tourism Organization (UNWTO) is the agency responsible for the promotion of responsible, sustainable and universally accessible tourism. According to their research, the hotel sector is one of the tourism industry's largest drivers of employment and economic revenue but at the same time it is one of the most energy-intensive with hotels and other types of accommodation accounting for 2% of the 5% global CO2 emitted by the tourism sector. The UNWTO identify that many of the issues in the sector arise from:

- Out-dated technologies
- Lack of human and financial resources
- Limited awareness and knowledge of greener alternatives
- Larger proportion of SMEs, which are usually less proactive about the environment in comparison to larger hotel chains.

Currently the volume of bodies created to focus on Environmental, Social and Governance (ESG) reporting or sustainability reporting has become quite confusing. However, what is clear is that jurisdictions around the world are developing guidance on ESG disclosures. This is being reinforced by regulatory pressures impacting on the accounting profession in both the United States and Europe, which is now driving the sustainability agenda for many organisations.

The International Sustainable Standards Board (ISSB) completed a consultation in 2023 which focused on four potential priorities for sustainability-related risks and opportunities associated with:

- Biodiversity
- Ecosystems, and ecosystem services
- Human capital and human rights
- Integration of financial reporting and sustainability reporting.

The European Sustainability Reporting Standards (ESRS) were finalised in 2023 with disclosure requirements applicable for the first companies in scope as early as 2024 (filing in 2025). The ESRS apply to all companies listed on EU-regulated markets. The Standards require the reporting of Scope 1,2 and 3 emissions, with Scope 3 focusing on the supply chain, which will have far-reaching impacts on those non-EU based companies supplying the companies required to report within the EU. Increasingly the accounting profession is focusing on developing their role in collecting, accurate measurement of, and verifying information for reporting, to avoid the accusation of greenwashing.

Asset management

In recent years there has been a growth in the role of the hotel asset manager. Hotel asset management focuses on the management of a specific asset class – hospitality real estate. Real estate investors are seeking to maximise the income and the value of their assets, and realise that the hotel asset differs from other property assets, in that the revenue and cost streams tend to be more complex compared to the letting of retail or office space.

A survey conducted in 2015 by the Hospitality Asset Management Association (HAMA) found that asset managers work across three broad categories:

- Private ownership groups for private equity investors
- Independent advisors
- Institutional owners

In these roles, asset managers will engage directly with unit and group accounting teams to monitor the asset performance.

Summary

Preparing future managers in the hospitality, tourism and leisure industries with the skills to effectively manage business resources includes enabling them to understand the developments currently impacting on the long-term future of the industry, and to be able to harness these changes to drive the industry forward. This is certainly true in the teaching of the finance function, where the education should be relevant and specific to the individual needs of the industry, to provide the graduate general manager of the future with the multi-skills required to manage the business effectively. Effective education needs to be supported by research, and yet historically the application of research effort to the field of hospitality and tourism finance has been sadly under-subscribed. Therefore, it is exciting to note the emergence of some new projects focusing on specific issues relating to the accounting and information systems. There is clear evidence that effective performance measurement systems are of paramount importance for the future, with a range of specific areas which still merit further investigation, including sustainability measurement and reporting, and market segment accounting.

Questions

1. What factors do you think are reshaping the role of the financial controller and the finance function in the hospitality, tourism and leisure industries?
2. To what extent does the finance function have involvement in measuring and managing quality and customer value?
3. What type of role do you see the financial controller taking in ten years time?

Practical activity

4. Research the following terms:
    a. Asset Management
    b. Benchmarking
    c. Environmental cost management
    d. Sustainability accounting
    e. The changing role of the accountant

References and further reading

Atrill, P. and Mclaney E. (2021) *Accounting and Finance for Non-Specialists*, 12th Edition, Pearson.

Castells, M. (1996) *The Rise of the Network Society,* Boston MA: Blackwell

Fitzgerald, S, Willman, T., O'Connor, J. & Ferguson S. (2023) Define your digital world class operating model, The Hackett Group, www.thehackettgroup.com

Hayes, D. K. and Miller, A. (2011) *Revenue Management for the Hospitality Industry*, John Willey & Sons

Hodari, D. and Sturman, M. (2014) Who's in charge now? The decision autonomy of hotel general managers. *Cornell Hospitality Quarterly* 55(4) 433-447

ICAEW Thought Leadership (2018) Artificial Intelligence and the future of accountancy, https://www.icaew.com/-/media/corporate/files/technical/technology/thought-leadership/artificial-intelligence-report.ashx

Institute of Internal Auditing (2023) 2023: Risk in Focus, https://www.iia.org.uk/media/1692515/risk-in-focus-2023.pdf

Lesser, E. L. and Storck, J (2001) Communities of practice and organizational performance *IBM Systems Journal*, 40(4), 831-842.

Musgrove, R.E., Raleigh, L.E. and Singh, A.J. (2016) *Hotel Asset Management: Principles and Practices* 3rd edition. AHLEI & HAMA

PWC Viewpoint (2023) Navigating the ESG landscape Comparison of the 'big three' sustainability frameworks. https://viewpoint.pwc.com/dt/us/en/pwc/in_the_loop/in_the_loop_US/navigesglandscape.html

Ransley, J., Ingram, H. and Adams, D. (2022) *Developing Hospitality Properties and Facilities*. Routledge

Roper, A. (2017) *Vertical Disintegration in the Corporate Hotel Industry*. Routledge

Schmidgall, R. (2016) *Hospitality Industry Managerial Accounting*. Educational Institute of the American Hotel Motel Association.

Seely Brown, J. and Duguid, P. (1991) *Organisational learning and communities of practice: Towards a unified view of working, learning and innovation*, Institute of Management Sciences

Senge, P. (1990) *The Fifth Discipline: The art and practice of the learning orgnaisation*, New York: Doubleday

Wenger, E. (1998) *Communities of Practice; Learning, Meaning and Identity*, Cambridge University Press.

Useful websites

www.finance4hospitality.co.uk An online community with bite sized content and resources developed by experts in hospitality accounting.

www.aicpa-cima.com/resources/download/the-changing-role-and-mandate-of-finance

www.unwto.org

https://ghgprotocol.org/corporate-standard

Appendix: Tables

Present Value of £1

Discount Factor

Year	1%	2%	3%	4%	5%	6%	7%	8%	9%	10%
0	1.000	1.000	1.000	1.000	1.000	1.000	1.000	1.000	1.000	1.000
1	0.9901	0.9804	0.9709	0.9615	0.9524	0.9434	0.9346	0.9259	0.9174	0.9091
2	0.9803	0.9612	0.9426	0.8890	0.9070	0.8900	0.8734	0.8573	0.8417	0.8264
3	0.9706	0.9423	0.9151	0.8548	0.8638	0.8396	0.8163	0.0000	0.7722	0.7513
4	0.9610	0.9238	0.8885	0.8219	0.8227	0.7921	0.7629	0.7938	0.7084	0.6830
5	0.9515	0.9057	0.8626	0.7903	0.7835	0.7473	0.7130	0.7350	0.6499	0.6209
6	0.9420	0.8880	0.8375	0.7599	0.7462	0.7050	0.6663	0.6806	0.5963	0.5645
7	0.9327	0.8706	0.8131	0.7307	0.7107	0.6651	0.6227	0.6302	0.5470	0.5132
8	0.9235	0.8535	0.7894	0.0000	0.6768	0.6274	0.5820	0.5835	0.5019	0.4665
9	0.9143	0.8368	0.7664	0.7026	0.6446	0.5919	0.5439	0.5002	0.4604	0.4241
10	0.9053	0.8203	0.7441	0.6756	0.6139	0.5584	0.5083	0.4632	0.4224	0.3855
11	0.8963	0.8043	0.7224	0.6496	0.5847	0.5268	0.4751	0.4289	0.3875	0.3505
12	0.8874	0.7885	0.7014	0.6246	0.5568	0.4970	0.4440	0.3971	0.3555	0.3186
13	0.8787	0.7730	0.6810	0.6006	0.5303	0.4688	0.4150	0.3677	0.3262	0.2897
14	0.8700	0.7579	0.6611	0.5775	0.5051	0.4423	0.3878	0.3405	0.2992	0.2633
15	0.8613	0.7430	0.6419	0.5553	0.4810	0.4173	0.3624	0.3152	0.2745	0.2394

Discount Factor

Year	11%	12%	13%	14%	15%	16%	17%	18%	19%	20%
0	1.000	1.000	1.000	1.000	1.000	1.000	1.000	1.000	1.000	1.000
1	0.9009	0.8929	0.8850	0.8772	0.8696	0.8621	0.8547	0.8475	0.8403	0.8333
2	0.8116	0.7972	0.7831	0.7695	0.7561	0.7432	0.7305	0.7182	0.7062	0.6944
3	0.7312	0.7118	0.6931	0.6750	0.6575	0.6407	0.6244	0.6086	0.5934	0.5787
4	0.6587	0.6355	0.6133	0.5921	0.5718	0.5523	0.5337	0.5158	0.4987	0.4823
5	0.5935	0.5674	0.5428	0.5194	0.4972	0.4761	0.4561	0.4371	0.4190	0.4019
6	0.5346	0.5066	0.4803	0.4556	0.4323	0.4104	0.3898	0.3704	0.3521	0.3349
7	0.4817	0.4523	0.4251	0.3996	0.3759	0.3538	0.3332	0.3139	0.2959	0.2791
8	0.4339	0.4039	0.3762	0.3506	0.3269	0.3050	0.2848	0.2660	0.2487	0.2326
9	0.3909	0.3606	0.3329	0.3075	0.2843	0.2630	0.2434	0.2255	0.2090	0.1938
10	0.3522	0.3220	0.2946	0.2697	0.2472	0.2267	0.2080	0.1911	0.1756	0.1615
11	0.3173	0.2875	0.2607	0.2366	0.2149	0.1954	0.1779	0.1619	0.1476	0.1346
12	0.2858	0.2567	0.2307	0.2076	0.1869	0.1685	0.1520	0.1372	0.1240	0.1122
13	0.2575	0.2292	0.2042	0.1821	0.1625	0.1452	0.1299	0.1163	0.1042	0.0935
14	0.2320	0.2046	0.1807	0.1597	0.1413	0.1252	0.1110	0.0985	0.0876	0.0779
15	0.2090	0.1827	0.1599	0.1401	0.1229	0.1079	0.0949	0.0835	0.0736	0.0649

Annuity Factor

Year	1%	2%	3%	4%	5%	6%	7%	8%	9%	10%
1	0.9901	0.9804	0.9709	0.9615	0.9524	0.9434	0.9346	0.9259	0.9174	0.9091
2	1.9704	1.9416	1.9135	1.8861	1.8594	1.8334	1.8080	1.7833	1.7591	1.7355
3	2.9410	2.8839	2.8286	2.7751	2.7233	2.6730	2.6243	2.5771	2.5313	2.4869
4	3.9020	3.8077	3.7171	3.6299	3.5460	3.4651	3.3872	3.3121	3.2397	3.1699
5	4.8534	4.7135	4.5797	4.4518	4.3295	4.2124	4.1002	3.9927	3.8897	3.7908
6	5.7955	5.6014	5.4172	5.2421	5.0757	4.9173	4.7665	4.6229	4.4859	4.3553
7	6.7282	6.4720	6.2303	6.0021	5.7864	5.5824	5.3893	5.2064	5.0330	4.8684
8	7.6517	7.3255	7.0197	6.7327	6.4632	6.2098	5.9713	5.7466	5.5348	5.3349
9	8.5660	8.1622	7.7861	7.4353	7.1078	6.8017	6.5152	6.2469	5.9953	5.7590
10	9.4713	8.9826	8.5302	8.1109	7.7217	7.3601	7.0236	6.7101	6.4177	6.1446
11	10.3676	9.7869	9.2526	8.7605	8.3064	7.8869	7.4987	7.1390	6.8052	6.4951
12	11.2551	10.5753	9.9540	9.3851	8.8633	8.3838	7.9427	7.5361	7.1607	6.8137
13	12.1337	11.3484	10.6350	9.9857	9.3936	8.8527	8.3577	7.9038	7.4869	7.1034
14	13.0037	12.1063	11.2961	10.5631	9.8986	9.2950	8.7455	8.2442	7.7862	7.3667
15	13.8651	12.8493	11.9379	11.1184	10.3797	9.7123	9.1079	8.5595	8.0607	7.6061

Annuity Factor

Year	11%	12%	13%	14%	15%	16%	17%	18%	19%	20%
1	0.9009	0.8929	0.8850	0.8772	0.8696	0.8621	0.8547	0.8475	0.8403	0.8333
2	1.7125	1.6901	1.6681	1.6467	1.6257	1.6052	1.5852	1.5656	1.5465	1.5278
3	2.4437	2.4018	2.3612	2.3216	2.2832	2.2459	2.2096	2.1743	2.1399	2.1065
4	3.1025	3.0374	2.9745	2.9137	2.8550	2.7982	2.7432	2.6901	2.6386	2.5887
5	3.6959	3.6048	3.5172	3.4331	3.3522	3.2743	3.1994	3.1272	3.0576	2.9906
6	4.2305	4.1114	3.9976	3.8887	3.7845	3.6847	3.5892	3.4976	3.4098	3.3255
7	4.7122	4.5638	4.4226	4.2883	4.1604	4.0386	3.9224	3.8115	3.7057	3.6046
8	5.1461	4.9676	4.7988	4.6389	4.4873	4.3436	4.2072	4.0776	3.9544	3.8372
9	5.5371	5.3283	5.1317	4.9464	4.7716	4.6065	4.4506	4.3030	4.1633	4.0310
10	5.8892	5.6502	5.4262	5.2161	5.0188	4.8332	4.6586	4.4941	4.3389	4.1925
11	6.2065	5.9377	5.6869	5.4527	5.2337	5.0286	4.8364	4.6560	4.4865	4.3271
12	6.4924	6.1944	5.9177	5.6603	5.4206	5.1971	4.9884	4.7932	4.6105	4.4392
13	6.7499	6.4236	6.1218	5.8424	5.8315	5.3423	5.1183	4.9095	4.7147	4.5327
14	6.9819	6.6282	6.3025	6.0021	5.7245	5.4675	5.2293	5.0081	4.8023	4.6106
15	7.1909	6.8109	6.4624	6.1422	5.8474	5.5755	5.3242	5.0916	4.8759	4.6755

Index

www.ingramcontent.com/pod-product-compliance
Ingram Content Group UK Ltd.
Pitfield, Milton Keynes, MK11 3LW, UK
UKHW051847100926
8556IPUK00005B/501

9 781911 396703